Violence, Culture and ...

Violence, Culture and Censure

Edited by

Colin Sumner

Taylor & Francis
Publishers since 1798

UK   Taylor & Francis Ltd, 1 Gunpowder Square, London EC4A 3DE
USA   Taylor & Francis Inc., 1900 Frost Road, Suite 101, Bristol, PA 19007

First published 1996

A Catalogue Record for this book is available from the British Library

ISBN 0 7484 0554 2
ISBN 0 7484 0555 0 (pbk)

Library of Congress Cataloging-in-Publication Data are available on request

Cover design by Barking Dog Art

Typeset in 10/12pt Times
by Graphicraft Typesetters Limited, Hong Kong

Printed in Great Britain by SRP Ltd, Exeter.

Contents

Preface

In this volume, we hope to make a small contribution to the historic and cultural process of taking violence out of the behaviourist textbooks of abnormal psychology and putting it into an historical sociology of censures. These essays continue the work in development over the last twenty years on the sociology and jurisprudence of censures (see Sumner, 1976, 1990a and 1994; also Roberts, 1993; Sparks, 1992; Wing Lo, 1993). Growing organically from a core of social-theoretical themes and bound by continuous discussion, they have emerged from a series of graduate seminars held by the editor in the Institute of Criminology at the University of Cambridge from 1993–5. All the contributors are graduates of that Institute's Master's programme and all of them are guilty of giving the editor a rough ride in his seminars or of making him think too much – which is another way of saying that, whilst he still loves them all for making his last days in Cambridge interesting, the editor does not necessarily agree with all the youthful wisdom expressed herein.

My thanks go to Mark Fenwick for all the assistance he has provided in the preparation of this volume; to Richard Jones in helping to produce the reference list; Comfort Jegede, for her confidence in this project from the outset; Keith Hayward for compiling the index; and Alison Chapman and Fiona Kinghorn for their patience and for helping to turn this into a publishable product.

Colin Sumner
University of East London
May 1996

Chapter 1

Introduction:
The Violence of Censure and the Censure of Violence

Colin Sumner

The essays in this volume are reflections upon our understanding and moral judgment of violence at the end of the twentieth century. We think they show that even a serious matter like violence is not a simple fact which speaks loudly for itself. They illustrate the theory of social censures as two-sided phenomena, partly passionate categories of blaming, reflections of anger, *angst* and frustration, and partly attempted descriptions of their targets. Violence is thus partly a censorious categorization of aggression and partly a form of aggression. Moreover, it is often an outcome of the social censure of others' violations; it can be described as either offence or punishment, depending upon the standpoint of the describer.

These essays take topics of contemporary interest as illustrations of the two-dimensional character of violence. They indicate that there is an uncomfortable proximity between the politically legitimized practices of censure, trial and punishment and the practices of socially proscribed violence. They bear in mind the Nietzschean interlinking of good and evil, peace and violence, and consider the nihilism at the end of a violent century. In particular, they stand as our own small commemoration of the Holocaust.

The world of unreason was once hidden from view by its signification in dominant ideological discourses as pathological. The authoritative world of reason, embedded historically within the practices of state, capital accumulation, imperial domination, conventional masculinity and ethnic arrogance, reconstituted unreason within a scientistic grid of negative categories purporting to denigrate and exclude the integral role of unreason within the human condition. That of course by its very nature appears perfectly reasonable, for what sense would it make to celebrate the 'dark side' of human practice? But sights require our eyes to see them, and if our vision is already structured by a cultural sediment which limits our view of what is light and what is dark, then we need somehow to reveal that cultural structuration – for it may make us blind to the significance and nature of the world of unreason.

It may even prevent us from distinguishing dark from light. The sun shades of 'reservoir dogs', in Tarantino's movie, may make such a distinction difficult.

Historically, as Foucault has implicitly and explicitly suggested in *Madness and Civilization*, unreason has come to signify, negatively, the non-rational, the feminine, the dark, the child-like, the perverse, the bestial and the passionate. Reason has thus marked off and downgraded, or censured, much of what gives life its deeper meaning, its fundamental vitality, and its intrinsic quality as nature as opposed to machine. The unpredictable and messy natural character of the human condition is over-run and glossed over by a scientized reason determined to effect an anodyne McDonaldization of social relations, in the interests of profit, convenience, practicality, realism, stability, predictability and global domination. Nature is abducted and raped by reason, and then reason has the nerve to turn round and accuse nature of being abnormal, deviant or criminal. However, despite the crimes of rationality, masculinity and bureaucratized capital, we must not forget: Foucault did not suggest, nor did anyone else, that reason was inhuman simply by its existence, nor that masculinity and science were faulty by definition. What Foucault regretted was that we had attempted to marginalize, confine, exorcize and delete one half of the human condition – not that the other half was any more or any less 'natural'. The romanticism of excess, passion, illogic, bestiality, femininity and childishness is not one of the more palatable features of late modern thought.

We could close ourselves off to the unreasonable desires and practices we have inside us or see around us, but what good would that do? Avoidance and denial, so evident in the amnesia of the Holocaust, never achieved any forward movement, merely a *stasis* of ignorance as we spin webs of anodyne discursive artifice in defence against our unending and searing pain. Intellectualization and distanciation provide no soothing or healing, but only freeze our horror in an impractical and perpetually wounding silence. Of course, it may often be hard to confront what has been censured, divided off and marginalized in this world, that tabooed topic or event which is spoken of in the hushed tones of obsessive gossip and vicariously devoured in the X-files, those X- and triple X-rated products of a media that knows only too well the fallibilites of its market (but understands absolutely nothing about its impact upon it in human terms). Few of us relish the embrace with pain or the embarassment of revelation, but just to begin to identify and classify the phenomena of 'the dark side', to unravel the issues and to discuss what could be different soon reveals that the unthinkable is often more thinkable than we assumed. To take some simple examples: yesterday's 'terrorist' often becomes tomorrow's leader; the slum culture's 'delinquent' turns out to be less reprehensible than the corrupt politician; the responsible bread-winning husband transforms into a wife-beating 'bully'; and the 'deviance' of many, when put under the spotlight of research, reappears as an editorial selection from a choice of a thousand normalities.

In fact, the world of unreason is subject to much moral, emotional and ethical judgment or filtering before it is constituted as substance, and there is, therefore, every reason for us to suspect that it may not be all that it seems. Unreason is perhaps, in part, an illusion or trick, for it is clearly defined so often by so much passionate, non-rational, infantile and bestial (mis-)judgment, that is, by elements that it is allegedly composed of in the first place. The irony. There is so much unreason involved in the so-called rational social censure of what is called crime, deviance, violence and subversion, that if we have a healthy appreciation of the humanity of truth, and the truth of humanity, we must conclude that reason is not all it seems and neither is unreason. Both, as Foucault argued in Volume 2 of his *History of Sexuality*, can be seen as elements in what are well described as moral problematizations. The present text can thus be seen as an exploration of the moral problematization of violence in the twentieth century.

This volume is premissed neither upon the value of the rational nor the celebration of its opposites. It is underpinned by scepticism about a hard distinction between the violent and the non-violent; the reasonable and the insane; the healthy and the sick; abuse and use; civilized and barbaric. It is of course thus conditioned by the passing of the twentieth century, which has done so much to make us question what is mad and what is normal – and how, and who is, to decide which is which. The focus of the book is upon the serious matter of violence, and its standpoint is that there is a latent violence in censure and a latent censure in violence; reason and unreason married as one, for better and for worse.

It may be that ethologists like Ardrey and Lorenz were right to highlight the constancy of aggression in human practice, but we cannot logically infer from this that violence is a universal feature of human behaviour. Aggression and violence are not the same. Aggression is action we accept, violence is action we do not normally condone. But, if this is true, the difference between aggression and violence resides not in physical action but in the meaning which we attribute to the two actions. Violence, it seems to me, is best understood as the censure of some forms of human practice as unacceptable forms or levels of aggression. Violence is a cultural and historical sign, subject to the usual human filters of interest, prejudice and principle; as a sign of disapproval, it is more arbitrary and capricious than a simple effect of its referent or target. Of course, this does not mean that its target or referent does not precipitate the censure or that such a censure would not command popular assent, but it does mean that what counts as violence is subject to the acculturated or political understandings and standpoints of the viewer. One man's 'healthy aggression' is another woman's 'mindless violence'; one society's blood feud is a system of social control, another's is dangerous vigilantism; one country's civilization is another's barbarism; one country's ethnic cleansing is another's war crime.

Some censures of violence may be agreeable to us but that would not alter one iota the fact that they are still signs lodged within a culture's moral orthodoxy or political creed; signs of human passion, interest, custom and disorder. They remain moral or ethical judgments of practice which are mainly legitimized through reference to the manifestations they condemn, the criteria and procedures of ethical judgment used, the explanations they suppose of the apparent violence, and the context in which they are made. In practice, as we know from everyday life, very often the facts of the case are more complex than they first seemed, our ethics are rarely consistently and abstractly applied, our implicit explanations are structured more by our desire to condemn than the facts of the case, and the context in which judgment is made can colour all. Thus it is that one person's 'necessary law and order' is another person's state violence, and the victim's perception of 'animal violence' is the assailant's attempt to 'cleanse' the world of evil.

Enforcing the law is in many cultures a legitimate form of state aggression; aggressively challenging state officials or policy is frequently an illegitimate violation of the peace. Or so the conventional theory of the state tells us. Violence is thus built into our politics as part of the unlawful, the illegitimate and the politically unacceptable. It is inherently a censure; it is not innocent of political theory nor moral judgment. It is culturally loaded in its meaning. Any social science which approaches the phenomenon of violence must therefore start by disentangling the sign from its referents, the signification from the logic and context of its practice, and the signifying agency from the case. Explanation of violence cannot proceed without this first step of cultural and political deconstruction – cultural studies, sociology of law, political theory – but, equally, it cannot rest there and must move on to explanation and ethics, a sociology of aggression and a normative jurisprudence, if it is to get to the heart of the matter. So little existing work completes each step of such a research programme; so little deconstruction of violence has begun, so much deconstruction stops with media imagery or the self-interest of legislators. Analysis of media metaphor and rhetoric needs to be combined with the search for the varied social and psychic roots of the desire to kill or to hurt, and with educated moral judgment about what is acceptable as healthy aggression and what is unacceptable and a sign of dis-ease.

Throughout, the book attempts to illustrate the way that violence is very much a social censure of perceived aggression or offence and thus a theme lodged within certain cultural ideologies of domination, namely those which specify what is legitimate violence and who should have the monopoly over it. Claire Valiér's essay in Chapter 2 emphasizes the violent character of censure through an analysis of the censorious discourses of sadomasochism. She demonstrates that both the censure of violence and the violence of such a censure are inseparable from its constituent ideological formations. Drawing upon literature and social history, she exemplifies the power of Foucauldian analysis in this field, and also reassesses the social role of blaming practices in the light of existentialist considerations. In particular, she attempts to portray censure as a means of extending the field of the norm and to rethink the moral problematization of sexuality.

The essays on the Holocaust by David Craig, in Chapter 3, and Anthony Amatrudo, in Chapter 4, penetrate deeply into the psychological and ideological formation of German Nazism. Drawing on psychoanalysis and the history of art, they trace the origins and character of the violent potential of certain ways of thinking and being. They observe the horrific violence that can flow from certain types of censure and reflect upon the fact that even what many would see as the most censurable of violence is itself subject to considerable variety of explanation, interpretation and representation. Craig's work is concerned with the merits of a renewal of psychoanalytic sociology and assesses the arguments of writers such as Freud, Fromm, Parsons, Marcuse and Reich in attempting to understand the mental set and social conditions which might enable some understanding of the incomprehensible horror of the Holocaust. Amatrudo demonstrates that a fascist aesthetics were an integral part of the Nazi viewpoint and that even a 'bestial' violence such as the Nazis perpetrated was a deeply cultural form; indeed, it was rooted in a rewriting of the cultural script of German-ness and German history.

Chapters 5 and 6, by Laurence Grant and Ethan Raup respectively, draw upon theories of hegemony and authoritarian populism to interrogate the roots of state violence in Argentina and the United States. They illustrate the popular support often fuelling state policies which are severely violent, and the way that such popularity is politically constructed in particular historical and political situations. In many ways, they link our shock or horror at the forms of violence discussed in the earlier chapters with our familiarity with, and acceptance of, forms of violence which we see in the contemporary world as 'law-and-order'. Grant's piece draws upon Hall, Poulantzas and Laclau to explain the economic, political and cultural bases of Perón's authoritarian populist régime in Argentina. In so doing, he interrogates the meaning and value of the category of populism for social-scientific analysis, and provides a useful illustration of the value of the concept of hegemony for critical criminology. Raup applies Hall and Poulantzas also, to explain the rising American prison population and the disproportionate censure of inner-city black people; but he develops their work significantly in drawing upon Lash and Urry's analysis of disorganized capitalism to offer an account of the scape-goating of black crime, especially in relation to drugs, as a reflection of the processes of postmodernization. Social censure of crime is thus portrayed as a violent reflection of social-structural change and the need to maintain a conservative political hegemony.

What is culturally taken for granted as normal is thus an integral part of the violence of censure. The violence to other possible truths inherent in our commonplace representations of violence is the subject of the final two essays of the book. In Chapter 7, Vicki Harbord discusses the recent representations of violence in contemporary films such as those of Tarantino and questions again the 'imitation' thesis so popular within media debates about media violence. Her work presents an important development of recent studies of 'crime stories' in the mass media by arguing that some contemporary film contains a drastically different narrative from that of conventional television crime drama and that this amounts to nothing less than the fictional disappearance of the detective and thus the demise of a mythically successful criminal justice. The loss of the hero reveals our loss of faith in the world's ability to return us to peace. In addition, Harbord's essay, in considering such matters as the role of special effects and product placement, in the context of film theory and psychoanalysis, sheds new light on the relationships between violence, social anxiety, commerce and moral panics in a radicalized modernity, or postmodern world. Violence, *à la* Tarantino and Baudrillard, becomes an aesthetic outside of a formulaic moral context, rather than a situated and meaningful representation; a movement that deeply disconcerts us and adds to the fear quotient already endemic in postmodernization.

So have postmodernist ideas of violence had a bad press too? The book ends with a consideration of the fact that the twentieth century has thrown considerable philosophical doubt over the idea that violence is unequivocally bad, and indeed has sometimes celebrated it as a cathartic or emancipatory form of release, or, in other contexts, has revealed the violence of language itself. Steve Goodman's essay in Chapter 8 reviews the philosophy of violence in the twentieth century and interrogates the conventional, dismissive, reading of Nietzsche as a mere nihilist. Drawing upon the writings of Bauman, Sorel, Fanon, Forgacs, Cotta, Derrida, Baudrillard and Benjamin, Goodman shows nihilism to be a much more complex form than is usually thought, and its appeal to people, or its value, at the end of the century is disturbingly illustrated in a spirited defence of postmodernist philosophy.

The positive role of nihilism in the 1990s may constitute an uncomfortable thought perhaps for what some may find to be an uncomfortable book. However, as all the contributors would agree, we end a violent century with yet more severe violence all around us and with little evidence that it can be attributed to a minority of strange, diseased, people or even that it can readily be described as a behavioural abnormality.

With dis-ease ubiquitous and immorality so tightly in the hands of power, there is no better time to reassess the roots of civility and the ethics of force; or to question the very meanings of violence as a category within the social sciences and humanities.

Chapter 2

On the Violence of Censure

Claire Valiér

In *The Gay Science*, Friedrich Nietzsche writes that 'what we do is never under-stood but always only praised or censured' (1887: 219). This essay asks two ques-tions: firstly, what place do certain blaming practices have in the mechanisms of power operating in modern Western societies? My inquiry will primarily use as its medium an analysis of the 'talk' about sadomasochism (see the exchange between Foucault and Alain Grosrichard in Foucault, 1980b: 221). The other question con-siders how else sadomasochism could operate within a moral problematization of sexuality.

Censure Seeks to Extend the Effective Field of the Norm

The theoretical framework of this essay draws in particular on the formulations of Nietzsche, Sartre, Beauvoir, Sumner and Foucault. I am going to start by discussing several essays from Mary Douglas' 1992 collection *Risk and Blame* in order to elaborate my use of Sumner and of Foucault. Douglas sees the different ways in which 'in all places at all times the universe is moralized and politicized' as func-tional to the organization of societies (1992: 5). She admits that her perspective is close to that of Durkheim, with the response to perceived dangers fulfilling the purpose of shoring up group cohesion. Here blaming practices are important to the making of communities – are an almost necessary part of culture. In seeking intel-ligibility, in asking the question 'what was, or is, the meaning of this practice?', there is a danger of the pragmatic question 'how did, or does, this work?' collaps-ing over into the functionalist question 'what purpose did, or does, this serve?'. It is my argument that the work of Douglas described above has not evaded that trap, and that further it is in the work of Michel Foucault that this is most effectively problematized.

Douglas sees dangers as 'weapons to use in the struggle for ideological dom-ination' (1992: 13). While working from the basis of social conflict rather than 'the public good' or shared values, Sumner (1990c) theorizes censures as 'negative ideological formations'. First of all, this asks the question 'ideology in the interests of whom?'. Sumner identifies the white, male bourgeoisie as the framers of the dominant values and ideas of capitalist societies. Secondly, for Sumner censures are practical, emerging from and having their existence within, historically specific social practices. Finally, censures legitimate and guide interventions directed at the deviant.

Foucault suggests another approach with his ideas about the use of strategies in which knowledge and power are inseparable in disciplinary societies. These strategies are seen as arising from contingencies, unlike Douglas' explanation of how misfortunes are explained, a: 'fixed repertoire of possible causes among which a plausible explanation is chosen, and a fixed repertoire of obligatory actions follow on the choice. Communities tend to be organized on one or another dominant form of explanation' (1992: 5). Sumner (1990c) however sees censures as relatively autonomous, as in no way reducible to a predetermined relationship with social relations such as class conflict. Paul Roberts (1993) theorizes a primary sex/gender censure that is fundamental to the constitution of society. My use of the theory of social censures does not see any censure as primary, or censures as functional to social organization. In Foucault's formulation various strategies are certainly useful to power, but not wholly assimilated by it. Power, according to Foucault, exists in a complex and reciprocal relationship with resistance. This means that some of the mechanisms of resistance become useful to power, in the sense that insubordination is produced through resistance to discipline and simultaneously attracts a more intense application of discipline. Sumner writes that censures are subject to resistance from opposing groups, and as such are unstable. There are of course counter-censures (e.g., 'vanilla' (non-s/m) or 'breeder') and also identifications that seek to subvert the operation of censure itself ('queer' being a recent instance of this).

Finally, the most effective ways in which power works in contemporary Western societies are not those which could be designated by the term 'domination'. Instead of operating primarily by repression, power moulds, shapes, and seeks to render its objects more useful to itself. It is in this sense that the title of this chapter is to be understood.[1] The question asked here is: 'what is the relationship of censure to the norm?'. The abnormal is that at which censure is directed. Difference refers to a measure of the distance between the normal and the abnormal, and is as such a relationship, a space, the construction of which is historically contingent (as illustrated by Foucault's genealogies). The extent to which the norm is able to be held sacred, inviolable, provides the degree to which difference can mark something as alien, bizarre, distant. It is perhaps here that censure finds its activity, and why censure does not exist as a thing-in-itself but must be deployed as a strategic device repeatedly and with a banal monotony. The norm seeks to subsume all within its reach, nothing is to exist in a relation of exteriority with it: this is the action of censure (to extend the effective field of the norm).

And what of my use of Sartre and Beauvoir? I disagree with the approach of Mary Warnock, who sees existentialism as something that is now quite defunct and that should instead be relegated to a chapter in the history of philosophy (Warnock,

1995). For me, existentialism remains a useful way of asking some questions about the self-evidence of certain categories. Warnock's comment that we should no longer view existentialism as 'a means of salvation . . . [nor] as a doctrine of commitment' (1995: xviii) seems important to thinking about what I have set out to do. Philosophy for me should be a mode of problematizing certain assumptions about our current modes of living, not a search for universal truths nor the elimination of conceptual errors from a system that should aim towards being all-explanatory. It should be neither a way of closing off certain questions as having received sufficient answers nor a way of erecting simple rules by which everyone can live (we do not need another Ten Commandments). By its identification of the individual as the source of values in any situation existentialism questions the morality of rules, but does not avoid asking the question 'how can choices made by the individual be justified?'. This is the marking out of the terrain of a problem, not the presence of an error in a philosophical system.

I want to conclude my preliminary comments by saying a little about a problem with interpretation. We might like to understand the hermeneutic move according to an explanation offered by Paul Ricoeur: 'to make one's own what was initially "alien" . . . the aim of all hermeneutics is to struggle against cultural distance and historical alienation. Interpretation brings together, equalises, renders contemporary and similar' (1981: 185). This chapter does not drive towards such equivalence, and most of all does not attempt to provide that in which one's face can be seen. I am not telling bedtime stories for those who find difficulty in sleeping. This is highly significant to my attitude to the forms in which sadomasochism has been censured, and not only to psychoanalysis, which may be seen as a most evident instance.

Just as it would be impossible to discuss psychoanalysis without talking about Sigmund Freud, I think that it will be profitable to start by saying a little about the figures of D. A. F. de Sade.[2] A contrast between two texts that discuss Sade's life and work will introduce the area that this chapter problematizes. Ronald Hayman (1978) interspersed the ideas of Krafft-Ebing and Freud to impose a sexological interpretation on his biographical account of Sade. Following Maurice Heine (1931–5), many commentators have focused on the psychiatric or psychoanalytic character of Sade's *The One Hundred and Twenty Days of Sodom*. Jean Paulhan for example described the work as an 'enormous catalogue of perversions', and Gilbert Lely saw it as a 'medical treatise'. Simone de Beauvoir's 1955 essay 'Must we burn Sade?' took another approach. Beauvoir noted that: 'The memory of Sade has been disfigured by preposterous legends, his very name has buckled under the weight of such words as "sadism" and "sadistic"' (1990: 3). She argued that Sade should not be understood through terms like 'algolagnia', as his eroticism was much more complex. Instead of a medico-psychiatric understanding of Sade, Beauvoir wrote that we must always see the ethical significance of Sade's peculiarities. For Beauvoir, the significance of the Marquis lay in the manner in which he made of his psychophysical destiny an ethical choice. She explained that the way in which he took responsibility for his aberrations and made of his sexuality an ethic was of interest. According to Beauvoir, at a young age Sade found it difficult to reconcile his pleasures and his social existence. He came to subordinate his existence to eroticism because he believed that eroticism was the only way of fulfilling his existence. Beauvoir wrote that for Sade virtue was tied to the world of appearances, and as such it was swallowing up the authenticity of existence. Virtue led to inertia, so crime became a duty. Beauvoir therefore sums up Sade's ethic as follows: 'In a criminal society one must be a criminal' (1990: 58). She wrote that Sade faced the problem of difference and also of membership of the community, which is a problem for all.

The tension between Hayman's approach and that of Beauvoir frames this chapter. I will firstly explore how sadomasochism has been censured in a variety of discourses, and my account here will owe much to Foucault's ideas in *The History of Sexuality, Volume One*. We can think here for example of the 'four great strategic unities' that Foucault identified in the deployment of sexuality. I will then make some gestures in the direction of an alternative ethical understanding of sadomasochism. This second area of concern is haunted by the following two questions: firstly, if the Superman is an ethical ideal how will we recognize him, and secondly, how will he recognize himself?

A Genealogical Excursus

Let us start by asking the question 'what mediums has sadomasochistic fiction taken, and what effects has this had?'. Until the second half of the nineteenth century there were three major mediums: tales of religious flagellations of various kinds, stories of the chastisement of children, and brothel tales. Other more minor mediums included accounts of torture and judicial punishment, and a few medical treatises. Let us commence with the presentation of sadomasochism in stories of religious flagellation. Jean Louis DeLolme's (1783) *The History of the Flagellants* presented itself as commentary on Boileau's *History of the Flagellants* (1701). DeLolme framed his work as an account of the self-discipline practised by Christians to conquer their lustful appetites. However, he also discussed flagellation before Christian times, including the *flagratores* of Roman times who allowed themselves to be whipped for money. DeLolme noted that the word *flagrum* signified both the whip and lustful passion, as these were both derived from the verb *flagrare* (to burn). He condemned naked whipping, particularly emphasizing the dangerous temptations that would arise from seeing one's own body.

Later a certain suspicion arose that ascetic practices claiming to extinguish lust were actually the expression of perverse vices. Ivan Bloch wrote in 1908, 'In a certain sense, the history of religion can be regarded as the history of a peculiar mode of manifestation of the human sexual impulse' (1908: 97).

Our next medium for depictions of sadomasochism is one that was particularly popular in nineteenth-century England. Ashbee's *Index* (1877) listed many tales and stories of domestic discipline, correction and chastisement. These stories often had salacious titles such as 'The cabinet of fancy' by Timothy Tickle-Pitcher and 'Venus school mistress' by Miss R. Birch, or a licentious frontispiece, such as that of 'Lady Termagant Flaybum going to give her stepson a taste of her dessert after dinner'. There were also many flagellation poems, for example 'The Rodiad' by George Coleman the Younger. Bertram (1868) stated that the majority of this poem was too impolite to reproduce. These writings presented whipping as pedagogic. Several of them took the form of a sort of *bildungsroman*, for example Capel Loft's autobiographical account of his whipping at school titled *Self-formation; or, the History of an Individual Mind* (1837). However, this was almost a bawdy sort of joke about just what they were teaching (a taste for the rod).

This material also later became the object of concern for sexology. In Albert Moll's *The Sexual Life of the Child* (1912), in a section titled 'The child as an object of sexual practices', there was a discussion of the flagellation of children to sate perverse lusts. Moll presented a lengthy discussion of 'educational advertisements' in the newspapers. He identified as suspicious advertisements for instruction bearing such catchwords as 'energetic', 'severe', and 'English instruction'. This interest in correctional chastisement was later to take the form of books arguing for the prohibition of corporal punishment in schools.

Our third category of writings depicting sadomasochism is brothel tales. Most of the 'brothel discipline' was coded in the form of the chastisement of (adult) naughty boys, for example the card addressed to 'gentlemen flagellants' inserted in the *Sublime of Flagellation* (Ashbee, 1877: 258–9).

So, until the late nineteenth century the talk about sadomasochism did not censure it in the ways to which we are now accustomed. However, this talk did exist in a relationship with power. Firstly, there was censure through humour and ridicule. Where this took the form of direct repression it was largely directed at immoderation. Secondly, there was also through the practice of sadomasochism in asceticism its codification into a set of relationships between sex and the subject, discussed by Foucault in the three volumes of *The History of Sexuality*. Sadomasochism here would take the form of a specific kind of work that would lead to the hermeneutic understanding of the self, and later take the form of a constant injunction to tell the truth about one's desires.

The Ruse of Enlightenment

Ridicule has been directed at corporal punishment as a stimulant of 'sexual emotion' in children for over two hundred years. However, there was not the suspicion that such practices were in some way linked to psychological problems. From Krafft-Ebing's *Psychopathia Sexualis*, first published in 1886, this accusation entered psychiatric and criminological discourse. Blaming practices seek to attribute some social problem or dysfunction to an individual or group. As such they are often interested in cause, and over the mid-nineteenth century what has been called the medicalization of deviance became interested in the aetiology of sadomasochism. What caused this aberrant condition, and how could it be cured and prevented? First of all I want to address the way in which the presentation of sadomasochism was codified in nineteenth-century medical jurisprudence and sexology. This was much more than a mere change in rhetoric, as a whole catalogue of sexual practices took on a new significance and was opened up to a wide range of corrective measures. The main bibliographies in which tales of sadomasochism were listed are 'Pisanus Fraxi's' (the pseudonym for Henry Spencer Ashbee) *Index, Catena*, and *Centuria*. These late nineteenth-century bibliographies of erotic works were presented as guides for he who would study the sexual aberrations in a scientific manner. Ashbee wrote: 'As little, it is my belief, will my book excite the passions of my readers, as would the naked body of a woman, extended on the dissecting table, produce concupiscence in the minds of the students assembled to witness an operation performed upon her' (1877: lxx). In his Introduction to the *Index*, Fraxi framed the task on which he had embarked, and in doing so he made use of the Rev. R. A. Willmott's *Pleasures of Literature*:

> Books, of which the principles are diseased or deformed, must be kept on the shelf of the scholar, as the man of science preserves monsters in glasses. They belong to the study of the mind's morbid anatomy. But they ought to be accurately labelled. . . . We may admire the brilliant spots and eyes of the viper, if we acknowledge its venom and call it a reptile. (Ashbee, 1877: xxvii)

The title 'Index' was one that was frequently used by the Roman Catholic Church from the time of the fifth century to list publications that should not be read by the faithful. This was undoubtedly satirical, as Ashbee was overtly anti-clerical, seeing in his *Centuria Librorum Absconditorum* the opposition of the church to scientific progress as one of the abuses of an ignorant and bigoted priesthood. Ivan Bloch similarly presented his *The Sexual Life of Our Time and its Relations to Modern Civilization* (1908), his 'complete encyclopaedia of the sexual sciences', as scientific enlightenment for the 'earnest' about research into the 'problems of sex'.[3] Ashbee discussed the difficulties involved in producing a bibliography of improper books, for example authorship was likely to be anonymous, writing under a pseudonym was common (which Ashbee himself did), the publisher would affix a false date, and a misleading title would be used (Ashbee's subtitle identified his subject as 'curious and uncommon books'). The circumscription of these tales within a whole range of rhetorical conventions should certainly lead us, with Foucault, to ridicule those who would insist upon the simple pervasiveness of a 'repressive hypothesis', and similarly the promise of freedom through sexual enlightenment should arouse our suspicions.

Nineteenth-century medical jurisprudence and alienism had already begun the codification of sexual aberrations within the discourses of medicine. This was to reach its zenith with sexology and psychoanalysis. Foucault's *Herculine Barbin* (1980a) presented the memoir and documents relating to the case of a nineteenth-century

French hermaphrodite for whom the doctors and lawyers set out to establish a 'true sex'. The decision to require this individual to change civil status from female to male was in large part based on information in the medical report of Dr Goujon, who noted Barbin's inclinations and habits (Barbin's sexual attraction was to women).[4]

Some theorists presented sadomasochism as a congenital condition. In his medico-legal work *Psychopathia Sexualis*, first published in 1886, Krafft-Ebing considered sadism and masochism to be congenital – manifestations of a hereditary psychopathic constitution. As a contrast, in *The Sexual Life of Our Time and its Relations to Modern Civilization*, published in 1908, Ivan Bloch saw the importance of Sade's *The One Hundred and Twenty Days of Sodom* as the refutation of the 'fable of modern degeneration'.

So, the codification of writing on sadomasochism by its presentation through mediums such as brothel tales, religious flagellation stories, and stories of correctional chastisement was replaced by another form from the late nineteenth century. The earnest monotony of this codification can be illustrated by the qualification that began to be carried by books from this time, for example: 'The sale of this book is restricted to members of the Medical and Legal Professions, Scientists, Anthropologists, Psychologists, Sociologists, Criminologists, and Social Workers' (Scott, 1938). This particular expression of concern regarding access framed a book that argued against corporal punishment as being the cause of 'unhealthy sexual excitation' in the child. Scott presented a similarly forceful argument:

> Every sexologist knows that the number of cases of individuals who have experienced sexual feelings while being whipped is a considerable one, and in nearly every instance where the anomaly has persisted in adult life the victim is able to trace the beginning of his perverse interest in flagellation to a flogging received at school or elsewhere. (Scott, 1938: xx)

The quest for causes has also manifested itself in empirical research. Christopher Gosselin presented a survey of 141 male masochists who were members of an SM club. This tabulated the sources from which they believed their masochistic inclinations to have arisen (see Gosselin, 1987: Table 10.2).

Dis-ease: Compulsion and Escape

Anthony Storr sums up for us an image of the sadomasochist as a victim of a terrible compulsion that is a common feature of the writings on sadomasochism from the late nineteenth century. The purpose of this was clearly the demarcation of sadomasochism as a malady that could be the object of medical intervention:

> Sadomasochistic fantasies are unwillingly entertained by a variety of highly respectable people who would never act upon them and are sometimes

deeply distressed by them. A compulsive interest in flagellation or bond-age is often felt as a horrifying preoccupation by sensitive people and may drive them to seek psychiatric help. (Storr, 1991: 92)

Richard von Krafft-Ebing had written anyway that those people such as 'uranians' (homosexuals) who did not seek medical help to be cured were just ignorant of the pathology of their condition. The strategy here is to deny the intensity of pleasures and instead to designate certain sexual practices as an obsession to which the individual only submits under duress. More recent psychiatric writing also makes an effort to identify sadomasochism as an unwanted compulsion. The American Psychiatric Association's latest *Diagnostic and Statistical Manual* (1994) describes the diagnostic criteria of sexual masochism as follows: 'The fantasies, sexual urges, or behaviors cause clinically significant distress or impairment in social, occupa-tional, or other important areas of functioning' (American Psychiatric Association, 1994: 593). So what is this 'distress' and 'impairment'? Well, we are told that 'Some individuals are bothered by their masochistic fantasies', and that these un-pleasant fantasies are usually rape fantasies. Finally we are given a relatively lengthy discussion of a 'particularly dangerous' practice, 'hypoxyphilia', or sexual arousal by means of oxygen deprivation (the danger appears to be referring to the possib-ility of accidental deaths). The concluding sentence tells us that some practitioners increase the severity of their acts 'over time or during periods of stress' which may eventually lead to injury and death.

1994 saw a media fascination with two deaths as a result of erotic strangula-tion in England. John Major remarked with regard to Stephen Milligan, 'What does seem probable is that he must have been pretty unhappy, pretty miserable'. Fellow MP Emma Nicholson, a close friend, said, 'I am terribly sad he should have been so lonely without any of us realising it' (*Daily Star*, 10 February 1994: 7; *The Sun*, 9 February 1994: 4). James Rusbridger, who committed suicide during sexual strangulation while wearing fetish clothing and surrounded by bondage pictures, was characterized as a 'lonely and unhappy man' (*Guardian*, 23 March 1994: 4). The media coverage of the Milligan and Rusbridger deaths depicted sadomaso-chism as a compulsion.

Sadomasochism has also been censured within psychoanalytic writings. With the increasing primacy of the Oedipus complex in Freud's works, psychoanalytic theory came to reveal masochism as a defence against castration anxiety. An oedi-pal drama to be subjected to rigorous analysis: 'It is surprising how often people who seek analytic treatment for hysteria or an obsessional neurosis confess to having indulged in the phantasy: "A child is being beaten"' (see Deleuze, 1991 on Freud's psychoanalytic theorizations of masochism).

More normative strains of post-Freudian psychoanalysis read masochism as, in varying forms, an expression of a deep sense of suffering in the unconscious. Wilhelm Reich (1933) theorized masochism as a defence against oedipal anxieties – the masochist as hurt during childhood, as a victim of aggression. Similarly, Berliner (1958) drew attention to parental cruelty in the psychogenesis of maso-chism, with masochism as a defensive response to a disturbance of object relations resulting from the love of a person who gives ill treatment. Finally, Edmund Bergler (1961) stated the position of masochism as suffering categorically. He claimed that masochism was the basis of all neurosis, and that it was the manifestation of self-aggression, a form of self-destruction. Allen's (1962) *Textbook of Psychosexual Disorders* presented a much-simplified Kleinian version of sadomasochism, which originated in infantile aggression, and especially that directed towards the breast of the mother.

The lament that life is suffering led some theorists to construct masochism as an escape. Karen Horney (1937) theorized masochism as a defensive strategy against fears of intrinsic weakness and insignificance, in which not guilt but a Dionysian oblivion is primary: 'abandoning oneself to excessive suffering may serve as an opiate against pain' (Horney, 1937: 265). Robert Baumeister (1991) constructed masochism, alcoholism, and spirituality as forms of self-forgetting. Masochism here is a narcotic against the burden of the modern self via an escape from identity into the body. Masochism as a panacea against a 'culturally constructed constraint' is not to be recommended though:

> Sexual masochism, despite its somewhat unsavoury reputation and deliberate bizarreness, appears to be neither helpful nor harmful. Most people who engage in it don't end up injured or sick. Nor does it make them better people. It simply provides an effective escape that is treasured by a certain minority. (Baumeister, 1991: 17)

The medical discourse on sadomasochism, as Sumner's (1990c) formulation of the sociology of censures would suggest, accuses rather than explains. It presents masochism as an enigma to be investigated and we should be as interested in this construction of a riddle as we have been in Freud's question: 'What does a woman want?'.[5] How can it be that a person could choose to be a masochist – could actually enjoy such suffering? This is not a question, it is an accusation. A journalist describes his experiences of watching edited highlights of the video on which the Spanner men recorded their practices: 'I find it impossible not to be repulsed by the bloody scenes that flicker before me' (*Guardian Weekend*, 28 November 1992). Perhaps we could hear from Sacher-Masoch's *Venus In Furs*, in which Severin declares to his mistress: 'I want your power over me to become law; then my life will rest in your hands and I shall have no protection whatsoever against you' (von Sacher-Masoch, 1991: 195). Such slavish devotion, absolute submission, and surrender to the law of the mistress that is merciless tyranny involves an exorbitant deprivation of liberty. Severin signs a contract, as did Sacher-Masoch, that hands himself over totally to the possession of his mistress. This contract includes her right to dispose of him as she wishes, including killing him if she so desires. Such an ultimately anti-egalitarian eros, although taking a different form, is also common to Sade. A rejection of such delight in submission is the starting point of numerous readings. The other strategy is to accept the enjoyment, but see it as the sign of something deeper, and quite terrible.

Claire Valiér

Critical Over-determination I: Anti-fascism

In writing about all manner of things from degeneracy to nationalism it is all too easy to fall into a negative teleology that culminates with the atrocities of National Socialism. Sadomasochism has been no exception. Adorno and Horkheimer claimed that Sade was in a way a prophet of fascist domination. Similarly, six months after the Allies' liberation of Buchenwald, Dachau, and Ravensbruck, Raymond Quenau asserted that Sade's imaginary universe was a 'hallucinatory precursor' of the tortures of the concentration and extermination camps ('Lectures pour un front', in Quenau, 1965: 216). An example may be instructive here. A slippage to violence, to self-harm, to the extravagances of fascist persecution: Ian Brady, 'Moors murderer', owned a collection of books that included bondage, fetish, and flagellation pornography, books about Sade, and about Nazi Germany including *Mein Kampf*. A passage from Sade justifying murder was read out at the trial of 1966, and it was claimed that the defendants wished to imitate Sade.

Despite a recent fashion for total indictment of radical feminism, it is still possible to respect the importance of its contributions to the women's movement. Radical feminism restored pride to women, and its problematic creation of a universal category of women was in its practical effects important to the mobilization of a collectivity of women. Additionally, as the slogan went, we should acknowledge that it did much to personalize the political, extending feminist critique and action to new domains. As such I do not locate my observations here within a general rejection of radical feminism that is today seen perhaps too frequently. However, several aspects of radical feminism's politicization of sexuality must be criticized, in particular its quest to identify domination in sexual behaviour in wholly inappropriate areas. The challenge that I am making here is to say: 'choose carefully what you seek to denounce', and 'think of what you are doing when you judge'.

Sheila Jeffreys (1994) presents a passionate denunciation of sadomasochism as 'the erotic cult of fascism' from a radical feminist perspective. Jeffreys elides together sadomasochism and fascism by claiming that sadomasochism was on the increase in pre-Nazi Germany, that lesbian sadomasochists have worn swastikas in public, that Hitler was a sadist . . . Jeffreys juxtaposes a description of a sadomasochistic practice with an account of the torture and murder of a gay concentration camp prisoner from Heinz Heger's *The Men with the Pink Triangles* (1980), thus claiming that sadomasochistic practices emerge from oppression and torture.

In *Male Fantasies* (1987), Klaus Theweleit presented an analysis of the novels and memoirs of the *Freikorps*, armed counter-revolutionaries in 1920s Germany. He focused on the attractiveness of the 'white terror' that he saw as overlooked by the Frankfurt School. Denying any connection between sadomasochism and fascism, Theweleit also employed the passage from Heger to illustrate his case. He considered that maintenance of the self was more important than that of specific object relations, and suggested abandoning use of the term 'sadism' in the context of fascism.

Theweleit rejected the Frankfurt School's analysis of adherence to fascism as linked to an oedipal internalization of authority.[6] Instead he stressed the pre-oedipal, with violence emanating from a fear of the feminine, a fear of dissolution of the self and a desire to maintain an armoured, self-contained body. Turner and Carter (1986) pointed out that Theweleit's analysis was not to be restricted to a demonization of the *Freikorps*, as the forms of proto-fascism he identified represented historically specific but reproducible formations of masculinity. If masculinity becomes associated with aggression, violence, and sadism, then it is unsurprising (if analytically disappointing) that relations between the sexes have been read as sadomasochistic.

Critical Over-determination 2: Feminism

Feminist criticism has had a tortured relationship with the connection between sexual relations and sadomasochism.[7] Perhaps if I tell you a story it will set the scene a little for us. Milan Kundera published a short story called *The Hitchhiking Game* in 1991. In this game, a girlfriend pretends to be a hitchhiker, her boyfriend picks her up, humiliates her verbally in the car and in a restaurant and takes her to a hotel room. He orders her to strip, commands her to climb upon a table and move about, uses obscene language, drags her to bed, and refuses to kiss her during intercourse:

> Hatred cleansed his sensuality of any sentimental coating. . . . Now he longed only to treat her as a whore. . . . She called him by his first name, but he immediately yelled at her that she had no right to address him so intimately. And so eventually in confusion and on the verge of tears, she obeyed . . .

The girl's response is ambivalent. She is reluctant to obey, and the boy's commands elicit tears, but:

> She knew that she had crossed the forbidden boundary, but she proceeded across it without objections and as a full participant – only somewhere, far off in a corner of her consciousness, did she feel horror at the thought that she had never known such pleasure, never so much pleasure as at this moment – beyond that boundary. (Kundera, 1991: 23–4)

The question of concern to feminism has largely been whether sadomasochism is an expression of male domination over women. In the terms of our story above, the questions would probably be: 'is this story just the product of the (male) pornographic imagination?', 'is this sadomasochism or sexual abuse?'.

Firstly, there is the question of whether women actually engage in and enjoy sadomasochism or not.[8] Bartky writes that '. . . standard heterosexual desire in women has often a masochistic dimension' (1990: 47). This assertion had been strongly denied by Caplan (1985), who described women's masochism as a myth – the myth that women seek out pain as a satisfaction of their innate masochism.

The sadomasochism of Kundera's *The Hitchhiking Game* could be written off as male fantasy alone, wrongly constructing an idealized image of the masochistic woman. However, female masochism in fiction written by a woman is less easily dismissed. Anaïs Nin's collection of erotica, *Delta of Venus* (1969), constructed a desire for submission to male brutality as normative of the 'Pandora's box of female sexuality'. In her introduction to the collection, Nin explained this enjoyment of masochism as a result of the identity of sex, emotion, and love in the 'feminine point of view'. This account was echoed in Robin Norwood's best-seller *Women Who Love Too Much* (1986), and is also propagated by the plethora of women's magazine advice pages. *Delta of Venus* typically presents scenes which commence with non-consensual sexual advances by the male, an attraction which the woman is unable to resist, and as the scene unfolds rapturously submits to. The collection also, highly contentiously, includes rape fantasies, as does Nancy Friday's *My Secret Garden*, and Madonna's *Sex*.

In 'Pauline Réage's' *L'Histoire d' O* (1954), written by Dominique Aury, O is trained as a slave at Chateau Roissy. She then leaves, and has masochistic relationships with her lover René and with Sir Stephen. Benjamin (1983) referred to the evasions in readings of *The Story of O* where masochism was interpreted as victimization:

> Such a viewpoint cannot, of course, explain what satisfaction is sought and found in submission, what psychological motivations lead to oppression, humiliation, or subservience. Instead it seeks to deny *the unpleasant fact* that people really do consent to relationships of domination, and that fantasies of domination play a vigorous part in the mental lives of those who do not actually do so. (1983: 297, my italics)

The publication of the novel under a pseudonym led critics to speculate on the likely sex of the author. Antony Storr (1991) and Maria Marcus (1978) considered that the story was a product of male fantasy. In *Sexual Politics* (1969), after denouncing the sadism of Mailer and Miller, Kate Millett read *The Story of O* as an extreme statement of the normative masochism of Freudian femininity that legitimated domination of women on the grounds that they enjoyed it.

How else could this text be positioned within feminist discourse? Amalia Ziv (1994) reads *The Story of O* as a critique of sexual relations. She experiences the text as a drama that exposes the hidden assumptions of patriarchal ideology and compels the reader to confront them. Ziv considers that masochism is a reaction to the social construction of femininity, enacting the tension between identification with, and frustration with objectification by, patriarchal culture. Denunciation is then necessary for Ziv:

This, of course, is not to say that we should advocate masochism as a form of resistance, but that works like *Story of O* should not be regarded as complicit in the patriarchal construction of womanhood since, mixed in with the poison, they already contain a dose of antidote. (1994: 68)

Women in Sade have received considerable critical attention. In *A Taste For Pain*, Maria Marcus pointed out that Justine was not a masochist, but was 'stupid' because she relied on virtue. Indeed the complete title of Sade's novel is *Justine, or the Misfortunes of Virtue*. However, in *The Sadeian Woman*, Angela Carter wrote that Justine was '. . . the heroine of a black, inverted fairy-tale and its subject is the misfortunes of unfreedom' (1979: 39). Justine became the model for a self-piteous female masochism, and Carter created a Marilyn/Justine figure. Despite describing the passage from Sade where Justine plays 'cut-the-cord' – in which the libertine who is victimizing her indulges in erotic strangulation from which only Justine can release him, which she duly does, Carter insisted on her lack of agency: '. . . if any of the Sadeian victims seem to incite their masters to their violence by tacitly accepting their right to administer it, let us not make too much of this apparent complicity. There is no defence at all against absolute tyranny' (1979: 139). As Carter associated 'tyranny' with masculinity and 'martyrdom' with femininity, she read Juliette as a dehumanized 'monster', and constructed the modern female executive as her inheritance.

Sexologists and psychoanalysts including Krafft-Ebing and Storr (1991) claimed that women were rarely sadists for their own sexual satisfaction. Less of an omission than an erasure leads Mandy Merck (1993) to inquire, 'where is sadism in these accounts?' She describes Eugenie of *La Philosophie dans le Boudoir* as the 'top girl' (1993: 256, 259). Other Sadeian female libertines included Delbene, the lesbian abbess of *Juliette* who has 'had' 22 out of 30 of her nuns. Little critical attention has been paid to Wanda in *Venus in Furs*, who comes to relish her sadistic treatment of Severin, and even subjects him against his will to a flogging administered by her new lover. In all the accounts that document sadistic male personalities such as Dostoevsky's Raskolnikov in *Crime and Punishment* and Wilde's Dorian Gray, the cruel libertine Marquise of Choderos Laclos' *Les Liasons Dangereuses* is conspicuous by her absence.

If the taste for pain and yearning for subjection were to be a characteristic of woman, from whence does it emanate? Krafft-Ebing described masochism as a morbid degeneration of feminine mental qualities, a pathological exaggeration of the female character. Describing childbirth as 'an orgy of masochistic pleasure', Helene Deutsch (1930) considered that as menstruation, defloration, and childbirth were painful, female masochism was a functional necessity for the survival of the species. Marie Bonaparte (1953) also considered that masochism was biologically determined and must be accepted by the female.

The practice of sadomasochism by some lesbians problematizes a simple equation of masculinity with sadism and femininity with masochism. Anthony Giddens (1992) claims that lesbian sadomasochism may be interpreted as the return of the phallus 'in a somewhat obnoxious form' (1992: 143). However, Parveen

Adams (1989) theorized lesbian sadomasochism as deconstructive of gender and the perversion/pathology linkage in psychoanalysis. This was based on her reading of lesbian sadomasochism as choice and mobility of desire. Her framework was still though very much tied to Oedipus, with the centrality of the phallus still rendering 'vanilla' lesbianism a form of perversion.

The Sensuality of Sex Crime

The term 'sadism' was prominent at the murder trial of Neville Heath in 1946. The World Health Organization's latest *International Classification of Diseases* advises that: 'Sexual sadism is sometimes difficult to distinguish from cruelty in sexual situations or anger unrelated to eroticism. Where violence is necessary for erotic arousal, the diagnosis can be clearly established' (World Health Organization, 1992: 220). The American Psychiatric Association's latest *Diagnostic and Statistical Manual* opens its discussion of sexual sadism with the comment that this involves suffering of the *victim*. Sadism is designated here as sometimes practised with a consenting partner, and sometimes with a non-consenting victim. According to the manual, in the case of sadism with non-consenting partners the acts are likely to be repeated until the individual is apprehended, and the severity of the acts usually increases over time. The manual's account concludes as follows: 'When Sexual Sadism is severe, and especially when it is associated with Antisocial Personality Disorder, individuals with Sexual Sadism may seriously injure or kill their victims' (American Psychiatric Association, 1994: 530).

Writing on sex crimes often elides together sadism, serial murder, lust murder and cruelty to animals and children.[9] De River's *The Sexual Criminal* (1956) was one of the books that did this most powerfully, presenting the sadist as a psychopath, and writing that 'The acme of sadism is murder' (1956: 8). De River's book presented itself as 'A Psychoanalytic Study', and did indeed diagnose murderers as sufferers of various complexes, but it is perhaps more noted for its 222 out of 353 pages on sadism and masochism. These presented police photographs of sadistic murderers, photographs of the corpses of the victims that they mutilated, and transcripts of interviews where they described their crimes.

The 'Spanner' prosecutions – part of a criminal investigation costing so far over £3 million – took sadomasochism out of the realm of sexual behaviour and into the realm of offences against the person.[10] The custodial sentences given were in some cases longer than those given to rapists: a zealously interested Obscene Publications Squad, an inordinate application of retribution. The penalties were additionally excessive in context, given that in 1988 a man was fined £100 for 'sadomasochistic assaults on women' at Carlisle Crown Court, and in Dublin a man was jailed for three years after the accidental strangling of another man during consensual sadomasochistic sex (newspaper report in Higgins, 1994: 280–1). In 1993 a local newspaper reported that a Portsmouth magistrate directed the jury to acquit a defendant once his former girlfriend had admitted to consenting to sado-masochistic activities with him in which he had inserted sewing needles into her ⌐nipples, which were then clipped with clothes pegs during bondage sessions (*The News*, Portsmouth, 6 January 1993: 40–1). In a consultation paper inspired by the Spanner convictions, *Consent and Offences Against the Person* (1994), the Law Commission elicits comments on the idea of a change in the law to enable sado-masochistic sex to be indulged in, but only up to the level of transient and trifling, non-serious injury. The Law Commission might like to listen to one response made at the Countdown On Spanner Conference, 1994: 'I get off on extreme pain. It's fine for you sitting there and saying we'll draw the limit here if it's just above you, but it's way below me'.

So, we can see that most of the talk about sadomasochism to date has sought to censure it in a variety of ways. None of us live easily with the norm. We might pause briefly here to consider how Sartre saw evil as a projection. In an attempt to eliminate anxiety, 'right-thinking' man relates his impulses to reject (which are the normal exercise of his freedom) to an external cause, the will of the Other. Evil is 'the Goodman's' own freedom, an enemy he must quell: 'Right-thinking people have developed the myth of Evil by depriving human freedom of its positive power and reducing it to its negativity alone' (Sartre, 1988: 27). The case of Genet provides an example here:

> In the case of those who condemn Genet most severely, I would say that homosexuality is their constant and constantly rejected temptation, the object of their innermost hatred, and that they are glad to hate it in another person because they thus have an opportunity to look away from themselves. And I do not mean, to be sure, that this constantly rejected homosexuality seems to them an inclination of their nature. Quite the contrary, it is diffuse, it is a shifty something about persons and things, it is a certain disturbing appearance of the world that might very well open up suddenly and become dizzying, it is an inner uneasiness, it is the dim and constant consciousness that there is no recourse within themselves against themselves. (Sartre, 1988: 29–30)

Sartre provided another example of this idea in *Being and Nothingness*, when he discussed the state of bad faith of the 'champion of sincerity' who wants his friend who engages in homosexual acts to admit that he is 'a homosexual', to identify himself as 'a paederast':

> Who can not see how offensive to the Other and how reassuring for me is a statement such as, 'he's just a paederast,' which removes a disturbing freedom from a trait and which aims at henceforth constituting all the acts of the Other as consequences following strictly from his essence. (Sartre, 1995: 64)

In *Being and Nothingness* Sartre discussed sadism and masochism as part of his thinking about the dynamic and reciprocal relations between the Self and the Other.

These relations are analogous to a Hegelian master/slave dialectic, as relations with the Other are characterized by conflict. For example, masochism for Sartre was an attempt to make myself be fascinated by my objectivity-for-others, by my self-as-object, which fails because objectivity eludes the masochist. The influence of psychoanalytic theories of object relations is evident here. Similarly in *The Second Sex* Beauvoir questioned the assumption that women are by nature masochists and instead wrote that women are more liable to be tempted towards masochism than men because of their positioning as passive object within the sphere of (hetero) sexuality. She saw women's passivity as a performance that creates conflicts in the woman but can be transcended because the woman can attain her own (and different) pleasure and in so doing uphold her own subjectivity. For Beauvoir masochism was not the expression of normal and mature feminine eroticism, and here she slid into censure:

> The fact could not be better expressed that masochism belongs among the juvenile perversions, that it is no true solution of the conflict created by woman's sexual destiny, but a mode of escaping from it by wallowing in it. (1988: 421)

Because she saw reciprocity as the goal of a mature feminine eroticism, what Beauvoir saw as the polarized relations of sadism and masochism became subsumed into her overall theorization of relations between the sexes. Her understanding of lesbianism followed a similar trajectory of thought, as she saw homosexuality as 'for woman a mode of flight from her situation or a way of accepting it . . . one attempt among others to reconcile her autonomy with the passivity of her flesh' (1988: 426–7). She saw the lesbian as first of all a woman having to live in a society in which women are positioned primarily as objects and men as subjects. This form of explanation may or may not be useful to an understanding of how female heterosexuality arises and of the forms that it can take, but the assumption that it can just be mapped onto the lesbian, the sadist, or the masochist, is highly problematic. Questions that initially arise here are: 'to what extent do sexual games act out psychic conflicts?'; 'to what extent does the alterity of other modes of sexual pleasure render their explanation along the lines of what can be seen as a norm applicable?'. Beauvoir concluded that 'homosexuality is no more a perversion deliberately indulged in than it is a curse of fate. It is an attitude chosen in a certain situation – that is, at once motivated and freely adopted' (1988: 444). We may like to follow the sexual radicals and co-opt the term 'perversion' to designate homosexuality and sadomasochism or we may not. We may additionally see both homosexuality and sadomasochism as pleasures deliberately indulged in. We may finally see both as freely adopted and not in any way as coping strategies – which the accounts of Beauvoir and Sartre do seem to suggest. We can look elsewhere if we want to have some insight into the relationships between forms of sexual alterity and the vertigo of freedom. Certainly we can agree with Beauvoir that the significance of such practices lies in precisely how they are expressed in actual living. We can think about how the various problematizations of modes of sexual conduct have produced the individual as a sexual subject – of 'the games of truth and error through which being is historically constituted as experience; that is, as something that can and must be thought' (Foucault, 1987: 6–7) – and of what relations there can be between sexual practices and modes of conduct. Sadomasochism is something that can prompt us to think about what kind of values we can recognize as useful without following a merely negative agenda. I am now going to suggest a different sort of relationship between sadomasochism and ethics.

An Ethics without a Domination

Firstly an omission must be noted: nowhere in the rash of articles on sadomasochistic practices that were inspired by the Spanner case is the practice of sadomasochism as an art of the mind considered. It appears that this possibility is not to be admitted. An unpublished essay by Mick Carter (1994) presents sadomasochism as a form of meditation. He draws comparisons between the techniques of the two arts and refers to 'the calmness and lack of aggression of members of both groups'. This tranquillity is equally applicable to both dominant and submissive practitioners. Mark Thompson's collection *Leatherfolk* (1991) includes several articles that explore sadomasochistic practices as the key to mystical experience.

The discovery of the Villa of Mysteries of 79 AD Pompeii earlier this century provides an insight into a possible historical antecedent for such experiences, and it has certainly been seen in this light by the contributors of several articles to the magazine *Skin Two*. Hall (1988) presented a commentary on Linda Fierz-David's (1988) manuscript which described the fresco depiction of women's initiation rites into the cult of Dionysos in the Villa of Mysteries. In the frescoes, ten scenes presented 'a complete set of images that expresses the complicated path of the psyche as it moves through the tortuous process of coming to know itself' (Hall, 1988). In scene seven, an angel raises a whip to strike the initiate, and the priestess appears to move the initiate's robe to expose her back for the blows. In the next scene, the woman is transformed into a Bacchante. The whipping has produced transcendence. It is here that we should be careful to make it clear that this does not of necessity involve a eulogy. Dionysos was a god of ecstasy, but also a god of terrors.

Sadomasochism has also been seen as the key to a new political spirituality. I am going to use Foucault's ideas about the possibility of a history of ethics that would not be a history of moral codes, interdictions and prescriptions. The final chapter of Mitchell Dean's book *Critical and Effective Histories* (1994) can be recommended for its discussion of how we might understand Foucault's political engagement in the last two volumes of *The History of Sexuality*. I am going to quote from this at length:

> In what ways could it prove amenable to the contemporary ethical situation? Above all, perhaps, it offers us the means and the possibility to

undertake a comparison of the contemporary search for liberation. Thus the analytic of ethical practices provides a kind of serial history of different ways in which it has been possible for humans to constitute themselves as ethical subjects. This serial history provides several dimensions for comparison: of the four aspects of the analytic of ethical practice, of the relation between moral codes and practices of the self, and the different formulae for the problematisation of sexual behaviour in the relation between acts, pleasure, and desire. It is thus a resource that allows one to 'think otherwise' about questions of ethics and morality, of the self, and of liberation. (Dean, 1994: 200)

Miguel Morey's article 'On Michel Foucault's philosophical style' (1992) addresses the relationship between 'telling of the present' and 'thinking differently' as an activity that could work against the normality of the present. This would operate by attempting to avoid the assumption of the normal as the criterion of the real, and also by undoing the primacy of the normal as an *a priori* and a given within the present. How might thinking about sadomasochism be useful here? In *Truth and Eros* (1991) John Rajchman describes the ethic of a 'concern for oneself' in the late Foucault. In this rethinking of eros, contemporary sex liberation movements were to have an important place. Rajchman writes:

In particular we should see S/M in this light: not as an intrinsic 'deviancy' rooted in infancy, of which the neurotic would dream in horror, but as a precise experimental game people choose to play in order to discover new 'virtualities' and augment the singularity and intensities of their pleasures. (1991: 97)

This new 'political spirituality' would involve a 'questioning through which people might start to depart from the historical limits of their identifications, taking their particularities as so many historical specificities' (Rajchman, 1991: 108). The significance of the alterity of sadomasochism here is that it offers to contemporary thought the possibilty to think itself differently. What is of importance here is not the banal specification of sexual behaviours, but the moral problematization of sexuality.

Beauvoir's essay 'Must we burn Sade?' addressed various ways in which we could think about Sade outside of a medical paradigm and in terms of an ethic of freedom and action. It is important for us to ask with Sartre the question: 'In what respects can we be said to be free?', but we can also find some dissatisfaction with his belief in a universal human condition (and ask him whether in this respect he has really followed the death of God to its ultimate implications). However, Sartre's demonstration that responsibility is the concomitant of freedom is of much interest. We can take as a starting point the observation that 'We cannot decide a priori what it is that should be done' (Sartre, 1995: 49). We must invent the law for ourselves in each instance, we must choose a morality. Additionally, when we act in doing what we have chosen to do we put forth into the world an ethical ideal:

Of all the actions a man may take in order to create himself as he wills to be, there is not one which is not creative, at the same time, of an image of man such as he believes he ought to be. (1995: 29)

When an action is made the actor is by that action 'a legislator deciding for the whole of mankind' (Sartre, 1995: 30) and as such responsibility is the concomitant of freedom. In each instance there will be no proof or sign, no *a priori* reassurance on which we can rely to guide us, and from thence arises anguish. Unfortunately Sartre's guidance – that we ask ourselves 'what would happen if everyone did as one is doing' (1995: 30–1) is ultimately unsatisfying. He also pointed out that we can judge that a choice is based on an error in some cases because we can judge by saying that the person deceives themselves (*mauvaise foi*, self-deception or bad faith is an error). However, there are three objections here. Firstly, we can ask: 'where is the angst about being legislator here?'; then we can ask, 'is *mauvaise foi* the only source of error?', and finally, 'is "error" the creation of a new morality?'. Our guide as to whether the individual acts in bad faith is to remember that: 'The one thing that counts, is to know whether the invention is made in the name of freedom' (Sartre, 1995: 53). But how do we know for ourselves whether we are acting 'in the name of freedom'? Is resisting the norm a sufficient guarantee? In *Being and Nothingness* Sartre presented several critical reflections on the idea of bad faith. Firstly he explained that bad faith is not to be identified with lying in general, as the liar intentionally withholds a truth which he possesses when he speaks, whereas the man of bad faith dupes himself, he is mistaken himself. This is also not to be given a psychoanalytic explanation by means of the unconscious. Secondly, the opposite of bad faith is not sincerity, in fact Sartre demonstrated that sincerity is itself a phenomenon of bad faith. He argued that the ideal that 'one must be what one is' makes sincerity an impossible demand because one can only play at being something (Sartre gave here the example of the man playing at being a waiter). So far bad faith had largely been characterized negatively. So, what can be said of the characteristics of bad faith? Bad faith involves a decision on the nature of faith – its aim is to pursue a particular way of believing that is in opposition to the tendency of critical thought of good faith:

With bad faith a truth appears, a method of thinking, a type of being which is like that of objects . . . a particular type of evidence appears; *non-persuasive* evidence. Bad faith apprehends evidence but it is resigned in advance to not being fulfilled by this evidence, to not being persuaded and transformed into good faith. . . . It stands forth in the firm resolution *not to demand too much*, to count itself satisfied when it is barely persuaded, to force itself in decisions to adhere to uncertain truths. (Sartre, 1995: 68)

This is why bad faith has been a risk potential in all human consciousness, and why forms of sexual alterity present to thought the opportunity to question itself – a challenge that has been rarely taken up to date.

An important objective of this chapter is to see whether it is possible to think beyond good and evil. Avoiding censure of sadomasochism is probably not the hardest of our tasks, but avoiding apology, domestication and eulogy could be.[11] I do not wish to suggest that sadomasochism is something that could ever be returned within the scope of the law, and within the range of society's norms, unproblematically – if for no other reason than that sadomasochism perceives law with a certain contempt. Additionally, such 'extreme' and 'unique' acts certainly ask us to suspend any idea of the norm. And so we return to Nietzsche's comment with which I started. My question here is: 'is that the best that we can do?'. Surely we can sail with both wind and steam?

Notes

1 Unlike Roberts I do not see censure as a masculinist act. Censure may take a multiplicity of forms, including gossip, ostracism and other practices that are certainly not usually associated with the masculine. Similarly, violence does not always manifest itself in extravagant gestures, but can take insidious, banal and subtle forms.

2 Much less has been said about Leopold von Sacher-Masoch. Robert Eisler's *Man Into Wolf* presents a biography of Sacher-Masoch (1951: 66–71). See also Deleuze (1991).

3 The edition of Bloch's book that I read in Cambridge University Library has a note appended inside the cover, informing the reader that 273 copies of the book were seized and ordered to be destroyed by Mr Curtis Bennett.

4 Among the important works in nineteenth-century medical jurisprudence that discuss hermaphrodites are Beck and Beck (1838) and the tracts by Male and Farr collected in Cooper (1819). See Thomas Laquer's book *Making Sex* (1990) for a discussion of changing attitudes to hermaphrodites, and also Donaghue (1993).

5 'Throughout history people have knocked their heads against the riddle of the nature of feminity' (Freud, 1991: 413).

6 In *The Fear of Freedom* (1942) Erich Fromm used Hitler's *Mein Kampf* to illustrate the 'authoritarian personality', which was characterized by the simultaneous presence of sadism and masochism. According to Fromm, Hitler employed a crude Darwinism to legitimate domination of the weak, and a doctrine of self-denial and self-sacrifice among the masses, who were urged to subordinate their desires to those of the leaders, and to make themselves insignificant. Fromm considered that both sadism and masochism arose from a fear of loneliness and a subsequent desire to overcome this by means of a symbiotic relationship with the group.

7 Two contrasting quotations may be useful here. Linda Williams comments that: '. . . masochism remains a thorny and shameful issue, an unspeakable testament to a certain state of feminist false consciousness in women, or painful proof of the conspiracy which has caused us to pragmatically to enjoy our lot' (1992: 15–16). Sheila Jeffreys raises a rallying cry: 'We can fight back against all the pressures that encourage us to love the boot that will kick us into submission' (1994: 232).

8 For empirical studies that document that women are not rare in the sadomasochistic subculture, see Breslow *et al.* (1985) and Levitt *et al.* (1994).

9   On the sadistic murderer, see Brittain (1970), Bartholomew *et al.* (1975), Power (1976). On sadistic fantasy and behaviour, see MacCulloch *et al.* (1983).

10 The paper 'The Criminalisation of Consensual Sex' by E. Phillips given at the British Criminology Conference held at Loughborough University from 18 to 21 July 1995 analysed the 'Spanner' case.

11 The most recent plea for tolerance comes from Bill Thompson, a libertarian. His *Sado-masochism: Painful Perversion or Pleasurable Play?* (1994) is a popular treatment of the subject that aims to attack state interference in the sphere of sexual morals.

Chapter 3

Psychoanalytic Sociology and the Holocaust

David Craig

Voids

There exists a plethora of academic work on the Holocaust. Historians, theologians, and the literati have all attempted to explain the most horrifying manifestation of the murderous process of modern history, that orgy of technologized killing that occurred in the Third Reich. Yet there remain serious gaps in the literature – there are few, if any, psychoanalytic, sociological or criminological texts on the Holocaust.

Regarding criminology, Rock has commented that it has neglected many of the key components of crime. Instead, 'The sociology of crime may then be represented as an activity which has been punctuated by the continual burial and exhumation of mundane conceptions of law-breaking' (1977: 326). The failure of criminology to address the Holocaust is a criticism that can equally well be levelled at sociology, which has also suffered something of a Holocaust amnesia. Indeed,

> the contributions of professional sociologists to Holocaust studies seem marginal and negligible. Such sociological studies as have been completed so far show beyond reasonable doubt that the *Holocaust has more to say about the state of sociology than sociology in its present shape is able to add to our knowledge of the Holocaust.* (Bauman, 1989: 3)

Psychoanalysts, too, have rarely ventured beyond their consultancy rooms in order to reflect on the human enterprise and the human condition in light of the Holocaust, giving psychoanalysis a 'chilling sense of conceptual unpreparedness' (Erikson, 1964: 208). As Luel and Marcus note: 'A dark cloud hovers over the psychoanalytic enterprise – the Holocaust and its haunting legacy' (1984a: 1). Although there is now a fairly extensive literature on first- and second-generation Holocaust survivors, psychoanalytic reflections on the Holocaust *per se* utilizing psychoanalysis not primarily as a clinical therapeutic tool, but, rather, as a systematized body of knowledge about human behaviour and psychological functioning, generally remain unavailable (Luel and Marcus, 1984a; 1984b).

This chapter attempts to redress the balance, to inject the Holocaust into the consciousness of a social science academia that has largely – in the psychoanalytic sense of the term – 'denied' the Holocaust. Perhaps this denial stems, at least partially, from the fact that 'the horror of the Holocaust lies in a horror of recognition: that the crimes were committed by our *Doppelgangers*, our doubles, and that the monstrosities were committed by Europeans in the name of *Kultur*' (Hanson, 1984: 35). It was among the hypercivilized that the impulsiveness of the pogrom was transformed and systematized into a liquidation, and postwar Western society is still haunted by that seemingly inexplicable question: How did the Holocaust happen? The following exposition will address that central question – the ability of ordinary men and women to become party to the perpetration of the 'final solution'.

Psychoanalytic Sociology

In spite of the close relationship between them, sociology and psychology have developed to an amazing degree independently of each other since they emancipated themselves from their common matrix – philosophy (Alexander, 1937). A partial explanation of this phenomenon can be ascertained from Freud's somewhat imperialistic contention that, 'sociology ... dealing as it does with the nature of people in society, cannot be anything but applied psychology. Strictly speaking there are only two sciences: psychology, pure and applied, and natural science' (1967: 216). This over-exuberance in the climate of optimism which characterized the early years of the psychoanalytic movement in Vienna was undoubtedly wrong – indeed, Freud later wrote about culture as a phenomenon *sui generis* – but it undeniably served to encourage the distantiation of the two disciplines.

Perhaps more important, however, as an explanation of the increasing separation and specialization of the two disciplines (see Wallerstein and Smelser, 1969) lay in the fact that psychoanalysis fundamentally challenged and undercut the dominant sociological emphasis on rational, cognitive and conscious aspects of human behaviour, and, indeed, subverted the emphasis in Western philosophy on the power of reason and rationality, of reflexive and conscious control of the self (e.g., Giddens, 1990, 1991; Thompson, 1990), and on the conscious mind as the source of knowledge and originator of action. Psychoanalytic propositions absolutely displaced the primacy of consciousness, and elucidated that what we knew of our selves (our conscious ego) and our behaviour was marginal at best. The Cartesian *cogito*, whose first truth was 'I think therefore I am', was shattered by the psychoanalytic assertion that the essence of life lies not in consciousness but in the unconscious vicissitudes of desire (Elliott, 1992; Craib, 1989). Perhaps this 'ego displacement' more than any other factor accounts for the marginalization of psychoanalysis within academia, despite its occasional fashionable upswings, such as within feminist theory (e.g., Mitchell, 1975; Rose, 1986; Chodorow, 1989; Brennan, 1992).

It is not surprising then, that many sociologists (see Berger, 1963) and psycho-analysts have taken a *separatist* position, contending that it is impossible to be both a social scientist and a psychoanalyst simultaneously and that these are separate and even contradictory pursuits: the former concerned with social structure, conflict and change, and the latter with the analysis of the internal processes of individuals (Alexander, 1937; Endelman, 1981; Prager and Rustin, 1993). Craib is surely right to assert that 'to be a sociologist is often to engage in, implicitly or explicitly, a more or less immense, more or less maniac denial of the internal world, an attempt to avoid an inner reality' (1989: 196). Thus, 'the separation of sociology and psychology is both correct and false. False because it encourages the specialists to relinquish the attempt to know the totality which even the separation of the two demands; and correct insofar as it registers more intransigently the split that has actually taken place in reality' (Adorno, 1967: 76).

It is the contention of this chapter that a rapprochement between the two disciplines must be effected, because together sociology and psychoanalysis may provide an overarching social science that neither neglects the intra-psychic depths of individuals nor the complexities of interactive processes in society, nor the intricate symbolic processes of culture (Endelman, 1981). Modern social processes interconnect in complex and contradictory ways with unconscious experience, and therefore with the self. As Wallerstein and Smelsner correctly point out, 'human life is simultaneously both psychological and social . . . both types of forces con-tinuously interpenetrate as they impinge upon human behaviour' (1969: 693). Certainly one discipline cannot and must not be reduced to the other, but 'an adequate psychological theory is not possible unless it is, at the same time, social; and an adequate social theory is not possible unless it is, at the same time, psycho-logical' (1969: 694; see also Smelsner, 1967).

The need for a 'complementary articulation' between the disciplines is not just a utopian luxury, but increasingly a scientific necessity as we approach the limits of explanatory power within our customary frameworks (Alexander, 1937). Initial attempts to fuse the two disciplines were undoubtedly characterized by grave methodological errors, with a tendency towards psychoanalysing society (when economic, political or technical facts provide a real and sufficient explanation of sociological questions: Fromm, 1989), or towards constructing an average abstract individual (Alexander, 1937). However, Sumner's assertion (1994) that psycho-analysis has a great deal to offer sociology – to an understanding of social processes and culture – and that pathological tendencies and social structures in modern societies might best be explained by a historically informed social theory with a built-in psychoanalytic dimension, is fundamentally correct. Sociology and psy-choanalysis, although superficially somewhat contrasting, must be viewed as two parallel and complementary attempts to theorize and understand the transition to a modern social order, with the ability to relate social-structural relations to the subjective–objective experience of those relations, and vice-versa. As Marx himself stated: 'History does nothing, it possesses no immense wealth, it fights no battles.

It is *instead the human being, the real living person, who does everything, who owns everything, and who fights all* battles' (quoted in Fromm, 1989: 39, no italics in original). Assertions of Freudian revisionists, such as Weinstein and Platt (1973; 1975), that psychoanalytic propositions are not easily accommodated to sociology or history because psychoanalysis is 'inherently ahistorical' and characterized by 'a radical devaluation of the external world' (1973: 1), reflect a fundamental misunderstanding of Freudian theory, which is at once both individual psychology and social psychology (Marcuse, 1956), and demonstrate a proclivity to view (falsely) psychoanalysis as a monolithic enterprise.

Freud and Social Theory

> In an age when systems theories, rational-choice theory, neo-functionalism and a Foucaultian critique of the sciences of man seem to dominate the field, Freud's peculiar mixture of nineteenth-century mechanistic psycho-biology and a romanticism of unconscious wishes and fantasies seems to be both scientifically discredited and sociologically irrelevant. (Kaye, 1991: 87)

Thus, Freud is often marginalized and more or less exists in sociology today as a figure for ritual dismissal. This is perhaps partially explained by the fact that his work is riddled with paradoxes that offer the basis for numerous (and contradictory) social theories. However, as both celebrators and critics of Freud agree, the dominant social theory articulated across Freud's analytic and social texts is based on the repression of instinctual desires and on the irremediable antagonism between the demands of instinct and the restrictions of civilization. For Freud, it was 'impossible to overlook the extent to which civilisation is built upon a renunciation of instinct, how much it presupposes precisely the non-satisfaction of powerful instincts' (1985: 286–7).

Two ambivalent positions within Freud's work have often been taken as his dominant social theory: a Hobbesian social contract perspective, and a Rousseauian 'noble savage' stance. The 'noble savage' theory, that man is born free but everywhere is in chains, essentially posits that humans are restrained by social organization from free and good expression of their drives, and that this leads to neuroses and psychoses. This position is frequently appropriated by 'radical' theorists (e.g., Marcuse, 1956; Reich, 1970) who emphasize the restrictive and oppressive nature of social institutions, and will be examined in more detail below. However, the majority of Freud's social writings tend towards a Hobbesian position, in which it is contended that the free gratification of man's instinctual impulses (under the rule of the *Nirvana* principle) is wholly incompatible with civilized society, and in which renunciations and delays in satisfaction of instinctual demands (under the rule of the reality principle) are the very prerequisites of cultural and civilizational 'progress'. Society therefore serves to restrict the destructive nature of both *Eros* (life instincts) and, primarily, *Thanatos* (death instincts).

Freud's development of *Thanatos* and the *Nirvana* principle necessarily led to a formulation that men are:

> ... creatures among whose instinctual endowments is to be reckoned a powerful share of aggression. As a result, their neighbour is for them not only a potential helper or sexual object, but also someone who tempts them to satisfy their aggressiveness on him. ... The existence of the inclination to aggression ... is the factor which disturbs our relations with our neighbours and which forces civilisation into such a high expenditure of energy. In consequence of this primary mutual hostility of human beings, civilised society is perpetually threatened with disintegration. ... Civilisation has to use its utmost efforts in order to set limits to man's aggressive instincts and to hold the manifestations of them in check by psychical reaction formations. Hence, therefore, the use of methods intended to incite people into identification with aim-inhibited relationships of love, hence the restriction upon sexual life, and hence the ideal's commandment to love one's neighbour as oneself – a commandment which is really justified by the fact that nothing else runs so strongly counter to the original nature of man. (1985: 302–3)

And yet there exists a fundamental ambivalence in the Freudian conception of the death instincts, because although they may be wholly destructive of civilization, they are also fundamental in its construction and maintenance through the formation of the superego, loosely translated into 'conscience' or morality – the principal vehicle by which the demands of civilization are carried. Moreover, the life instincts are also considered to be destructive of civilization. The sexual instinct tends towards the formation of couples and is therefore inherently subversive of civilization because it renders a third person superfluous or disturbing, preventing the development of a social nexus. Sexual instincts, therefore, also have to be inhibited in their aim, to enable the development of civilization. For Freud, then, the meaning of civilization is the fundamentally ambivalent struggle between *Eros* and *Thanatos* as it works itself out in the human species (Freud, 1985: 251–340).

A particularly astonishing contention was that 'what we call our civilization is largely responsible for our misery, and that we should be much happier if we gave it up and returned to primitive conditions' (Freud, 1985: 274). Yet here too we find an ambivalent position in Freud's conception of the nature of societal repression of instinctual demands, paralleling the Marxian concept of everything being pregnant with its opposite. On the positive side, social life provides regular opportunities for the gratification of instinctual demands, and more importantly, the absence of suffering – the avoidance of unpleasure.[1] But, on the negative side, social life structures the occasions for frustration and deprivation of instinctual needs. It is this fundamental ambivalence in Freud's dominant social theory that differentiates it from a strict Hobbesian position. Kolakowski's (1975) criticisms of

Freud, therefore, derive from a fundamental misunderstanding of Freudian theory, attributing to logical contradiction what Freud asserts to be the ambivalent reality of human nature (cf. Kaye, 1991).

Kolakowski, for example, states that there is 'a contradiction in the attempt to interpret culture simultaneously as a functional extension of instinct and as an antagonist of instinct' (Kolakowski, 1975: 45). By failing to recognize the simultaneous presence of conflicting desires in the human psyche, Kolakowski can only dismiss the contradictory idea of the simultaneous satisfaction of id and superego, of individual desires and cultural demands. Most glaringly, Kolakowski fails to consider the civilizing effects of Eros which for Freud (in contrast to Hobbes) renders humans naturally social *and* asocial. It is love – borne of dependency and desire – which, together with external material necessity, provides the foundation for communal life both by binding together numbers of people with positive feelings of affection and by transforming their equally natural feelings of hostility and fear into a compelling and socially creative sense of guilt – generating fraternal feeling, religion and morality in its wake. Freud may take for granted that patricidal sons are enemies of their father (Freud, 1960), but because of the both-ness of human nature he takes equally for granted that they are also loving and remorseful sons who crave reinstatement of order and control (Kaye, 1991).

Freud's social theory is undoubtedly, therefore, far more subtle than most sociologists allow, and perhaps the greatest point of convergence between Freud and Hobbes is their contention that reason is the servant, not the master, of fear and desire. As Kaye cogently argues, 'Freudian theory has been rendered superfluous by faulty and incomplete sociological interpretations and its central concepts and cultural theory have been emptied of meaning' (Kaye, 1991: 102).

Parsons and the Parsonians

Freud's work certainly drew attention to elements of social behaviour which optimistic, rational, interest-based theories of individual and society could not adequately explain (Prager and Rustin, 1993). However, criticisms of Freudian social theory as biologistic and manifesting a tendency towards a universalism that negates the social and historical specificity of identity (e.g., Rieff, 1964) became prominent amongst North American ego-psychologists, who attempted to displace the primacy of the non-rational unconscious and replace it with the concept of an independent and primary rational ego as the most important component in any understanding of the social order. To my mind this reflected/reflects an obsession to emphasize the optimistic elements of psychoanalysis within the 'healthy' and 'positive' personal growth paradigm prevalent in North American culture, thereby robbing orthodox psychoanalysis of its most apposite insights and, indeed, its revolutionary potential, merely perpetuating at the conceptual level the exaggerated illusions of autonomy and selfhood that mirrored, and still mirror, the optimistic gloss of North American society.

Parsons' (1951, 1952) cybernetic 'theory of action' which is often hailed as a major connecting work of sociological (particularly Durkheimian) and psychoanalytic propositions, is in actuality a demonstration of such 'Freudian revisionism' and illustrates the worst dangers of sociological approaches. Centrally concerned with the problem of social order and the prevention of a Hobbesian 'war of all against all', Parsons emphasizes cognitive aspects of personality development – those more or less conscious social role-learning processes. In short, Parsons posited that people's expectations of what we should be and do are 'internalized' in the ego, and that we act according to such expectations and feel dissatisfied if we fail to meet them. As such, it comes close to a Meadian conception of the growth of the conscious self through the internalization of the 'generalized other', although, unlike Mead (1970), Parsons stresses the primary importance of the family in the socialization process, asserting that parents provide children with clear and differentiated role models based on the *expressive* mother and the *instrumental* father, which he considers to be features of families in all societies (although existing in their purest and most specialized form in North American society). Reversing the Freudian metaphor of a somewhat beleaguered rider (ego) on horse (id), Parsons considers an independent and autonomous ego absolutely central to man's harmonious socialization into the community.

One of Parsons' major divergences from Freud is his claim that all structural elements of the psyche, including the id, are modifiable by cultural influences – which therefore requires the abandonment of the most crucial, structural, features of Freud's theory. Parsons reduces the id to a simple supplier of energy for the personality system, in which the ego directs the personality, the superego integrates the personality into the wider social system, and the ego-ideal integrates the personality into general cultural values (Craib, 1989). This ultimately leads Parsons to an 'oversocialised concept of man' (Wrong, 1961; 1976), emphasizing an effective and simplistic harmony between personality and society and treating internalization as a relatively conflict-free and stabilizing form of socialization (denying the ambivalent nature which Freud attributed to this process). He thereby renounces the central conflict between instincts and culture articulated in Freudian theory that delivers its special appositeness in dealing with the conflictual and troubled nature of life in society. Effectively, Parsons renders any intra-psychic conflict and/or tension between individual and society abnormal and pathological, arguing that any conflict that does occur is due to 'deviant' socializing influences with which every culture must grapple. As such, Parsons' theory condones 'the subordination of the individual into the social system' which is considered to be 'perfect and final' (Bergmann, 1967), and in which 'the human being appears as a rubber manikin which must fit itself into the contours of society' (Mitscherlich *et al.*, 1970: 36).

The utopian optimists

Marcuse and Reich engaged in a social theory which was allied far more closely with Freud's central propositions, more accepting of Freud's conceptions of the identity between ontogeny and phylogeny, of Eros and Thanatos, and of the primacy of unconscious id processes in understanding personality development and contemporary society. However, they also envisaged the possibility of a utopian society in which the conflict between life and death instincts was mitigated. As such they adhered to the 'noble savage' position that can be ascertained in Freud's social theories. Marcuse asserted, for example, that increasing production promises a better life, but 'intensified progress seems to be bound up with intensified unfreedom' (1956: 4). Both saw the development of an 'administered society' as fundamentally subversive of individual autonomy – transforming mind and body into an instrument of alienated labour (a point that will be returned to in more detail in the discussion of Nazism). Marcuse distinguished between 'basic repression', due to the unavoidable constraints of life and the conflict between instinct and civilization, and 'surplus repression' due to the imposition of specific social forms of repression in the interest of continuing domination and asymmetrical relations of power (paralleling Marx's distinction between necessary and surplus labour). In capitalist society, the reality principle appears as a *performance principle*, which requires surplus sexual repression in order to ensure that people will spend most of their time working for capital rather than pleasure, and that such sexual activity as does occur is aimed at reproduction. The performance principle, therefore, perpetuates the monogamic-patriarchal family, the hierarchical division of labour, public control over private existence and so on.

Marcuse argued, then, that Freud generalized the structure of psychological repression from a specific form of the reality principle, based on scarcity, and extended it to all types of social organization – although this does not vitiate the basic truth in Freud's generalization that a repressive organization of instincts *does* underlie all historical forms of the reality principle. As Marcuse stated: 'If he [Freud] justifies the repressive organisation of the instincts by the irreconcilability between the primary pleasure principle and the reality principle, he expresses the historical fact that civilisation has progressed as organised domination' (1956: 34). Both Reich and Marcuse saw liberation in terms of the freeing of the sexual instincts, although Reich saw it in terms of the freeing of genital heterosexuality, and Marcuse saw it in terms of freeing polymorphous perversity, enabling highly civilized human relations in which sexuality would be integrated with work and play, and would enable the final defeat of Thanatos.

However, for Freud, Eros and Thanatos *imply each other, they continuously interpenetrate, and indeed at the most general level are united with the same aim* (Nirvana principle), and therefore the removal of conflict between the instincts formulated particularly in Marcuse's *Eros and Civilisation* seems to run counter to Freud's basic assumptions, and indeed to his general pessimism (Freud, 1985).

The prophets of reality

Although Freud and Jung had fundamentally distinctive conceptions of the human psyche – Jung generally maintaining a far more optimistic approach to the unconscious – both wrote prophetically in the 1930s of the impending disaster that was to confront mankind in Nazi Germany.

Jung stated that: 'we can no longer deny that the dark stirrings of the unconscious are effective powers – that psychic forces exist which cannot, for the present at least, be fitted in with our rational world order' (1933: 233–4; see further discussion in Sumner, 1994). Freud more ominously stated:

> The fateful question for the human species seems to me whether and to what extent their cultural development . . . will succeed in mastering the disturbance of their communal life by the human instinct of aggression and self-destruction. . . . Men have gained control over the forces of nature to such an extent that with their help they would have no difficulty in exterminating one another to the last man. They know this, and hence comes a large part of the current unrest, their unhappiness, and their mood of anxiety. And now it is to be expected that the other of the two 'Heavenly Powers', eternal Eros, will make an effort to assert himself in the struggle with his equally immortal adversary. But who can foresee with what success and with what result? (1985: 339–40)

Dialectics

Freud elucidated the fact that the development of every civilization and all culture, based as they are on the sublimation of instinctual desire, is infused with both Eros and Thanatos. The dialectical and ambivalent nature of the unconscious, therefore, finds its reflection in the civilization process itself. Like the human psyche, modern society is dialectical – it has both a 'dark' and a 'light' side that continuously interpenetrate – and the very neutrality and ambivalence of reason (so central to Western development) facilitates the ability of society to manifest different shades of light and dark (Adorno and Horkheimer, 1973).

It is my contention here that when the dark side of the human unconscious and the dark side of society (including reason) gain ascendancy over their coexistent light sides, and merge with one another, their inherent potential for destruction may be actualized. To argue that the Holocaust demonstrated the manifestation of dark and diabolical forces that were alien to modern 'democracies' and belonged to the dark ages (e.g., Chiaromonte, 1962), is therefore to misunderstand fundamentally the very nature of all society. A wild man lives within every civilized one, and civilization is infused with barbarism. Equally as inaccurate is the assertion that man is essentially good and simply manipulated by an evil system. The extraordinary destructiveness of the Holocaust is surely better explained by looking towards the dominance of Thanatos. The system was 'evil', yes, but a barbaric man was also able to surface from his imprisonment in the unconscious – cajoled and directed by the energies of Thanatos.

The Holocaust, undoubtedly and fundamentally, challenged the unbridled faith in science as an unmixed good and the assumption of an inherently positive relation between reason and freedom (the light side of modernity). Furthermore, it demonstrated that the empowering agencies of modernity had turned in on themselves, changing from means of freedom into means of domination and submission. The Holocaust, more than any event this century, uprooted the association of the passage of time with the triumph of virtue and progress, and the optimistic belief in a necessary human inclination towards freedom and good. It is precisely this challenge to the belief in the light side of the Enlightenment that calls the theory and practice of psychoanalysis into the picture. The poison within us (Camus) and within our civilization requires a thorough rethinking of modern life. Psychoanalytic sociology can function as a tool enabling the exploration of the deepest sources of human motivation and the gleaning of hermeneutic insights previously beyond our field of vision.

However, it must be realized that working within the disciplinary boundaries of psychoanalytic sociology means that any 'truth claims' that this chapter asserts are inevitably limited. It does not, therefore, attempt to provide a definitive, overarching theoretical and substantive explanation of the Holocaust, nor a universal theory of fascism and genocide, but rather seeks to present an explanation of the Holocaust from the view of psychoanalytic sociology. As such it entertains the questions of why the German people were attracted to Nazism and how they were able to perpetrate genocide – focusing predominantly on the psychic mechanisms and processes involved, and exploring how these mechanisms emerged and how they were implicated in the Holocaust. Adorno is surely right to point to the fact that we do not even have the discourse to deal with the Holocaust (no poetry after Auschwitz), an assertion reiterated by Derrida:

> Of course silence on Auschwitz will never be justified, but neither will the fact that people speak of it in such an instrumental way and to say nothing, to say nothing that is not self-evident, trivial, and that does not serve primarily to give themselves a good conscience, in order not to be the last to accuse, to take positions or to show off. (in Kaplan, 1994: 6)

It is with such thoughts in mind that I enter, with some trepidation, an arena that presents more questions than it offers answers – the Holocaust.

Towards an Understanding of Nazi Genocide

On Fascism

In any discussion which attempts to explicate the rise of National Socialism in Germany, a distinction must be made between latent structural conditions which created an underlying potential for Nazism, and the immediate conditions which actualized that potential. As such this enables the construction of a simple heuristic that the latter may be associated with specific economic, social, cultural and political factors that precipitated fascism,[2] whereas the former may be associated with underlying psychical predispositions to Nazism and the latent potential within modernity to flip onto its 'dark side'. Central to such a division is Fromm's assertion (1941: 180) that 'Nazism is a psychological problem, but the psychological factors themselves have to be understood as being moulded by socio-economic factors; Nazism is an economic and political problem, but the hold it has over a whole people has to be understood on psychological grounds'. National Socialism had a mass basis; it secured not only the frightened submission but also the active cooperation of the great majority of the population (positive and negative power), a feat that it accomplished in part by appealing to the population's most primitive and irrational wishes and fears (Adorno *et al.*, 1950).

The Frankfurt School assumed the task of identifying tendencies that linked liberal capitalism with its totalitarian abolition, and perceived the roots of fascism in capitalist socio-economic crises that were given a totalitarian solution in order to protect the relations of production and to secure the continued domination of the ruling classes: institutions in bourgeois affirmative culture such as the family, and repressive socialization processes which created personality types who conformed to, accepted, or actively desired socially imposed domination; and culture and ideologies that defended or transfigured the existing society while mystifying the social relations of domination (cf. Kellner, 1984). However, a detailed examination of the work of the Frankfurt School inevitably leads to the conclusion that these elements were analysed somewhat separately, and there was a failure to properly integrate them at the level of an analysis of structural and precipitant factors of fascism.

Many of the Frankfurt School tended towards a somewhat vulgar Marxist position, contending that Nazism was simply the result of the protection of capital during the transition from private to monopoly/state capitalism (Marcuse, 1968; Horkheimer, 1975, 1982).

> Under a totalitarian form of state capitalism, the state is the power instrument of a new ruling group, which has resulted from the merger of the most powerful vested interests, the top-ranking personnel in industrial and business management, the higher strata of the state bureaucracy and the leading figures of the victorious party's bureaucracy. Everybody who does not belong to this group is a mere object of domination. (Pollock, 1975: 73)

This reflected the pronouncement of the Third International Executive Committee (1933) that 'Fascism is the unconcealed, terroristic dictatorship of the most reactionary, chauvinistic, and imperialistic elements of finance capital' (in Sinclair, 1976: 884). Fascism was therefore seen simply as a political system which propped up capitalist society by totalitarian means.

Such a position, however, must be criticized for its failure to address the middle-class roots of fascism, its somewhat overstated polemic that the whole population was absolutely mystified, and its failure to confront the very real fact that Nazism actually appealed to a great number of people who actively desired such a system – that is, its psychological underpinnings (Reich, 1970). The vulgar Marxist approach completely separated economic existence from social existence as a whole and stated that man's ideology and consciousness are solely and directly determined by his economic existence, thereby ignoring the 'subjective' factor of history.[3] However, more convincing within this approach was the elucidation of links between liberal capitalism and fascism which demonstrated that the fascist state was not a monstrous rupture with the past, but rather that there were continuities between the two systems, and, indeed, that liberal capitalism had already sown the seeds for its own destruction by fascism.

Marcuse argued that the fascist state was the fascist society, and that totalitarian violence and totalitarian reason came from the structure and tendencies of existing liberal society (Marcuse, 1968). He posited that bourgeois affirmative culture prepares the way for its abolition in fascist society by teaching submission and deflecting individuals from demanding material well-being and social change (see Marcuse, 1968: 19, 125).

Bourgeois culture projected the spiritual realm as essential to individual autonomy and health, automatically serving an escapist function, encouraging the individual to transcend the toil and tribulations of the everyday world into the refuge of a higher spiritual realm. Although superficially championing individuality, bourgeois culture prevented the development of critical thinking and collectivities and thereby aided the mystification of social antagonisms and contradictions systematically carried out by cultural education and reflected in the 'naturalistic interpretation of society' and 'liberalist rationalism that ends in irrationalism' (Marcuse, 1956). Bourgeois culture therefore demanded a new type of personality – the great soul, as opposed to the 'Renaissance man' who sought happiness in worldly action and sensual experience (cf. Marcuse, 1956, on the performance principle).

However, Marcuse recognized that there were new elements in Nazi 'heroic-folkish realism' that went beyond the old liberal social order and its mere negation, and in which a clear dialectical reaction against liberalism was perceptible (1956). These were:

1. universalism – which maintains the priority and the primacy of the whole over its 'members', claiming that the whole is an organic unity and the destiny of its members is to serve the whole, to fulfil themselves through participation;

2. naturalism – which idealizes the fascist 'folk community' and fetishises natural properties of folk, blood, soil, homeland, racial purity and the *Führer*. Here class conflict is veiled by the ideology of the nation's destiny and individuals are urged to submit to poverty and to die for their country or their highest duty; and,

3. political existentialism – which supported the ideology of heroic-folkish realism by championing the existential as something beyond the normative and outside the sphere of conventional morality, and allying it with anthropological activism which glorifies action for action's sake – radically devaluing the *logos*. The total politicization of existence in the fascist state defined the existential as political and directed activism into a total mobilization dictated by 'the folk', thereby annihilating individual existence and the force of reason. It submerged in the hidden darkness of 'blood' or 'soil' contradictions that would be recognized in the light of conceptual knowledge.

Thus the fascist state actually abolished the individuality, freedom and subjectivity that were the foundations of existentialist anthropology: existentialism collapsed the moment its political theory was realized. The heroic man, bound to the forces of blood and soil, was the man who travelled through heaven and hell, without reasoning why but went into action to do and die, sacrificing himself not for any purpose but in humble obedience to the dark forces that nourished him (Marcuse, 1968).

However, Kellner (1984) is surely right to assert that Marcuse's critique of fascism lacks a theory of the ideological apparatus and ideological transmission, and the aesthetic dimension of fascism. His thesis is limited to analysing and criticizing written pronouncements of fascist ideologues, and fails to address the way fascism is transmitted through the mass media and a whole cultural ideological apparatus. This is a criticism that cannot so easily be levelled at Adorno, who also sees fascism and its controlled violence as a culmination of enlightenment rationality developing along its 'dark side';[4] civilization as a whole, far from lapsing into barbarism was progressing towards it.

For, Adorno, fascism was a possibility built into the very fabric of modernity, and there existed numerous homologies between fascism and the culture industry (Adorno, 1991). Adorno and Horkheimer posited that the commodification of cultural forms has atrophied the capacity of the individual to think and act in critical and autonomous ways (1979; see also Adorno, 1991).

> What people read, see and hear is familiar and banal, and into this symbolic sphere of repetitive familiarity is inserted a string of homespun slogans – 'all foreigners are suspect', 'a pretty girl can do no wrong', 'success is the ultimate aim of life' – which appear as self-evident and eternal truths. (Thompson, 1990: 99–100)

The development of the culture industry, then, is part of a process of increasing rationalization and reification, rendering individuals progressively less capable of independent thinking, and increasingly dependent on social processes over which they have little or no control, thereby facilitating manipulation by dictators and demagogues. Those swept along by the rhetoric of fascism had already been crumpled beneath the footsteps of the culture industry. Human beings had become not the masters, but the servants of their technological, bureaucratic and rationalized society, and their consciousness had been fettered by the products of the culture industry. Adorno argued:

> It may well be the secret of fascist propaganda that it simply takes men for what they are: the true children of today's standardised mass culture, largely robbed of autonomy and spontaneity.... Fascist propaganda has only to reproduce the existent mentality for its own purposes; it need not induce a change. (1991: 129)

The gratifications which fascism offered were, to Adorno, wholly irrational and illusory, because they offered no real pleasure or joy, but only the release of feelings of unhappiness, and contradicted the material interest of the vast majority. Its propaganda, therefore, had to be orientated psychologically, and had to mobilize irrational, unconscious, regressive processes. However, Adorno did not locate the success of Nazism solely within the uncritical 'automaton' (cf. the 'authoritarian personality'). Not only would such an approach overstate the destruction of individuality, critical thinking and the extent to which individuals were integrated into the social order, it would also fail to address the actual psychological appeal of Nazism, explaining it, rather, as if the masses had simply been duped.

Psychoanalysis and Fascism

It is in the critique of the culture industry that the links between the Frankfurt School's analysis of fascism most explicitly joins with their work on the psychological underpinnings of fascism. In particular, it concurs with Fromm's (1941) concept of the automaton personality type who adopts the kind of personality offered to him by cultural patterns, substituting a pseudo-self for his 'real' self. The automaton personality type may believe he is 'he', and that his thoughts, feelings and wishes are his own, but this is an illusion. In reality he simply follows the internal or external pressure of having to want what he is going to do. 'The automatisation of the individual in modern society has increased the helplessness and insecurity of the average individual. Thus, he is ready to submit to new authorities which offer him security and relief from doubt' (Fromm, 1941: 178). The repetitive slogans of modern advertising and propaganda increased the individual's feelings of insignificance and dulled his critical capacities. Thus Fromm argued that one part of the German population bowed to the Nazi regime without admiring or resisting it.

Fromm's *Fear of Freedom* contends that the transition from a feudal to a capitalist order was a dialectical process: on the one hand it increased the potentiality for man to attain positive freedom, but on the other hand it increased his isolation and made him feel helpless and insignificant and thereby increased his potentiality to escape from positive freedom by completely submerging himself in the outside world (negative freedom). Men could

> not go on bearing the burden of 'freedom from'; they must try to escape from freedom altogether unless they can progress from negative to positive freedom. The principal social avenues of escape in our time are submission to a leader, as has happened in Fascist countries, and compulsive conforming. . . . [I]n our effort to escape from aloneness and powerlessness we are ready to get rid of our individual self either by submission to new forms of authority, or by a compulsive conforming to accepted patterns. (Fromm, 1941: 116)

Jung (1958), also keenly aware of the dialectical nature of modernization, argued that man had become the slave and victim of machines, was intimidated and endangered by the might of the war technique, and 'his spiritual and moral freedom . . . is threatened with chaotic disorientation. . . . All his achievements and possessions do not make him bigger; on the contrary, they diminish him' (1958: 41–2). Jung posited that one of the chief factors responsible for psychological mass-mindedness was scientific rationalism, which robbed the individual of his foundations and his dignity and made him 'a mere abstract number in the bureau of statistics' (1958: 16). The individual, overwhelmed by the sense of his own impotence, was already on the road to state slavery, and without knowing it, had become its proselyte. Individual judgment grew increasingly uncertain of itself and responsibility was therefore collectivized as much as possible. It was just that banding together and the resultant extinction of the individual personality that made it succumb so readily to a dictator. 'A million zeroes joined together do not, unfortunately, add up to one' (Jung, 1958: 55).

The Authoritarian Personality

For Fromm (as for Adorno *et al.*, 1950), the character type that was central to the emergence of National Socialism in Germany was the sadomasochistic authoritarian, particularly prevalent among the lower middle class.[5] The sadomasochistic character admires authority and tends to submit to it, but at the same time he wants to be an authority himself and have others submit to him. The middle-class admiration of and subservience to authority, and at the same time their need for their own authority is excellently exposed by Bettelheim's description of the inability of non-political middle-class prisoners to withstand the initial shock of the concentration camp:

> They could not understand why they, who had always obeyed the law without question, were being persecuted. . . . Their only objection was that

they had become objects of a persecution which must be just, since the authorities imposed it. . . . Their self esteem had rested on a status and respect that came with their positions, depended on their jobs, on being head of a family . . . (1986a: 120–1)

Fromm provides an excellent socio-historical critique of the pervasiveness of sado-masochistic character types in the German lower middle class, singling out Protestantism and capitalism as crucial in producing fearful, alienated individuals who sought cures for problems in Nazism. In particular, Protestantism prepared individuals to submit themselves readily to extra-human ends, and 'once man was ready to become nothing but the means for the glory of a God who represented neither justice nor love, he was sufficiently prepared to accept the role of a servant to the economic machine – and eventually a *Führer*' (Fromm, 1941: 96). With the transition from market to monopoly capitalism, the crisis of international trade, and the Wall Street Crash of 1929, it was the middle classes who felt most threatened by unemployment or slipping into the ranks of the proletariat ('social declassing' – Kuhnl, 1975) and who were seized with feelings of individual insignificance and powerlessness. The authoritarian personality sought to gain security in a symbiotic relationship provided by Nazism – masochistically submitting to a greater whole and a higher power, and sadistically dominating those lower in the hierarchy.

However, Fromm's psychoanalytic exposition on the roots of the sadomasochistic character in the Oedipal complex and the bourgeois family is covered far more comprehensively by Adorno *et al.* (1950). Indeed, the links between bourgeois and fascist society that the Frankfurt School addressed reaches its psychoanalytic sociological peak in the discussions on the authoritarian structure of the bourgeois family – the 'germ cell' of bourgeois culture (Horkheimer, 1982) – which produced the sadomasochistic personality type so crucial to the rise of Nazism.

The studies of the authoritarian personality (Adorno *et al.*, 1950; Ackerman and Jahoda, 1950; Bettelheim and Janowitz, 1950) revealed that the production of the sadomasochistic character and the resultant presence of extreme ethnic prejudice in such individuals, tended to be related to a complex network of attitudes within, and relating to, the (predominantly bourgeois) family (Frenkel-Brunswik, 1950a). Authoritarian subjects reported a relatively harsh and threatening type of home discipline which was experienced as arbitrary by the child, and family relationships 'characterized by fearful subservience to the demands of the parents and by an early suppression of impulses not acceptable to them' (Frenkel-Brunswik, 1950b: 257). Such families were also characterized by a high degree of status-anxiety, reflected in the adoption of a rigid and externalized set of values which were outside the child's scope of understanding, but none-the-less rigorously imposed on him. Conduct not in conformity with the behaviour/facade required by the parents had to be rendered ego alien and 'split-off' from the rest of the personality, with a resultant loss of integration.

For Adorno *et al.* (1950) the child's relationship to his parents is an ambivalent one, for at the same time as he is dependent on them and wishes to be taken care of by them, he also resents them and is hostile towards them. As a reaction against this hostility, the child often rigidly glorifies and idealizes his parents, and only this admiration is admitted and ego-accepted; the resentment and hostility is rendered ego-alien and externalized, thus rendering the ego narrow and constricted. Thus the authoritarian personality manifests a fundamental break between the unconscious and conscious layers of the personality – unwilling to become aware of the unacceptable tendencies and impulses in himself. However, their early repression hinders their mastery and the authoritarian individual is constantly threatened with being completely overwhelmed by them, especially because of his weak ego. A great deal of energy is therefore devoted to constructing rigid defences against these instinctual tendencies and to keeping them out of consciousness. Most important among these is the mechanism of projection by which much of what cannot be accepted as part of one's own ego (i.e., Thanatos) is externalized. Thus it is not oneself but others who are seen as hostile and threatening (also see Wangh, 1963). The sharp ingroup-outgroup dichotomy provided by Western culture made it possible for the authoritarian character to suppress his hostility against prestige figures, on whom he is dependent, by displacing it onto weak outgroups from whom no retaliation need be feared and whom he may feel superior to. If permitted to do so by outside authority, the same person may very easily be induced to an uncontrolled release of his instinctual tendencies, especially those of destructiveness.

Nazism provided the opportunity for submission both to a higher authority (masochistic) and to the domination and projection of hostile unconscious tendencies onto outgroups (sadistic). However, Fromm (1941) and Adorno *et al.* (1950) identified other character types that were also important to Nazism and, particularly, to the perpetration of genocide – the 'destructive' and 'manipulative' characters. Adorno (1950) posited that the manipulative type comes close to the Freudian concept of the 'anal' character and in this regard is reminiscent of the authoritarian syndrome. But he is differentiated from the latter by the simultaneity of an extreme narcissism and a certain emptiness and shallowness. The manipulative type divides the world into empty, schematic, administrative fields and treats everything and everyone as an object to be handled and manipulated, seized by the subject's own theoretical and practical patterns, with an emphasis on doing things. Many fascist, political, anti-Semites in Germany showed this syndrome: Himmler may be symbolic of them.

> Their organizational way of looking at things predisposes them to totalitarian solutions. Their goal is the construction of gas chambers rather than the pogrom. They do not even have to hate the Jews; they 'cope' with them by administrative measures without any personal contacts with the victims. Anti-semitism is reified, an export article: it must 'function'. (Adorno, 1950: 370)

The 'Jewish question' was to be solved entirely legally and the ingroup–outgroup relationship became the principle according to which the whole world was abstractly organized.

Fromm (1941) argued that, like the authoritarian character and the automaton, the destructive type was rooted in the unbearableness of individual powerlessness and isolation, but this character attempted to escape his powerlessness by destroying the outside world, rationalized as duty, love, patriotism etc. Again, Fromm linked destructiveness to repression and the blockage of spontaneity and growth, such that energy was directed towards destruction – '*destructiveness is the outcome of unlived life*' (Fromm, 1941: 158, italics in original).

The Mass Appeal of Fascism

It is this concept of psychical repression which forms the basis to Reich's *Mass Psychology of Fascism* (1970). Reich's sex-economic position asserts that fascist mysticism is orgastic yearning, restricted by mystic distortion and the inhibition of natural sexuality – the result of social conditions which man has himself created. Reich argued that ' "*fascism*" *is the basic emotional attitude of the suppressed man of our authoritarian machine civilization and its mechanistic-mystical conception of life. It is the mechanistic-mystical character of modern man that produces fascist parties, and not vice-versa*' (Reich, 1970: xiii, italics in original). Reich chastised sociologists for failing to recognize the importance of the irrational appeal of fascism and for perceiving it simply as an imperialistic interest or a 'prejudice'. Reich argued, rather, that race ideology, for example, is the pure biopathic expression of the character structure of the orgastically impotent man.

Like Marcuse, Reich argues that it was not until the establishment of authoritarian patriarchy that suppression of sexuality began – because it was at this stage that sexual interests began to enter the service of a minority's interest in material profit, and was given a solid organizational form in the patriarchal marriage and family (cf. Marcuse, 1956). Reich posited that the moral inhibition of the child's natural sexuality makes the child afraid, shy, fearful of authority, obedient, 'good' and docile in the authoritarian sense of those words.

> In short, morality's aim is to produce acquiescent subjects who, despite distress and humiliation, are adjusted to the authoritarian order [also see Foucault, 1961; 1980b]. Thus, the family is the authoritarian state in miniature, to which the child must learn to adapt himself. . . . *Man's authoritarian structure is basically produced by the embedding of sexual inhibitions and fear in the living substance of sexual impulses.* (Reich, 1970: 30, italics in original)

And this results in reactionary thinking. The notions of homeland and nation are notions of mother and family and are rooted in the child's fixated tie to the mother due to sexual suppression; among the middle classes the mother is the homeland of the child, just as the family is the nation in miniature (cf. Chasseguet-Smirgel, 1990).

When sexuality is repressed it seeks various substitute gratifications; natural aggression, say, is distorted into brutal sadism. Militarism is based on libidinous mechanisms (the soldier in uniform as sexually arousing – see also Theweleit, 1987, 1989). Thus sexual inhibition changes the very structure of the sexually and economically suppressed man, such that he acts, feels and thinks contrary to his own material interests. Thus Reich argues that fascism is organized mysticism (which derives its most active energy and, in part, its content from the suppression of sexuality), able to prey on the nation's fears and to create personality types who surrender to authority. He therefore interprets the *Führer* cult, swastika, goose-step, mass-mobilizations, race theory, sadism, militarism and imperialist adventures as substitute sexual gratifications which fascism provides for a repressed and anxious nation. The basic elements of Nazi ideology, then, are of a sex-economic nature.

Essential to the success of fascism, Reich argued, was the identification of the individual with the leader (also see Federn, 1990). The more helpless the 'mass-individual' had become, the more pronounced was his identification with the *Führer*, and the more his childish need for protection was disguised in the form of feeling at one with the *Führer*. This inclination to identify is the psychological basis of national narcissism, that is, of the self-confidence that individual man derives from the 'greatness of the nation'. The reactionary lower-middle-class man perceives himself in the *Führer*, in the authoritarian state. On the basis of this identification he feels himself to be the defender of the national heritage, of the nation, which does not prevent him from simultaneously despising the masses and confronting them as an individual. The wretchedness of his material and sexual situation is so overshadowed by the exalting idea of belonging to a master race and having a brilliant *Führer* that he ceases to realize how completely he has sunk to a position of insignificant, blind, allegiance. As such, Reich and Adorno come very close to espousing the same argument; Adorno (1994) also stressed the libidinal character of the link between the individual and the masses in fascism and fascist propaganda. Adorno outlined the concept of the fascist leader as the 'great little man', remaining enough like his followers to appeal to those elements of narcissism which remain attached to the follower's own ego, and his power and charisma functioning for the follower as a narcissistic projection of his own ego-ideal – a projection with which he then identifies.

The White Terror

Theweleit criticized the Frankfurt School for their lack of attention to the 'attraction of fascism itself' (although as has been demonstrated above, this criticism is somewhat overstated), an attraction which he understood as the passionate celebration of violence originating in the fear and hatred of the feminine, a fear of dissolution and decomposition of the self, and a consequent desire to maintain an armoured self-contained body. Allying himself with the work of Deleuze and Guattari (1983,

1988) on desiring-production, Theweleit (1987, 1989) argues that the Frankfurt School had no category for the desiring production of the unconscious, focusing on ideologies while omitting any discussion on the feelings of rejecting pleasure and the prohibition against using one's own body in a manner consistent with sexual needs and potential. What was central to any understanding of fascism for Deleuze and Guattari was that people 'actually want humiliation and slavery not only for others but for themselves' (1983: 29). They argue that Reich is at his profoundest when he refuses to accept mystification on the part of the masses as an explanation of Nazism, and demands an explanation that will take desires into account. But, they argued, Reich failed to provide a satisfactory account because he created a distinction between rationality as it ought to be in the process of social production, and the irrational element in desire, and regarded only the latter as a suitable subject for psychoanalytic investigation. He therefore 'gives up trying to discover the *common denominator or coextension of the social field and desire*. . . . There was a category that Reich was sorely in need of: that of desiring-production, which would apply to the real in both its so-called rational and irrational forms' (Deleuze and Guattari, 1983: 30). Deleuze and Guattari themselves claim that '*social production is purely and simply desiring production itself under determinate conditions. . . . There is only the desire and the social, and nothing else*' (1983: 29, italics in original).

In his study on the ideology of the *Freikorps*, Theweleit deals with fascism as a specifically masculine imaginary of violence, and found in the *Freikorps*' representations of real or imagined acts of violence against women many variations on the same imaginary: women as a threat to the male subject. An 'unnatural', devouring sexuality is ascribed to them; they are dirty, unruly, enraged, sluts or whores, sources of defilement, flowing and flooding which must be stopped and laid to rest; men must bind together in camaraderie to maintain their integrity, to police the boundaries of their own erect, column-like bodies against the threat constituted by the female body and its disorderliness, its uncontainable, engulfing flows. Theweleit emphasizes the distinctively sexual nature of these violent fantasies and specifically their links with masculine anxieties (fear of engulfment, of castration) and hence with patriarchal power, arguing that sexual anxieties are about regulating bodily boundaries and controlling or eliminating dirt (see Forgacs, 1994).

Theweleit argues that fascism places sexuality in the service of destruction, such that fascism is fundamentally anti-Eros and 'the core of all fascist propaganda is a battle against everything that constitutes enjoyment and pleasure' (Theweleit, 1989: 7). For the male, it is the woman within that constitutes the most radical threat to his own integrity, and the desire of the male ego is to be freed from all that can be identified with the female body: with liquidity, with warmth, and with a sensuality that is responsive to other human beings. These 'steel-hard' men 'struggle against the mass and femininity as a struggle to contain the soldier-male's fear of the desiring production of his own unconscious' (Theweleit, 1989: 6); their most urgent task being 'to pursue, to dam in and to subdue any force that threatens to transform him back into the horribly disorganized jumble of flesh, hair, skin, bones, intestines, and feelings that calls itself human' (Theweleit, 1989: 160). The warrior utopia of a mechanized body is therefore erected against the female self within, a process effected through a variety of mental and physical procedures: military drill, countenance, training operations which Foucault (1977a) identified as techniques of the self; 'the new man is a man whose physique has been machinized, his psyche eliminated' (Theweleit, 1989: 162).

Theweleit's thesis has obvious links with Sumner's (1990b) work on the gendered nature of social censure. Sumner argues that not just fascism, but the rise of capitalism and the mechanisms of disciplinary power are both concomitant with a negation and censure of women and femininity, and reflect an assertion of men and a military masculinity. Sumner quotes la Mesnardiere who in the eighteenth century posited that 'most men are censured . . . for having degenerated in contracting the softness, the habits, and the inclinations of women' (cited in Foucault, 1961: 170), demonstrating that a general notion of what masculinity men should display and the importance of the rejection of what was defined as femininity, was prevalent in Europe and reflected in state structures and institutions over 150 years before the emergence of the *Freikorps*. More importantly, however, Sumner recognized that since the fifteenth century, and intimately bound up with Enlightenment itself, the suppression of the unconscious was not solely a suppression of passion, but also of *what was supposedly feminine*. Thus, 'the definition and suppression of the feminine, and of unacceptable masculinities, is part of the historic censure of unreason which is itself . . . intimately connected with the rise of capitalism and the formation of disciplinary power' (Sumner, 1990b: 37).

Such censure is of course potently demonstrated in Nazi propaganda and Nazi art (see Amatrudo *infra*), which celebrates the rigid, steel, phallic Aryan who disavows any notion of femininity, and further, and perhaps most obviously, is reflected in the censure of homosexuality in Nazi Germany that ended in extermination. In a passage demonstrating remarkable parallels with Theweleit, Sumner argues that 'in this movement not only was softness, openness, flexibility, litheness, sensitivity, emotionality, warmth and passivity identified as feminine and censured, but these characteristics also became associated with their bedfellows in unreason, such as mental illness, black culture and the innocence of the child' (Sumner, 1990b: 34). Passion and its association with femininity and the 'dark' unconscious was considered subversive and threatening to the social order – it threatened hegemonic masculinity with flooding.

Thus, as Theweleit (1989) demonstrates in a more psychoanalytically rigid fashion, the *Freikorpsman* is constantly threatened with dissolution, thereby explaining his compulsion to violence in the external world as a reaction to the anxiety of the interior one. Only in the explosion of war can redemption from control and constraint be risked: war is a kind of rebirth, the apocalyptic moment of battle when the man longs for the moment when his body armour will explode. War allows him to achieve identity with his alien, primitive, bestial interior while at the same time avoiding being devoured by it.

Only war promises to animate the dead within him. War is rebirth, resurrection of the mass of his dead desires. And when those desires break out, they give the world their own form of life – which is death. . . . For every desire that had been put to death, a Jew, or a nigger, a nip, a communist, a woman, a child was made to die. (Theweleit, 1989: 25)

The anxiety over bodily contact so central to Theweleit's argument is of course paralleled by Reich's position on the sexual nature of fascism, and on Nazi race-ideology:

The creed of the 'soul' and its 'purity' is the creed of asexuality, of 'sexual purity'. Basically, it is a symptom of the sexual repression and sexual shyness brought about by a patriarchal authoritarian society . . . the core of the fascist race theory is a mortal fear of natural sexuality and its organism function. (Reich, 1970: 84, italics in original)

For Reich, more than anything else, it is the fear of sexual freedom, conceived as sexual chaos and sexual dissipation, in the mind of the reactionary fascist thinker which has a retarding effect on the yearning to be free of the yoke of economic exploitation.

However, despite the undoubted appeal of Theweleit's thesis, it must be subject to a number of criticisms. Historically, the *Freikorps* as a 'protofascist' group existent in the 1920s, was not directly linked with the NSDAP (Nazi party) and the militarism and right-wing radicalism of the *Freikorps* did not always lead to Nazism. Moreover, although locating the key to fascism in pre-oedipal desires (unlike the Frankfurt School), drawing heavily on the work of Klein and Mahler (an ego-psychologist, and therefore fundamentally antithetical to the whole discourse of desiring-production!), Theweleit fails to identify what distinguishes the childhood experiences of *Freikorpsmen* from other men (Benjamin and Rabinbach, 1989). Moreover, anti-semitism plays a relatively minor role in the *Freikorps* literature compared to fear and hatred of women, and this raises the question whether exclusive focus on the anti-feminine psyche diminishes the significance of anti-Semitism. Ehrenreich, in her foreword to Theweleit, 1987, outlines the problem that, if fascism was deeply male and misogynistic, it does not follow that fascism and misogyny are somehow the same thing: 'the Jewish (and Communist) men who fell victim to it were not substitute women, symbolic whores, or anything of the kind, but real men whose crime was their Jewishness, or their politics. Neither feminism nor antifascsim will be well served by confounding Fascist genocide with the daily injuries inflicted by men on women . . .' (Ehrenreich, 1987: xv). Theweleit (1989) avoids such a confusion, but none-the-less it is not clear where he stands on the relation between fascism and patriarchy, since in some places he recognizes the internal heterogeneity and complexity of fascism, disclaims a totalizing interpretation of it and stressing the exploratory character of his research, while in others he represents fascism as a historical subset of patriarchy, and insists that male – female relations are central to its imagery (Forgacs, 1994).

The problem with adopting a strong version of Theweleit's position is that, while it may work straightforwardly enough to explain fascism's oppression of women and homosexual men, it is harder to make it account in a non-reductive way for fascist oppression of other groups. However, as Forgacs cogently argues, what can be taken productively from Theweleit's work is the idea that oppression of these various groups contained an anxiety over the health of the imagined body and over the maintenance of bodily boundaries, and that this anxiety was an important element of fascism, without needing to make a case for this anxiety being the 'true' cause of all fascist oppression (Forgacs, 1994).

The Holocaust and Modernity

There exists an aetiological myth of Western civilization based on a morally elevating story of humanity emerging from pre-social barbarity. The myth enables an explanation of genocide as a failure of modern civilization to contain the morbid predilections of man's nature, i.e., not enough civilization (Bauman, 1989). Such reasoning is entirely fallacious. It fails to comprehend the ambivalent nature of society.

> Civilisation means slavery, wars, exploitation and death camps. It also means medical hygiene, elevated religious ideas, beautiful art and exquisite music. It is an error to imagine that civilisation and savage cruelty are antithesis. . . . Both creation and destruction are inseparable aspects of what we call civilisation. (Rubenstein, 1978: 92)

It is psychoanalysis that perhaps most clearly elucidates the ambivalent nature of society and of the human psyche, and of the resultant potential for the manifestation of a '*Thanatocracy*'. Marcuse (1956) cogently demonstrated that civilization is only rendered possible by the transformation and utilization of Thanatos. It is the diversion of primary destructiveness from the ego to the outside world that feeds the technological progress so central to the modernization process, and the formation of the superego that achieves the punitive submission of the pleasure ego to the reality principle, thereby assuring the development of civilized morality. When Thanatos is brought under the service of Eros it provides the energy required for the continuous mastery of nature to the advantage of mankind, and assures advances to even richer stages of civilization. But civilization therefore preserves throughout the mark of its deadly component. Indeed, the development of technics (so thoroughly infused with Thanatos) provides the very basis for progress, and technical rationality sets the mental and behavioural pattern for productive performance and power over nature that is almost synonymous with civilization. Indeed, destructiveness seems to be more directly satisfied in civilization than libido. Freud's metapsychology therefore comes face to face with the dialectic of civilization – the very progress of civilization leads to the release of increasingly destructive forces. Thus the process of civilization is heavily imbued with Thanatos, which serves a socially useful purpose when under the domination of Eros. But ultimately, and perhaps inevitably, if Thanatos gains the upper hand then the technological advances of mankind and the development of rationalized bureaucracies will by their very nature aim towards the annihilation of life. One surely cannot deny the correlation between technological advance and destruction.

The slaughter of the Holocaust was no fury of destruction; it is not represented by the traditional anti-Semitic pogrom, but rather by Auschwitz, that somewhat mundane extension of the modern factory system, where 'rather than producing goods, the raw material was human beings and the end-product was death. . . . The chimneys, the very symbol of the modern factory system, poured forth acid smoke produced by burning human flesh' (Feingold, 1983: 399–400). The Nazis applied death in its most alienated form, that of abstract numbers and abstract goals delivered by a technically abstract industrial process. The Nazis were scientistic with a vengeance – engineers of survival and extinction, their work expressed in the 'art form' of a statistical chart – so many 'pieces' per day marked carefully on the destruction 'targets' (Bauman, 1989; Kaplan, 1994). It is not, then, anti-Semitism alone which explains the Holocaust, although, as will be seen later, it undoubtedly facilitated genocide, and we must look to the structural features of society and the psychoanalytic 'make-up' of the perpetrators to further our understanding.

Arendt (1964, 1973), Rubenstein (1978), Sabini and Silver (1980), Hilberg (1985), and Bauman (1989), all locate the Holocaust within the very process of modernity itself; it was 'a legitimate resident in the house of modernity; indeed, one who would not be at home in any other house' (Bauman, 1989: 17); '*we are more likely to understand the Holocaust if we regard it as the expression of some of the most profound tendencies of Western civilization in the twentieth century*' (Rubenstein, 1978: 21, italics in original). For all the above authors, advances in social and political organization, and in particular the development of bureaucracies, made it morally and psychologically possible to realize dreams of destruction that had previously been confined to fantasy. Indeed, it was only when the genocidal project was taken out of the hands of 'hoodlums' and delegated to bureaucrats, that the Holocaust could be effected (Hilberg, 1985). Bureaucracy certainly enabled the viewing of society as a legitimate target for social engineering (cf. Bauman, 1989 – garden metaphors), but more importantly, such authors argued, it allowed the overcoming of an instinct of a disinclination to violence, of animal pity, which would have prevented the perpetration of genocide, by distancing people from the consequences of their actions and absolving them of any moral responsibility (a process facilitated by scientific reasoning). Thus the Nazis took moral agency from their own hands and moral identity from their victims, under the principle of bureaucracy – *sine ira ac studio* ('without scorn or bias'). Bureaucratic mass murder reached its fullest development when gas chambers with a capacity for killing 2 000 people at a time were installed at Auschwitz. As Arendt (1973) observed, the very size of the chambers emphasized the complete depersonalization of the killing process – a machinery devoid of love or hatred.

Certainly, to view the Nazis as pathological monsters would be fundamentally mistaken, and their caricature as faceless, mindless, banal cogs in a bureaucratic machine in which discipline and order substituted for moral conscience is a more apposite insight for any attempted explanation of the Holocaust (Arendt, 1964). Indeed 'the chronicler of this epoch stands almost helpless before the task of relating so much mediocrity and insignificance of character, intelligibly to the extraordinary results' (Fest, 1970: 291). However, the concept that 'a normal human being, at the sight of another's suffering, even at the thought of it ... will at least feel spiritual pain' (Kusnetzov, in Bettelheim, 1986a: 13) is a concept that must be associated with the light side of the human psyche, with Eros. The fundamental error that such authors make (which arises partly because of their failure to theorize the unconscious), when utilizing this concept of pity, is their failure to realize that it was Thanatos that had gained ascendancy in the unconscious, and *an instinct of an inclination to violence was thereby realized, not merely the suppression of pity*. The fusion of Thanatos with the potential for destruction inherent in civilization itself provides a far more coherent and realistic explanation of the Holocaust. However, such authors are right to argue that twentieth-century bureaucratized violence is an expression of contemporary Western civilization and not a rebellion against it. 'No assessment of modern culture can ignore the fact that science and technology – the accepted flower and glory of modernity – climaxed in the factories of death' (Greenberg, in Chalk, 1990: 325).

This is not to assert, however, that some perpetrators had no difficulty in killing. Lifton reports that as many as 20 per cent of the Einsatzgruppen had manifested psychological problems due to their 'work' (although 80 per cent did not), and the prohibition of unauthorized killings induced by desire, the insistence on adhering to the law, and the transition from mobile killing units to gas vans, to gas chambers, undoubtedly served to facilitate the perpetration of the Holocaust, supposedly through a process of psychical distancing. However, Browning (1992) demonstrates that the problems the perpetrators faced were not those of an admonishing conscience, as the above authors would like us to believe, but rather a fear of admitting cowardice and weakness. 'They pleaded not that they were "too good", but rather that they were "too weak" to kill' and thereby 'only reaffirmed the "macho" values of the majority – according to which it was a positive quality to be "tough" enough to kill unarmed, noncombatant men, women and children' (Browning, 1992: 185).

Fantasy and Illusion

Marcuse (1968) drew attention to the heroic-folkish realism that characterized Nazism, and such mythology undoubtedly served to facilitate the perpetration of the Holocaust.

> Official culture was used as a tool of social integration by offering a
> collective ego ideal in the form of anachronistic historical romances and
> a collective antithesis in the form of all those forces and figures that

disrupted the official picture of reality. Thus sociopathic tendencies could be sanctioned in the service of simplifying social reality: extermination could be transformed into chivalric quest, and art, deprived of its own imaginative mission, could be used to infiltrate the collective psyche. (Hanson, 1984: 37–8)

Historical amnesia and the disguise of primal anxieties enabled the tenets of Nazism to be internalized as a social fantasy that blocked introspection and allowed the average citizen to soar to the heights of group heroism. In particular, the discourse of Nazism was full of 'imagined acts of violence which heal and restore order where there has been a perceived state of disease and disorder . . . all manifestations of this imaginary have a displacement in common, through a sort of inversion or negation of the violent act from a hurting to a healing one' (Forgacs, 1994: 5).

In his study on Nazi doctors (1984, 1986, 1988), Lifton demonstrated that killing had become a therapeutic imperative: pointing to the chimneys at Auschwitz, a survivor asked an SS doctor how he could reconcile them with his hippocratic oath; the doctor replied: 'When you find a gangrenous appendage you must remove it' (Lifton, 1984: 14). There was, therefore, a loss of a boundary between healing and killing which removed the barrier between violent imagery and systematic liquidation. The Nazi 'biocracy', ruling in the name of a higher biological principle which it had to effect because civilization had prevented Nature from carrying out Her own natural selection, enabled sadism and bureaucratic killing as a healing process; collective violence became a perverse quest for the vitality and immortality of one's own group – mass murder in the name of more life.

The metaphor of surgery is to be found again and again in Nazi discourse – a discourse aimed at distinctly modern ills for which it claimed to offer efficient cures.

> The body of the state administration is bloated with bureaucracy, infested with parasites and must be cut out. The body of international politics is weakened by bad medicine and requires a blood transfusion. The boils that erupt on the body of modern society can be cauterised by the fascist party. In all these variations of the metaphor, it is assumed that modern society is sick and that appropriate forms of political intervention – by the state, the party, the movement – can make it well. (Forgacs, 1994: 7)

Sores or wounds in the social body, preventing its unity, had to be destroyed to make the body whole again. Nazism, and particularly the violence of Nazism, enabled the hierarchical separation of bodies and the preservation of the purity of the superior race.

The imaginary of this violence worked by displacement and non-recognition, by turning violence into something other than itself. 'Fascism thus presents itself as a modern form of heroism, a righting of a new kind of social and political wrong . . . converging on the notion of Fascist violence as therapy, as designed to make whole the imagined body of society and the state' (Forgacs, 1994: 8–9). The

Nazi genocide was therefore in part a response to 'a collective fear of pollution and defilement. It depends upon an impulse toward purification ... but it brings to that impulse a modern, much more deadly stress on health and hygiene – for the Nazis, racial hygiene' (Lifton, 1988: 481–2).

Chasseguet-Smirgel advances an interesting psychoanalytic explanation of this demand for unity as one body, based on her theory of the archaic matrix of the Oedipus complex – a primary wish of the infant to strip the mother's body of its contents in order to regain possession of the place it once occupied before birth – and to retrieve a mode of mental functioning governed by the pleasure principle. She argues that obstacles making access to and reunification with the mother's body impossible – represented by the father and the father's derivatives (penis, children) – have to be removed. The Nazi biocracy re-enacted this scenario on a world-stage in which the subject's body (the body of the German people) was to become one with the body of the mother (the Homeland, Mother Earth), and all obstacles preventing this union had to be eliminated. 'Ridding oneself of paternal obstacles by emptying the maternal body, fighting against reality and thought, form a single, identical wish: that of returning to a world without organisation, to prime-val chaos, to a universe marked by homogeneity and the continuum present before birth' (Chasseguet-Smirgel, 1990: 168).

Nazism held out the promise of absolute bliss, and insidiously aroused the hope of fusion with the mother and a return to the primary narcissistic state; it therefore possessed the capacity to incite individuals to remove all obstacles on that path. The first obstacle to be removed was the superego, which was replaced by an aspect of the ego-ideal which aims to bring down the barriers between the psychic agencies and abolish them in order to return to that time when the ego and ideal were one, to the time when the infant and mother were merged as one. This regression to the archaic matrix of the Oedipus complex allies itself all too easily, therefore, with destruction. Hitler had argued that it was the Jews who had created conscience and reason, and who were a parasite preventing the formation of the Aryans as a single body pure of all foreign elements – what worse obstacles to the return to the primary narcissistic state could possibly exist? Chasseguet-Smirgel situated her theory in a socio-historical context, positing that historical events in Weimar Germany reduced Germans to a state of profound dereliction, like that of a new-born infant abandoned by its mother, and this, combined with a long cultural tradition in German Romanticism of a longing for fusion with Mother Nature, impelled the German nation to accept the fantasies, illusions and myths that the Nazis constructed, and prepared them for the perpetration of genocide in order to effect those fantasies. As such, Chasseguet-Smirgel's thesis is wholly antithetical to that of Theweleit, who argues that the fascist wants to destroy the mother – to 'fuck the earth' – to rid himself of all those maternal qualities of warmth and sensuality and is therefore representative of a dramatic repudiation of her, rather than an identification with her as primal Nature, typical of Nazism.

Lifton (1988) argued further that part of the cure that Nazism offered was the experience of transcendence – a psychic state so intense that time and death dis-appear. The sense of transcendence merged with an image of immortality bordering on the omnipotent, and in that experience or promise of ecstasy its followers were willing to kill or to sanction killing. Death itself was embraced as a means of cure, in the name of purification, seeking to restore a past of perfect harmony and unity that had never existed. Here at least the individual self was no longer to be haunted by the fear of its own disintegration, or by conflicts over competing alternatives; rather, it became part of monolithic unit, bound together by blood and fate, and every act of mass murder could be connected to a vision of mystical unity (Lifton, 1988).

Thus, as Hanson (1984) recognizes, mythical nationalism and other enabling fantasies empowered by an amoral machinery had lethal effects. The social fantasies of Nazism were swallowed up by the masses. Their need to feel heroic and immortal hastened their entrance into the bloody world of genocide. 'The Nazis were able to tap the fear of freedom, the self-hatred, the anxiety over disorder experienced by the postwar Germans and to devise a liturgy of healing and resurrection that guided the populace out of history and into unconsciousness' (Hanson, 1984: 44). Seduced by the power of myth and fantasy, they remained blind to their needs and fears of self-destruction. A manifestation of the psychic problem, Nazism and genocide posed as its solution.

Aestheticisation and Language

Nazism offered a 'total solution', and was total also in its subjugation of all spheres of life, both public and private. The destruction and outlawing of communist, socialist, democratic, liberal, Jewish, decadent culture and the demand for national-socialist, Aryan, Germanic, heroic art stands testament to this subjugation (Stollman, 1978). Benjamin (1992) pointed out as early as 1936 that the true artistic accomplishments and successes of Nazism were to be found in its political methods – in the 'aestheticisation of political life' – that arena where the relationship between politics and art had become inverted (see Amatrudo *infra* on Nazi art).

The aestheticization of political life in Third Reich became apparent in the permeation of daily life with celebrations, ceremonies, artificially created customs and staged folklore, but soon all public life assumed an aesthetic shape. The window-dressers of Nazism created a public sphere from which all decision-making processes were removed through the *Führer* principle, and of which nothing remained but the mere ghostly but enduring shell, its grandiosely erected facade, created as a total work of art. The Nazis provided a 'beautiful illusion' in the place of reality (Stollman, 1978: 53).

The party conventions, the architecture built to last for the immortal Thousand Year Reich, the rituals and ceremonies, united the German body as one; the principle of beauty was a chief element of the political praxis of National Socialism. The folkish-realism made its appeal at the level of unconscious imagery, where symbols and fantasy replaced (external) reality. 'At this level, the strains of masochistic desire to be dominated, the destructive disease fantasies, and the dreams of aesthetic reintegration could be reached' (Hanson, 1984: 43). Everything political disappeared from the publicly established aesthetic illusion, as did all reflection. The ability for abstraction and aesthetic isolation in this shared fantasy served to protect the Germans not only from a knowledge of who they were but also from an appreciation of what they had become.

The aestheticization of all spheres of life and the ubiquity of fantasy and illusion distanced Nazi Germans from a critical perspective of their actions. The cold, bureaucratic, technocratic language of the Holocaust (cf. Levi, 1988), and its euphemistic nature (final solution, special treatment etc.) also served a distantiation purpose. Abstractions wear no flesh and are easier to kill. Moreover, the concentration camps manufactured sub-humanity, people reduced to their most base instinct of self-preservation (cf. Wiesel, 1981: 112–3), coming close to their portrayal as *Untermenschen*, as vermin, in Nazi propaganda films (e.g., *The Eternal Jew*). They became a strange psycho-physical product indelibly stamped with the words 'Made in Germany'. The transformation from human to non-human (and most often then to *musselman*) was the first and most painful death that the inmates of the concentration camps suffered, and their reduction to pitiful creatures undoubtedly facilitated the perpetration of genocide.

However perhaps the most pertinent explanation of genocide within the context of this discussion comes from Jung, who like Foucault was wholly sceptical of the development of reason and the splitting of reason from unreason, of consciousness from unconsciousness, so central to the project of modernity. Like Eissler (1975), who contends that the development of consciousness constitutes 'the fall of man' – burdening man with a task for which he was utterly unprepared and in which he was bound to fail – Jung argued that the splitting of the conscious from the unconscious, which he describes beautifully in the metaphor of a boundary line bristling with barbed wire running across the psyche of modern man, can lead the unconscious to explode into destructiveness if given an opportunity. 'It is the growth of consciousness which we must thank for the existence of problems' (Jung, 1933: 110). 'His reason has done violence to natural forces which seek their revenge and only await the moment when the partition fails to overcome the conscious life with destruction' (Jung, 1933: 278). The energy flowing off from the unconscious, because it is unused, strengthens the negative traits of the unconscious personality, and the separation inevitably plunges man into a conflict between conscious and unconscious, spirit and nature, knowledge and faith, and becomes pathological the moment his conscious is no longer able to neglect or suppress his instinctual side. However,

> in accordance with the prevailing tendency of consciousness to seek the source of all ills in the outside world, the cry goes up for social and political change which, it is supposed, would automatically solve the much deeper problem of split personality. . . . What then happens is a simple reversal; the underside comes to the top and the shadow takes the place of the light. (Jung, 1958: 81–2)

The evil that surfaces is aided by the incomparably effective means of modern man to destroy, and man is able to realize his proclivity to evil. Reason cannot prevent the emergence of such destruction; only the construction of a bridge across the psychic split can effect any positive outcome.

Psychoanalytic Sociology: Censure and Deviance

Censure

This discussion has focused relatively little on anti-Semitism. However, it was the Jews more than any other group who were considered to be the racial tuberculosis that was destroying the body of the German nation, and it was only the Jews who were singled out for complete annihilation across the whole of Europe at the Wansee conference. The Jews did not merely represent one danger among others, but the totality of evils confronting Aryan civilization, and their eradication was the condition for its future life (Wistrich, 1991). For Hitler, Judaism meant the triumph of anti-nature over nature, of disease over health, of intellect over instinct, and as has been demonstrated earlier, this mystical, biological and naturalistic racism was later used to sanction the eradication of the entire Jewish nation. The hostile tendencies of the German unconscious were projected on to the Jews in particular, such that they became the enemy, scape-goated as hostile and destructive, and against whom aggressiveness and destruction could now be justified as re-action, as self-defence.

Hilberg (1985) has argued that the Holocaust is best described as a tripartite process: definition, exclusion, and annihilation. Each part invoked a cut. The first was a censorious cut of the parasitic, capitalist, communist, and conspiratorial Jew from the good, upstanding, virtuous and pure Aryan. It created the scape-goat. The second cut involved the 'ghettoization' or forced emigration of the censured group, distancing Germans from the 'one good Jew' they all knew. The final cut was surgical and absolute – it removed the boils, the sores, and the infestations destroying the German body.

The first cut created difference. Perpetuated by the eternal need of scientific rationalism and of language itself to classify and to objectify, to centre, to fix and to pigeon-hole, the Jew was forced outside of the sameness of human life; he became different, sub-human. The very process of differentiation thereby intensified the sameness of the inside, that is, the German nation, facilitating the imaginary illusion of the single Aryan body. The scape-goated Jew served, in a Meadian sense, to unify and cement the German population against a common enemy, and he became the target for projected destruction. The Jews were a danger to the social body, and their removal was sanctioned as morally principled and justified, the Forces of Good defeating the Forces of Evil. The enormous Nazi propaganda machine facilitated this one-dimensional construction of the Jew as the devil incarnate. Freud had demonstrated that a group can only live together in an organized unit if they are able to turn their aggressiveness outwards to some external enemy outside the limits of the organized group, and the media/propaganda machine demonstrated its inherent and enormous ability not to reflect reality but rather to project an (unconscious) reality, and the German people now acting in self-defence could justify destructive power without restraint.

Deviance

Psychoanalysis challenged the entire concept of normality and of deviance – those considered socially normal, well-adjusted, successful and respectable could in fact be the most unhealthy psychologically, and vice versa. From the psychoanalytic point of view, there are very dysfunctional forms of conformity and compliance, and very syntonic forms of rebellion. More importantly, however, psychoanalysis brings to the sociology of deviance the insight that society needs to censure, to project unconscious fears, anxieties, wishes and aggressions on to groups that can be labelled as outside society, and by implication that 'deviant behaviour is behaviour that people so label' (Becker, 1963: 9). As Gilman notes: 'everyone creates stereotypes. We cannot function in the world without them. They buffer us against our most urgent fears by extending them, making it possible for us to act as though their source were beyond our control' (1985: 16).

Drawing on object-relations theory, Gilman (1985) and Rustin (1991) assert that the creation of stereotypes is a concomitant of the process by which all human beings become individuals, a differentiation – individuation process occurring in infancy which creates anxiety in the child as he realizes that the world is not simply an extension of himself, and which he overcomes by splitting objects (including people and 'part-people', e.g., good breast/bad breast) in the world so that they can appear good even if they behave badly. This is mirrored in the child's own psyche which is split into a good (free from anxiety) and bad (unable to control the environment and therefore exposed to anxiety) self. In this split lies the root of all stereotypical perceptions. An illusion of truth now descends on the distinction between good and bad world and self, control and loss of control, acquiescence and denial (Gilman, 1985). The split enables the bad self to be distanced and identified with the mental representation of the bad object, and

> this act of projection [which occurs when the self is threatened] saves the self from any confrontation with the contradictions present in the necessary integration of 'bad' and 'good' aspects of the self. The deep structure of our own sense of self and world is built upon the illusory image of the world divided into two camps, 'us' and 'them'. 'They' are either 'good' or 'bad'. (Gilman, 1985: 17)

The world is thus divided into binary opposites – good and bad, healthy and sick, normal and deviant – the former denoting characteristics of one's own group, and the latter of an outside negatively stereotyped group (Adorno, 1950a, Frenkel-Brunswik, 1950a, 1950b; Levinson, 1950a). Thus, hated self-attributes of members of the group gripped by prejudice are phantasized to exist in members of a stigmatized and stereotyped group.

Sumner (1990a, 1994), disrobing the concept of deviance, argues that what is censured as deviant reflects the political economy and culture of a society, and is irredeemably suffused with the ideology of dominant societal groups. But why do the majority internalize (to use Sumner's quasi-psychoanalytic use of the term) such censures? And is there a level of social censure that Sumner has not yet explored – namely that of a psychoanalytically informed sociological analysis of censure, which explores the role of the human psyche, and particularly the human unconscious as a major factor in the need to censure, but does not negate the moral-political ideology of censure, nor reduce it to a simple epiphenomenon of 'dark psychic forces'?

The potential for such an approach does not require an addition to Sumner's thesis, but rather a simple unfolding of it, as it already contains the seeds of such an analysis inherently within it. For example, Sumner argues that there is a correlation between the growth of social censure and the growth of social individuation and the emergence of industrial capitalism, and that social censure also supposes a high degree of fear of others' freedom. The parallels with Fromm's *Fear of Freedom* are glaringly obvious, and the concept that social censure may also suppose a fear of one's own freedom would not disrupt Sumner's line of thought. The over-zealously repressive nature of capitalism (so eloquently demonstrated by Marcuse and Reich); the splitting of reason from unreason (Foucault, Jung); the creation of unreflexive automatons subservient to the rules, mores and definitions of a hegemonic bloc; the realization that the social conflict that so often leads to the formation of censure often stimulates a great deal of psychic anxiety (and perhaps, thereby, fear of death); the need for projection as a mechanism to protect the ego from being overwhelmed by the unconscious, and the opportunity that censures provide for a morally sanctioned release (i.e., by the dominant groups) of unconsciously harboured aggressive and hostile tendencies; all surely have contributions to make to the development of the sociology of censure. Psychoanalytic-sociology may therefore enable a better understanding of the psychic appeal of and need for censure (why even a community of saints would censure), and its resultant resistance to rational argument.

Voids

The Holocaust was perhaps the most graphic demonstration of the hopes of the Enlightenment being destroyed, of life consuming itself, of the manifestation of a Thanatocracy. It was with a new ease that terror and normality became one, and construction and destruction were unified. Nazism and its controlled violence was a culmination of Enlightenment rationality developing along its dark side (control of nature and society by science and technology, bureaucratization, mass culture), and its merging with the dark side of the human unconscious (Thanatos). However, unlike the positions of Foucault, and Deleuze and Guattari who seem to glorify the unconscious, and who implicitly situate the blame for the manifestation of such atrocities as the Holocaust in the dominance of reason, this thesis has contended that the unconscious also harbours destructive forces. This is not, however, to glorify the value of reason over unreason. Deleuze and Guattari, Foucault and Jung all argue that the horrors ascribed to the unconscious could only really be those of consciousness, and of a belief too sure of itself. 'The unconscious has its horrors, but they are not anthropomorphic. It is not the slumber of reason that engenders monsters, but vigilant and insomniac rationality' (Deleuze and Guattari, 1983: 112). Freudian psychoanalysis in its formulation of the death instincts and Oedipality had therefore set itself up as the last priest, stamping on the unconscious the indelible print: 'guilty'. 'As if all that is good, reasonable, beautiful and worth living for had taken up its abode in consciousness! Have the horrors of the world war really not opened our eyes! Are we still unable to see that man's conscious mind is even more devilish and perverse than the unconscious' (Jung, 1933: 19). This chapter has contended that there are horrors both in reason and consciousness, and in passion and the unconscious. Both are ambivalent by nature. Both contain the seeds for liberation and for domination. Neither should be glorified. The poison that impregnated Hitlerism is within and around us. We cannot accept any optimistic conception of existence, any happy ending. This realization must be the precondition for any modern political thinking.

Almost all Holocaust survivors remember a dream which recurred during the nights of imprisonment: 'they had returned home and with passion and relief were describing their past sufferings, addressing themselves to a loved person, and were not believed. In the most typical (and most cruel) form, the interlocutor turned and left in silence' (Levi, 1988: 1–2). Such thoughts have also haunted the author of this essay. It was not to come to a definitive explanation of the Holocaust that the project was embarked upon, but to adhere to the protestations of the survivors ZACHOR (the phonetic spelling of the Hebrew word remember).

As Levi states, 'something one cannot understand constitutes a painful void, a puncture, a permanent stimulus that insists on being satisfied' (1988: 143). The void has been shaded but it has not been filled. As one Holocaust survivor stated: 'The professor would like to understand what is not understandable. We ourselves, who were there and have always asked ourselves the question, and will ask it until the end of our lives, we will never understand it because it cannot be understood' (Lifton, 1988).

Notes

1   Malinowski, for example, posited that social institutions are fashioned solely as a means of accommodating biological needs (1931).

2   See Sinclair (1976) for an interesting discussion on the roots of fascism in authoritarian populism.

3   This is not to suggest, however, that big business did not profit enormously from Nazism, for example the use of slave labour, Agfa photography (part of I. G. Farben that also manufactured Cyclon B pellets for the gas chambers), the arms race etc.

4   But see Adorno 1994 for a very dubious and unconvincing account of German anti-Semitism.

5   This is consistent with the substantive historical evidence that demonstrated a definitive middle-class base to National Socialism (cf. Hilberg, 1985).

Chapter 4

The Nazi Censure of Art:
Aesthetics and the Process of Annihilation

Anthony Amatrudo

'One way of preventing people from asking questions is by suppressing them. You give them dogmatic answers, and if they don't accept them you silence them. You don't allow people to question rules or opinions or institutions – you eliminate the very habit of questioning as subversive.'

(Isaiah Berlin, 1993: 141)

The Nazi Holocaust is the worst crime in human history, in its scale and its horror. Yet the academic study of the Holocaust by criminologists is largely neglected. Sumner has sought to draw attention to this neglect (Sumner, 1990a: 20–3). He makes the case, as Lopez-Rey (1970) does, that criminology has for too long neglected crimes of the state, war crimes, and genocide and focused upon 'juvenile delinquent behaviour'. At a more general level Rock makes the point that 'the erratic history of criminology has been marked by the organized neglect of many, if not most, of the phenomena that constitute crime' (Rock, 1973: 392). The point is that criminology needs to focus on the big crimes as well as the small. It must examine the political economy of crime; it must examine the cultural context of the censure of crime. It must seek to examine the ideology of censure. It must perceive crime in relation to history. Finally, a theory needs to be developed to note how art and culture contribute to crime. A need exists to examine further aspects of violent censure when such censure is legitimized by the state.

This chapter seeks to examine how the banal censure of anti-Semitism was nourished by the Nazi state. It is noted how such a censure once nourished led directly to genocide. The chapter will examine how the political and economic climate of the 1920s and 1930s positioned Germany to an anti-modernist and anti-Semitic ideology. It will show how that ideology was reflected in the art of the Nazi period. It is my aim to demonstrate the ideological role of National Socialist art in the plan to marginalize, and ultimately to annihilate, European Jewry. The historical analysis offered will be aimed at filling a gap which exists in the criminological treatment of genocide. In general, the social sciences have neglected aesthetics, and this focus on art in the study of the Holocaust may make a contribution to socio-logical studies. Because there is such a wealth of art historical academic writing to be evaluated, and because the art of the Nazi period has still not been penetrated, the perspective may be particularly fertile for the development of criminological theory.

The Cultural Ideology of Nazism

National Socialism destroyed German *Kultur* but it also furnished the German nation with a ideology with which to interpret the world. The German people were living through a period of great economic and political uncertainty following the 1918 defeat. The average German was without the education and insight needed to appreciate the legacy of the great cultural achievements of Germany. Instead the average German resorted to the hollow nationalistic catch phrases made available by the Nazis and others who chanted for a 'national culture' and who championed the mediocre. What Nazism offered was not a elevation of consciousness or an initiation into the glories of German culture but rather a cheapening of that cultural past until it was on the level of the banal, the impoverished and the easily under-stood. Nazism was in many ways a form of politics which set about erecting a cultural facade: it had no role for genuine culture.

The Nazis twisted Goethe, the great cosmopolitan, to serve their narrow na-tionalistic needs. The ideas of the past were reinterpreted. German cultural history was reassembled. As Glaser has argued the word 'German' was used to express an absolute value. 'Whatever was German remained unequalled whatever was unequalled was called German' (Glaser, 1978: 171). There was an insistence on national uniqueness. Modernism was said to be shallow when compared with the profundity of the German cultural depths. All that was not German was inferior. The period 1918–33 was said to be 'criminal' by Goebbels because it was a time when Germany had dabbled with internationalism (Bracher, 1991: 329). It would be the task of education to instil 'proper German values', especially through the teaching of the German language and music. History would be reduced to pure ideology.

The repression of imagination that this entailed showed itself in a twisted image of the hero, who was worshipped as saviour and as the fulfilment of German history. The hero was hardly human: the hero was an Aryan myth. The recruiting ground for both the heroes of tomorrow and their admirers was to be found in Nazi youth movements, but Hitler perverted them. Such organizations became breeding grounds for mob romanticism. Hitler circumvented the political process and ap-pealed directly to the masses. The hero's followers felt an affinity with the *Führer* that was not so much political as personal and emotional. Of course if Germany was indeed the home of a heroic race then her defeat in the First World War and the economic and political chaos following 1918 needed explanation, or better still, a scape-goat.

Followers of the Nazi credo needed a scape-goat to explain Germany's fate after 1918. The Nazi with his feelings of inadequacy in the teeth of an ever more complex and demanding world, compounded by a lack of comprehension of its *raison d'être*, sought after a scape-goat. The Jewish community in Germany was large enough to serve this purpose. The Jews would serve as the receptacle for Nazi resentments and as an outlet for the uncompensated feelings of Nazi inferiority. However, the Jewish community in Germany was also small enough for discrimination against Jews not to impact unduly upon the economy. The vacuum of ignorance about Judaism in Germany was in turn fed by a long history of ghettos and anti-Semitism. The Jewish community was slandered by tales of horror and terror. Moreover, such censures, as anything derogatory relating to the scape-goat anywhere, were relished. The 'crimes' and the 'failings' of the Jews were merely the product of myth and fabrication. The censure of the Jewish community by the Nazis was the post hoc response dictated by an ideology which needed to show itself as 'heroic'. The Jew was the dragon it had to slay. Fritz Stern has shown how this fierce ideology of censure at home distorted both the style and substance of German foreign policy (Stern, 1971: 24–33). Once locked into a *Weltanschauung* of conceiving the German nation as the home of some heroic race thwarted by the forces of Judaism, Bolshevism and modernism, the Nazis could hardly contain the dark forces that such an ideology unleashed. The enemies within would have to be destroyed. The enemies without would have to be conquered. This was the natural corollary to conceiving of Germany as the warrior who, once injured, had to revenge in order to restore dignity.

National Socialism was the outcome of certain cultural and sociological developments which were much older that Nazism itself. The ideas of National Socialism were in large measure borrowed from other times. The Nazis took them from the past but did so with great discrimination. They selected only those elements which accorded with their censorious policy of destroying all they considered un-German. The cultural vanguard of the Nazi state did not usher in new talent. The work of artists and musicians was in large measure corrupted by the publicness of their work. There was official support for art, but official art had to conform to an official standard, and so much of the energy that can only come through conflict and the desire to break with conformity was lost. The choice between types of art – in this case between traditional and modern styles – became a political one. The Nazis upheld, mistakenly, that abstract styles stood for modernity and progress and that representational styles stood for traditional values and conservatism. Such a conception of art meant that the Nazis were antithetical to anything novel. In architecture buildings were to represent authority. Architecture was to be blank and orderly. It expressed the power of permanence and was so conceived to crush the ordinary person. The was nothing accidental in this. Nazi ideology did not care for the spontaneous and it championed the strength of state institutions over the citizen (see *infra* Craig).

Nazism projected its ideology in every building, work of art, film, song and postage stamp. The ideological infiltration into every aspect of German life was total. It was often subtle though often crude. It was so conceived to take hold of the mentalities of the German nation. Culture, broadly defined, was the main vehicle for projecting Nazi ideology. It projected an art which was 'pure' and which would overcome class to forge a Germany that was strong once again. Art and culture were to be communal experiences. The other aspect of culture was to censure all that did not admit to the Nazi *Weltanschauung*. Nazi ideology was wedded to totalitarianism.

German Anti-Semitism

The Nazi super-race theory and its attendant race-conflict dogma and the breeding and extermination programmes proposed by Heinrich Himmler arose in response to the social and economic circumstances to be found in Germany after 1918. There was a rejection of traditional parliamentary ways of organizing a democratic society. Marxists and Jews were thought by many to be conspiring against the working man. Nazi ideology began to present the Jew as a parasitic creature. The Jew was to be both the brunt of Nazi attack and the distraction from its obvious failures to produce well-constructed social policy. The Social Darwinist theory of survival of the fittest found a ready partner in the notion of 'the superman' which Nietzsche outlined in his work (see *infra* Goodman). What Germany required, some argued, was the creation of a heroic race of Aryan heroes who would destroy the inferior races out of historico-political necessity. A nation of Aryan heroes, it was argued, would surely be a nation which displayed the characteristics of strength, racial purity and industry regarded as indispensable to a Nazi ideology which took its inspiration from a concept of the idea of 'the General Will' which cared little for the individual, instead conceiving 'the Will' as belonging to the masses.

Nazism made full use of Social Darwinism; it opened up the possibility of disregarding individuals and it could explain how the inferior Jew had succeeded. He had done so under the unnatural condition of urbanization where Jewish characteristics might flourish (Rosenberg, 1970: 149).[1] Nazism romanticized a mythical German past. Following Schiller and Kant, too sharp a distinction was drawn between the past and the state of modernity, allowing scathing critiques to be made. Nazism offered holism and a return to an idealized past: a past where the Jew had no place. Nazism offered a return to *gemeinschaft*: it offered a pseudo-spirituality based on myth.

Anti-Semitism has a well-documented history. In the middle ages the Roman Catholic Church practised this anti-Semitism. It was not confined to obscure theological texts and rhetoric. The Roman Catholic Church made decrees which anticipated the Nazi racial laws. The Synod of Elvira of 306 outlawed inter-marriage between Jews and Christians. The Synod of Claremont of 535 outlawed Jews from holding public office. The Fourth Lateran Council of 1215 decreed that Jews must mark their clothes with a special badge. The Council of Oxford of 1222 prevented the building of synagogues. The Council of Basel of 1434 prevented Jews from obtaining academic degrees (Axel, 1979: 135–6).

More pertinent still to Nazi anti-Semitism are the works of Gobineau, de Lapouge and Houston Stewart Chamberlain. Gobineau taught a bizarre doctrine of racial difference. He argued that the 'white race' has a monopoly of strength and creative power and that all the racial differences in the world are the result of the degree to which the white race, the engine of history, mixes with the lesser races to bring forth culture. Gobineau ascribed to German civilization the need to remove all that was not in accord with its reasoning. Though Gobineau never singled out the Jews, his work none-the-less offered the anti-Semite a framework within which to argue for the racial purity of the German peoples.

Vacher de Lapouge rejected much of the romanticism of Gobineau. His work rested upon the results of skull measurements and the like. There was no autonomy of the individual: the race was all there was. The Aryans were said to be the 'master race'. De Lapouge is of considerable importance, for he shifted anti-Semitic thought away from mythical sentimentalism concerned with a racially pure past and oriented it to 'science' and the future. He advocated selective breeding and rejected what he termed 'Christian mercy'. Through de Lapouge's work anti-Semitic writing enters the modern world.

In 1898 Houston Stewart Chamberlain penned his *Grundlagen des XIX Jahrhunderts*. This was an entirely new approach to history, one in which the interpretation of history is conceived solely in terms of racist doctrine. He raged against the race-destroying universalism of Roman Catholicism, and more especially the Jesuit Order with its 'overdeveloped and twisted intellectualism' (Copleston, 1993: 74–90).[2] Chamberlain conceived of his anti-Semitism in terms of Jewish conspiracies. Socialism, with its concern for economic planning was seen as one such conspiracy. It was argued that through socialist planning the Jews would destroy the hard fought for Germanic civilization and culture. Germany, Chamberlain argued, had to exterminate the Jews and socialists and do down the Roman Catholic Church in order to uphold the culture of the Aryan (Nolte, 1965: 285).

The Third Reich drew on this kind of European anti-Semitic writing. The legion of European anti-Semitic thinkers fell into step with the National Socialists in the march toward a greater, Jew-free, future. The European legacy of anti-Semitism, which was Hitler's, was in accord with the *Weltanschauung* of many Germans who were keen to find a scape-goat for the ills of Germany after 1918. The solution to the economic ills that beset Germany following her defeat in 1918 was straightforward: it was all the responsibility of the Jews; they must, surely, be eliminated in order for Germany to flourish. Such an analysis obviously did not find universal acceptance in Germany and the Nazis knew it. The German nation had to be systematically subjected to propaganda: it had to be given a systematically uniform vision of reality; the process of questioning the Nazi state had to be eliminated. Central to this process was the formation of a Nazi aesthetic.

Anthony Amatrudo

The Aestheticization of Political Life and the Politicization of Aesthetics

It was Walter Benjamin who argued that fascism was the aestheticization of political life (quoted in Adam, 1992: 21). Nazi government meant the organizing of people into geometrical patterns, the expression of party political functions through uniforms, the elevation of political rituals of submission and of adoration. It might be stated that all mass politics uses symbolism. In fascist politics such practices permeate all life; such practices are intensified and constant. Hitler, from 1933, practised one-party politics with the emphasis on the theatrical. He had an acting coach and practised his poses, as Hoffman's photographs testify (Adam, 1992: 90–1). Hitler became a media star. Great care was taken in the creation of Nazi symbolism. In *Mein Kampf* Hitler wrote of the Nazi flag:

> As National Socialists we see our programme in our flag. In red we see the social idea of movement, in white the nationalistic idea, in the swastika the mission of the struggle for victory of the idea of creative work, which as such always has been and always will be anti-Semitic. (Hitler, 1974: 452)

Nazi Party officials systematically set about creating new works of art, sculpture and architecture, music and design work to reflect National Socialist ideology. The Nazis did not conceive of art as decorative but as the moral projection of the Germanic ideal. In 1933, the House of German Art (*Haus der Deutschen Kunst*) was built which was to be an important National Socialist cultural bulwark. Lectures were given there by Alfred Rosenberg and Josef Goebbels against Jewish and 'Bolshevik' art. Art in Nazi Germany was conceived of as essential for the propagation of political ideology. The Nazi state afforded art, music and architecture a greater role in the formation of the national identity and consciousness than in other democratic states.

Hitler's regime was antithetical to capitalism. It instituted a planned economy which was ultimately geared to warfare. In 1936 a four-year plan was devised in order to prepare for war with Bolshevik Russia. One should be under no illusion: politics triumphed over economics in Hitler's Germany. Big business was a constant target for Nazi rhetoric. Jewish financiers and businessmen had contributed to Germany's defeat in 1918 and to the subsequent economic chaos of the 1920s. These neglected aspects of Hitler's programme are given prominence as Labour Theory in *Mein Kampf*:

> For the first time labour had sunk to the level of an object of speculation for unscrupulous Jewish businessmen; the alienation of property from the wage-worker was increased *ad infinitum*. (Hitler, 1974: 214)

It must be asked, however, whether this was genuine economic theory or a propagandistic attempt to exploit the anti-Semitic sentiments of workers and business people, who were suspicious of Jewish capitalists.

Economic history viewed in the light of developments within German civic life of the Nazi period is key to understanding the rise of German anti-Semitism and ultimately the Holocaust. After the First World War Germany suffered economically as the result of war reparations, the repayment of war debt and the cost of reorienting the economy to peace-time production. Politically Germany was fractured. Weimar Germany collapsed under the strain of trying to hold together a plethora of competing political parties; indeed Weimar Germany became synonymous with a fractured German political life which could not come to terms with its own internal confusion, save for raising the idea of the *Volk*. German national cohesion came about only by conceiving of a new enemy, namely, the international Jewish conspiracy (Hitler, 1974: 136, 155, 159, 210).

The German nation was resentful in defeat. National Socialism offered not merely a critique of the postwar situation in Germany following 1918 but the transformation of the political life of the nation. In becoming political, art was part and parcel of that transformation. Art took on more meaning for Germans in the pre-1939 period. Symbolism rose in its importance as people joined the Hitler Youth, the SS or the Nazi Party in its various forms in greater numbers. The need to forge a common identity was seen as vital. Individuals were expected to affirm shared values. The *Führer* cult and the virulent expression of anti-Semitic sentiment were the site of such a coalition of values. The Nazis exerted their ideological machinery through the theatrical direction of public life and the liturgy of political life and symbolism. The parades and publicity connected with the great staged events of the 1933–39 period were expressions of fascist aesthetic phenomenology. Such events both focused attention on the *Führer* and the aesthetic aspects of political life, and hid the failings of a credo that was contradictory, eclectic and illogical. Of course, none of this is to claim that art was used in an unproblematic way by the Nazi state. The *Führer* stood aloof from the machinery of government but he legitimated that machinery by rallying the German people to commit themselves to him, whose fate was the same as that of the nation. The *Führer* was projected as the saviour of the nation, whose vision was diamond sharp. This conception of the *Führer* was then echoed in Nazi political and theatrical rhetoric for sure, but it was also echoed in music, painting, sculpture and architecture.

Needless to say there was dissent and not all art genuflected to the National Socialist ideal. However, painters especially supported the Nazi cause: not by a simple process of producing images with a political sloganizing quality, as is the case with Soviet Socialist Realism, but rather by producing works which did not question the Aryan ideal. In Nazi Germany architects and artists had an elevated position and by and large they were satisfied by this. There was a great increase in the number of artists under the Nazi state which organized large numbers of scholarships, competitions and exhibitions for artists, sculptors and architects. These artists produced works for public spaces which echoed the National Socialist concerns for order, for the Aryan ideal and the elimination of dissent. National Socialist art was antithetical to modernity with its attendant notion of progress.

The Nazi Response to Modernity

Nazism wanted to marginalize Marxist ideas of class struggle as the revolutionary force in society, and to replace class struggle with notions of racial exclusion. Nazism built its mass support with the promise to overcome the alienation of capitalism by building an integrated community. The reality was, however, an intensification of alienation – so much so that society was ultimately destroyed. None-the-less one must underline the fact that Nazi propaganda sought to exploit a very real need for a socially coherent community in post-1918 Germany (Bracher, 1991: 66–71).

The Nazi period can only be understood properly by contextualizing it in the political history of twentieth-century Germany. Only by doing this can one hope to understand how Europe was plunged into barbarity. Germans were understandably dissatisfied at the end of the First World War by the Treaty of Versailles, whose chief drawback was that it made no provision for old adversaries to be reconciled; something the Nazis would exploit. It was obvious that postwar Germany would find itself in a dire economic situation and yet the Treaty of Versailles did not address this issue. The economic depression and soaring unemployment in Germany could have been foreseen. By the end of the Weimar Republic the German nation was ready to follow anyone who promised work to the six and a half million who were unemployed and the many others in low-paid part-time work. It is not surprising that people voted for the Nazis, but what is of interest is the nature of those voters. Certainly the Nazis did get the votes of many of the unemployed but they also gained the votes of the middle classes, who viewed the economic collapse with dismay and the breakdown of legal order with dread. Hitler made direct appeals to this fear in his speeches (Zeman, 1964: 36). The inter-war period was one of unrest in Germany. The period following the cessation of hostilities in 1918 until 1921 was one of political ferment and streetfighting. Some battled for dominance in an increasingly confused political discourse and others threw up their arms at the increasing disunity of Germany; still others deplored the growing divide between the poor and the well-off.

Hitler offered himself as the nation's saviour. At first, in an attempt to establish his respectability, he hid from the masses his devotion to a mystical idea of the *Volk* at whose heart lay a rabid anti-Semitism. Nazism originally wanted to gain legitimacy for its programme. It did this by talking about the united *Volk* and by incorporating into its *Weltanschauung* a view of society that had a long European tradition. The utopian anti-modernist notions, on which Nazi art was built, would colour the artistic imagination of the Nazi period and feed through to the imaginations of the German people. It was the function of Nazi propaganda to offer a plausible response to the realities of life in Germany after her defeat in 1918. We must never forget that there was an active Left in Germany. It was defeated in the war of ideology through the greater concentration upon ideas of German nationalism, which the Nazis made their own.

Nazism drew succour from a number of aspects of German history. It drew on an established tradition of nationalism, myth-making and anti-Semitism. Such factors were not however confined to Germany. There was, for instance, a far greater depth of anti-Semitism in Poland, the Ukraine, France and the Austro-Hungarian Empire (Carsten, 1967: 9–41). Nationalism was widespread in European political thinking in the first half of the twentieth century; it was by no means confined to Germany (Bracher, 1984: 90). Therefore, one must beware any thesis which argues that Germany alone was suited by its history and social psychological disposition to passive obedience and extreme racist politics. What Nazism did achieve however, was the appropriation of certain strands of German history to fashion an ideology which would prepare the ground for the annihilation of those persons it deemed to have been either absent in that history, or whose role in that imagined past was conceived of as being wholly negative. German history was manipulated by National Socialist ideology to popularize the Nazi agenda in a period of social and cultural turmoil. This was done by shaping certain aspects of Germany history to negate the status quo and to create a myth of the past which could gain the appeal of the masses and influence their political consciousness.

There is no denying that the crisis in German political and cultural life was part of a wider transformation in the political life of European nations. Essentially this transformation involved changing traditional authoritarian political structures into pluralistic democratic ones. In the inter-war period this transformation faltered in Germany. Until this period Germany had embarked upon the transition to modernity, and this process had a long history, going back some three centuries. In Germany, which had been hurriedly industrialized after the Franco-Prussian War, the transition to modernity was then accelerated by the abolition of the monarchy and the introduction of a republican, liberal-democratic constitution in 1919. This social change proved both too slow for the urban proletariat, who had little to lose, and too fast for the majority of the conservative middle classes who feared the loss of their material condition and who clung to the traditional order. The process of transition first produced frenzied ideological and social contradictions in the Weimar state but was, by and large, halted by the Nazis with the establishment of a dictatorship. The demagogy of National Socialism, however unconvincing to many workers, was none-the-less assured of public approval the more it could project a unified nation. The abolition of all party and ideological divisions and the promise of forging the German people into one unified 'blood' was at once a counsel of despair and a successful rallying cry.

During this period of transition Germany developed a modern class structure, with all that meant for class conflict. These class conflicts manifested themselves in the political, economic and cultural spheres. The German Parliament (*Reichstag*) may well have been overpowered by the Kaiser, his Chancellor and personal bureaucracy, but it none-the-less accrued power over time with the extension of universal male suffrage, and it did give expression to a plurality of political interests.

Oddly enough, despite the fragmented social scene, participation in elections rose to almost 90 per cent in March 1933. At the same time there grew up a demand to abolish parliamentary government which had not avenged the Treaty of Versailles. It had not provided the wage labourer with work, nor helped investors after the stock market crash of 1929.

Historians have often remarked how Germany was slower to industrialize than Britain and France (Taylor, 1954; Milward, 1965). When she was in the process of changing her economy from an agrarian one to one based increasingly on mechanization, Germany had both a level of rural backwardness and a large number of urban intellectuals versed in literary and philosophical material. They were to become a reservoir of reactionary anti-modernist sentiment (Glaser, 1978: 106–10).[3] In an earlier age, Germany had been made up of small towns and villages and had displayed a very strong sense of social cohesion. It did not want to give up this aspect of its nature. This sense of cohesion was perceived by the great Germans of letters and philosophy, notably Kant, Schiller and Goethe (Glaser, 1978: 58–76). Such men as these were concerned to preserve the Germanic idyll. In the nineteenth century Germans sensed a contradiction between modern production, with its urban context and mechanized production, with the attainment of a proper character. They railed against the fragmentation of human faculties through the division of labour and the elaboration of bureaucracy. Friedrich Schiller, as early as 1795, wrote *On the Aesthetic Education of Man* as a direct response to the French Revolution. Schiller was against the raw violence of the French Revolution but held to its ideals. Schiller, as did Kant, proposed an autonomous realm of the aesthetic imagination as a saviour from barbarism. He cleverly drew a radical divide between antiquity and modernity. In such a way he conceived the modern as that which alienates. Such tendencies were, at that time, more pronounced in the more developed nations of France and Britain. *On the Aesthetic Education of Man* was a call to preserve Germany from the same fate. Despite its failure to develop as early as Britain or France, Germany had none-the-less embarked upon a course of modern capitalist development. Yet Germany feared the modern in a way that other nations did not. It feared the alienating process of mechanization. In a country that had a devotion to medieval ways of thinking and living, the notion that societal interdependence was being marginalized seemed to the German mind to hold the threat of alienation. Little wonder that such a context gave rise to anti-modernist sentiment even prior to the onset of modernity. The fear of alienation and disconnection had been a part of German culture and political life since the eighteenth century: such a fear had become a mania by the 1920s. It is easy to see, against this particular background, how Nazi ideology was both exploiting a set of historical fears and was itself part of that history of fears (Glaser, 1978: 126–9).

Nazism offered a return to the values of *gemeinschaft*. It offered itself as the force to bring about a perceived long-overdue revision of the political and social sphere in order to reverse the alienating forces of modernity. As Nolte has noted:

The innate strength of the seemingly powerful prewar Germany was weakened – according to Mein Kampf – mainly by an 'industrialization which was unbridled as it was harmful', and which entailed a dangerous regression of the farming class. The aristocracy of the sword gave way to the aristocracy of finance. . . . This signalled an alienation of property as against the employee, and the internationalization of the economy. This mammonization led at the same time to the Hebraization of spiritual life. (Nolte, 1965: 403–4)

However, the Nazi analysis and its call for the reinstitution of *gemeinschaft* far from establishing the autonomy of persons merely reduced them to automatons. A vow to Germany became a vow to do the heinous work of Nazism.

The propaganda which streamed out of Nazi radio, film, architecture, art and posters repeated the same message: 'The Germans were united by blood'. It followed from this that those whose blood was not German were not entitled to the same respect or rights. This blood unity was supposedly summed up in the person of one man, Adolf Hitler. The psychology of Hitlerism was all about affording rights by blood (Laswell, 1933). It was all about getting people agitated at their failure to exercise those rights because of the Jewish conspiracy to thwart those rights and because of the alienating process of modernization. The German nation would be united into one single entity whose defining features would be racial purity and power. The various social classes would be affirmed as meaningful components of the corporate order. The central ideological appeal of Nazism was in this vision of a harmonious social order in which those who were included could feel secure; if only by looking down on those who were not included and who were thus fit only for enslavement, or, because they had no place in the Nazi social order, elimination from it.

The ideology of the organic National Socialist utopia was relayed by propaganda and by art which expressed its message of power, the rootedness of the individual to groups and racial solidarity. National Socialist art gave positive expression to sets of images which were in tune with Nazi political theory, but by excluding certain groups (Jews, the disabled, homosexuals, blacks) it also marginalized subjects it did not portray. This latter point, of exclusion, is central to understanding the role of art in relation to the Holocaust. After a period an absence is no longer noted and comes to be seen as normal. It became natural to think in the racially structured way the Nazis had in mind. By excluding the Jews from art, from theatre, from posters, it followed that they became excluded from the consciousness of ordinary Germans. Art was so conceived by National Socialism to present racial harmony as the goal of public policy; that is to say an homogeneous Aryan nation.

National Socialism was the outcome of the fractured political culture of Weimar. National Socialism defeated those forces loyal to democracy by countering with an anti-modernist chant whose chorus resounded the need for a powerful leader, who alone could banish the alienating tendencies of modernism. Needless to say, such a chant resounded throughout Europe in the 1920s and 1930s, but nowhere else was the inflection so racist in its tone. The longings for an integrated rural Germany were clearly reflected in the Nazi art and architecture of the Third Reich (Pinthus,

1948; Lane, 1968). All that was not German, all that was not heroic, was to be annihilated from National Socialist aesthetics. This desire for purity through annihilation was the same feature of the Nazi psyche which ultimately led to the deaths of millions.

The Nazi response to modernity was entirely negative. In architecture it looked backwards to Greece for its inspiration and to the Baroque and neoclassicism of Vienna (Adam, 1992: 207). In sculpture it took its themes from the myths of antiquity (Adam, 1992: 188). Yet the relationship of National Socialism to the past was not reverential but manipulative. It sought to esteem its present by playing with elements from the past. In this regard Nazi aesthetics were postmodern. The censures of the present were 'selected' from the wealth of imagery left by the past.

The Role of Art in Nazi Germany Before 1939

In 1937 the Nazis put on the most savage attack ever conceived against modern art. It opened on 19 July in Munich and was called the *Entartete Kunst* (Degenerate Art) exhibition, in which over 650 works of art – paintings, prints, books, sculptures – earlier exhibited in Germany museums were shown together, with the intention of demonstrating to the German public what was unacceptable to the Nazi state and to show public disapproval of modern art. All the exhibits were said to be 'un-German'. *Entartete Kunst* ran for four months in Munich and over two million people attended the exhibition. After Munich, *Entartete Kunst* toured throughout Germany and Austria and a further million people saw it after its Munich run was over. It has been noted that *Entartete Kunst* was the most popular exhibition of modern art ever. The free admission policy meant up to 36 000 people came to see it every day. It was five times as popular at the *Grosse Deutsche Kunstausstellung* (Great German Art Exhibition) put on by the Nazis to show Nazi-approved art in the *Haus der Deutschen Kunst* (House of Germany Art) also in Munich in 1937. *Entartete Kunst* was conceived and executed as an exercise in censure. It showed the German people what was not acceptable. As Sumner has noted:

> There was a systematic slandering of the vision of modern artists as similar to the vision of the mentally ill. Modernist artists were censured as being like the deformed, the homosexual, the black, the communist, the criminal – sick, socially useless mutants suffering from racial inferiority, who might have to be destroyed. (1994: 64–5)

Entartete Kunst shows us just how politicized the aesthetic realm became under Nazi government: a politicization without parallel in the modern era, even in fascist Italy. *Entartete Kunst* demonstrates to us how Germany's heroes and cultural history were given over to National Socialist ideology. All that was considered outside of that history was to be censured as un-German. All that was un-German was to be eliminated. Art under the Nazis was considered a topic central to propaganda but also to the ordering of German life. Art policy was integrated into Nazi social policy, which was itself inseparable from policy to the Jews. In 1933 when the Nazis came to power one of the first acts of the regime was to burn the books of modern authors. Thousands of books were publicly burnt, announcing to all the new policy towards the arts. This was a public declaration of war on the arts. *Entartete Kunst* was important but it must be seen in context for it was only part of a wider policy towards the Jews and towards modernist art. This policy was well planned, and coordinated in such a way that an examination of art shows up aspects of the meta-policy towards the un-German that is, the context of the Holocaust. In 1937 nearly 17 000 pieces of modern art were confiscated as 'degenerate' by a committee under the aegis of Josef Goebbels. Some of this art found its way into the *Entartete Kunst* exhibition, some was sold and some of it was burnt in a huge fire outside Berlin's fire department headquarters in a public act of censure (Adam, 1992: 127). Much later the world would learn that the Nazis did not burn only books and works of art in their insane policy of destroying the un-German.

The *Gesetz zur Wiederherstellung des Berufsbeamtentums* (professional Civil Service Restoration Act) of 7 April 1933, allowed the Nazis, aided by the Gestapo, to dismiss all non-Aryan government employees from their jobs. This Act impacted heavily on the arts where many Jewish art historians and other academics were dismissed from their university posts and over 20 museum curators and directors were sacked. The Act was conceived to give a racial and political basis to employment. It was important that the running of museums and galleries was given over to those persons who were disposed to attack modern art as Jewish, degenerate and Bolshevik and who would seek to mobilize prejudices against modern art and to ferment anti-Jewish and anti-communist sentiments. The language of these new arts administrators was all concerned to censure the 'degenerate' as Jewish and Bolshevik, and the denunciation embraced not only the art but also its intellectual basis. It was posited that modern art was implicitly radical and its meaning was ambiguous and thus could never be compatible with National Socialist notions of Aryan solidarity and racial purity. These new Nazi placemen were not crude and unschooled brutes, but highly educated men who knew their task was to implement Nazi policy and to justify it in their institutions to the public.

The Nazis did not want merely to have control over arts administration but also its production, and artists were required to join officially sanctioned groups where their work was overseen. Those considered 'undesirables' were forbidden to produce art or to be involved in artistic life. All modern art was censured – be it surrealist, expressionist or some other style. Emil Nolde's work was declared degenerate even though he was a member of the Nazi Party. Most of the artists who were persecuted were not Jewish, and of the 112 artists exhibited at the *Entartete Kunst* exhibition only six were Jews. In fact, the censure of modern art was conceived in more than simple anti-Semitic terms, and extended to embrace a total ideology, of which the espousal of anti-Semitism was only a part. Hinz has shown how Carl Einstein's *Die Kunst des 20 Jahrhunderts* (The Art of the Twentieth Century) was used by the Nazis as a guide to define what was and what was not 'un-German', and so to be vilified (Hinz, 1979: 24). Using Einstein's book as their guide the Nazis set about destroying the work of German modernist artists.

It is essential that the Nazi attitude toward modern art be seen as indicative of the wider spectrum of the cultural and political arena. All life was overseen by National Socialist bureaucracy. The Nazis paid enormous attention to the regulation of all aspects of cultural life in the Reich, establishing procedures whereby it decided what and who was acceptable. Nazi exclusion was essentially permanent disbarment. It was preoccupied with ideological matters and saw the disproportionate amount of bureaucratic attention given over to the paperwork and regulation aimed at an area of society that was politically, economically and militarily unthreatening – in other words the artistic realm – as necessary to the project of furthering Nazi ideology; the allocation to the arts of a major role in a totalitarian state society was without precedent, save for the Soviet Union. Lehmann-Haupt, the great chronicler of Nazi anti-Semitism in art, wrote:

> Such complete monopolization of the entire creative potential of a people, of every aesthetic instinct, such subjugation of every current of its productivity and its capacity for artistic experience to the purposes of the leaders of collective society does not exist before this century. (Lehmann-Haupt, 1954: 3)

It might be argued that this was connected with Hitler's own unsuccessful career as a painter in Vienna, but Lehmann-Haupt has shown, I think convincingly, that the Nazi concern for culture far transcended Hitler's own frustrations as a young man (Lehmann-Haupt, 1954: 45–6).

Both *Entartete Kunst* and the *Grosse Deutsche Kunstausstellung* show the fusion of political and aesthetic themes, and the use of the term *entartete* to designate inferior racial, sexual and moral types had been around for some time, at least until the mid-nineteenth century. *Entartet* is usually translated as either 'degenerate' or 'decadent' but was usually reserved for biology. The way the Nazis used it was to refer to art which is unclassifiable or so far beyond that which is acceptable that it is essentially 'non-art'. *Entartet* is a censure drawn from biology.

Prior to 1937 the elements of *Entartete Kunst* can be found in German culture. As a unified nation Germany became prone to an intense nationalism that manifested itself as a belief in the natural superiority of the Aryan people. The ideal of a blond, blue-eyed Nordic hero as the embodiment of the future civilization was promoted in the writings of many European authors. By the first quarter of the twentieth century this concept of racial superiority had popular support in Germany. By the 1920s some writers, notably Alfred Rosenberg, were arguing that the racial characteristics of the artist were linked to the art he produced, and that the style of a given artistic approach was to be derived from a racial origin. Therefore, if a non-Jewish artist worked in a modernist way, it was argued, he was none-the-less upholding the Jewish, or non-Aryan, ideal (Rosenberg, 1970: 126–74).

Before the Nazis came to power German art had displayed a great willingness to challenge conventions, and art, music, literature and film, later to be censured as 'degenerate', flourished. Intellectuals, like Christopher Isherwood, came to Germany to experience the spirit of German modernism. Artists formed groups like *Die Brucke* (the Bridge). Important new journals sprang up in the wake of the First World War to develop the ideas which were important to German Expressionism. Artists and intellectuals were increasingly drawn to anthropology and were influenced by African and Asian art. The art drawn by the mentally unwell was the inspiration for poets, like Hugo Ball. After 1918 German modern art came into conflict with simple nationalistic realism, a realism more easily understood by the average German. The country, after all, had suffered a crushing defeat and had been assessed for massive reparations which had the effect of undermining an already weak economy. Modern art movements such as Expressionism, Cubism and Dada were considered overly intellectual, elitist and 'foreign' by the bulk of a population demoralized by a defeat which was increasingly blamed on a conspiracy of Jews and Bolsheviks. Throughout the Weimar period Socialist thought was supported by many avant-garde artists who expressed their political sentiments in their art. As modern art came to be increasingly identified with the causes of internationalism and left-wing politics, it became a highly visible target for German nationalists.

At the same time as these modern artistic developments were getting underway so was a growing movement against them. Max Nordau, himself a Jew, penned *Entartung* (Degeneration) in 1892 and in it he lambasted Symbolism and the Pre-Raphaelites, as well as arguing that Henrik Ibsen and Emile Zola were inferior authors to those in the German canon. *Entartung*, and other works of its type, took the position that the nineteenth-century genre of representational realist painting was the culmination of a tradition of Aryan art. The avant-garde, the modern, the abstract were all considered the work of disturbed minds. German psychiatry had long held that the Jew was inherently degenerate and more likely to succumb to insanity. By the 1930s the idea that Jewishness was related to degeneration and mental illness was widely held. Modern art was linked to irrationality, to degeneration, to Jewishness. The Nazi theorists desired that these be eliminated. The censure came first and then the inevitable action; in this case destruction (Sumner, 1994: 63–6).

Modern art was opposed in German museums from the 1920s when the *Deutsche Kunstgesellschaft* (German art association) decried the corruption of German art and advocated an art which was in line with traditional German concerns. They especially disparaged the work of George Grosz with its social criticism. It was deemed 'Bolshevik'. Alfred Rosenberg wrote *Der Mythus des 20 Jahrhunderts: Eine Wertung der seelischgeistigen Gestaltenkampf* (The Myth of the Twentieth Century: An Evaluation of the Spiritual-intellectual Confrontation of our Age), in which modern art is damned. *Der Mythus* was a huge 700-page work which discussed such issues as Christ's racial origins, the Roman Catholic Church, the ideal Nazi state, aesthetic theory. However, it is best understood as a pseudo-intellectual attempt to justify Nazi anti-Semitism and anti-modernism. For Rosenberg, modernism represented a break with the German tradition in art.

Creative strength was broken because it had oriented itself, ideologically and artistically, towards a foreign standard and thus was no longer attuned

> to the demands of life. . . . A later age will prove whether the powers of the *Volk* and race were strong enough to create a syntheses out of chaos. . . . The task of the present is to prepare a Volkish unity or to sink into civilized barbarism. (Rosenberg, 1970: 154–7)

Wilhelm Frick was elected to the Reichstag as the Nazi representative for Thuringia in 1929. Frick was also elected *Innenminister* (Minister for the Interior) for Thuringia. Immediately after taking up his office Frick replaced most department chiefs and sent out directives on cultural policy. Frick appointed Paul Schultze-Naumburg, a qualified architect (like Rosenberg) and a racial theorist, to replace Walter Gropius who was dismissed from the faculty of the *Bauhaus* in Weimar. Schultze-Naumburg had previously published an attack on the *Bauhaus*, in 1925 and in 1928 he wrote the influential work *Kunst und Rasse* (Art and Race) which linked the 'excesses of modernist art' to Jewish influences. For Schultze-Naumburg an attack upon modern art was *de se* an attack upon the Jews. Schultze-Naumburg had a thorough training in aesthetics and art history and he set about systematically developing a theory, of sorts, which would uphold the Nazi ideal in art. He juxtaposed examples of modern art and photographs of the deformed and suggested that they were the inspiration for the elongated faces of Modigliani. A crude analysis but an effective propaganda.

In the 1920s Heidelberg had become a centre for the art produced by the mentally unwell, where art therapy was used to treat mental and emotional problems. In 1922 Hans Prinzhorn published an important work in psychiatry *Bildnerei der Geisteskranken* (*Image-Making By the Mentally Unwell*) which examined some 5 000 works of art by mental patients and which argued that they exhibited certain specific attributes.[4] This study gained widespread favour with the Nazis.

In 1934 there was something of a confusion about the attitude of the Nazis to Expressionism as expressing the spirit and vigour of Nazi youth. Goebbels collected Nolde's painting and Barlach's sculpture. Alfred Rosenberg had a quite different conception. He sought to promote *volkisch* art, that is the art of the German people. He rejected any type of modern aesthetic. Rosenberg and Goebbels built up rival camps and made speeches and wrote articles advancing their respective causes. Mosse (1966) and Lane (1968) have detailed how Rosenberg and Goebbels struggled against each other, especially in relation to German Expressionism and Italian Futurism. Rosenberg had been appointed by Hitler in 1934 to oversee all ideological and intellectual training. He was given the same rank as Josef Goebbels in his post as president of the Reich Chamber of Culture. This controversy continued until Hitler felt the need to make a personal intervention. Hitler cleverly rejected both positions after thinking through the arguments. In a speech at the Nuremberg Rally he condemned the dangers of the degeneracy of modern art and yet cautioned against retrograde German art. After the 1934 speech all art would be based on the German 'racial' tradition. All forms of modern art and art criticism would be outlawed. It must be noted that Hitler was less concerned with aesthetic theory and more with racial questions. What mattered was the perceived un-German elements in art and not so much the theoretical elements of art production. Censures of art and artists were then always, at root, racial statements.

It is only by conceiving of Nazi censures of art in this way that one can begin to understand properly the odd methodology of *Entartete Kunst* – an exhibition convened with the sole purpose of defamation. *Entartete Kunst* was ideologically about condemning the Jewish and Bolshevik enemies of the *Volk* and only second-arily was it about showing the deficiencies of modernist images. Hitler saw the attack on modernism as a chance to use the average German's distrust of modern art, which they did not understand, to further his objectives against the Jews, the Bolsheviks, the non-Aryans and the enemies of the *Volk*. The blanket charge of 'degeneracy' was made against music, art, literature and film. Such items as were said to be 'degenerate' were to be destroyed to ensure the purity of German culture. Confiscated items were placed in the *Schreckenskammer der Kunst* (chamber of horror of art) whose organizers decried the fact that public money had been wasted on buying such 'horrors' (modern art). They argued that such works had been purchased by Jewish intellectuals, who ran the museums, from Jewish art dealers, who had grown rich by selling such degenerate art to the state.[5]

In 1937 Goebbels set up a five-man commission to visit the museums to select works for an exhibition of 'degenerate' art. The commission was convened under one Professor Ziegler from Munich and included Count Klaus von Baudissin, an SS officer who had briefly run an art museum in Essen. Von Baudissin shows the link between concerns about acceptable modern aesthetics and the machinery of death. Interestingly, Hitler's personal adviser on matters of art policy was not Goebbels, Rosenberg or even Professor Ziegler, but SS Major Dr von Baudissin (Adam, 1992: 52). Therefore one should be under no illusion about Nazi policy towards the arts. It was inextricably tied up with those whose trade was murder. As Adam had chillingly noted: 'The new German art had the elimination of part of the human race written into its concept' (Adam, 1992: 15).

Censure, Exclusion and Annihilation

It is easy to detect a parallel between the fate of modern art under the Nazis and the fate of European Jewry. Both were publicly censured. Both were excluded from German civic life. Both were to be the focus of Nazi attempts to destroy them physically. In his article on Nazi policy towards musical composition and perform-ance, Erik Levi traces the censure of Jewish performers and composers before the war (in Taylor and van der Will, 1990: 158–82). Atonality was damned, as was the romanticism of Mahler and Mendelssohn and other Jewish composers (Bracher, 1984: 325). The Nazi's policy of anti-Semitism was carried out with efficiency. All elements which could be said to be Jewish were ruthlessly purged. The Nazis conceived that the moral foundation of art must be a heroic one. Their belief in the corrupting influence of race upon artistic values meant that they were bound to eliminate all that was not 'Aryan' (Adam, 1992: 33). The order (i) censure, (ii) exclusion and (iii) annihilation seems to be the way the Nazis dealt with their perceived enemies such as Jews, Bolsheviks, homosexuals and modern artists.

This process can be detected in relation to Goebbels' treatment of music in Germany. Goebbels wanted to rid the German music scene of Jewish influence. All Jewish elements in music were censured as un-German and degenerate. The anti-Semitic censure was ruthlessly executed. This was the first stage. Second came exclusion, and all Jews working in German musical life were expelled from their posts. This was done by using the new anti-Semitic laws brought in after 1933, notably the laws relating to the civil service. These laws sanctioned dismissal on either racial or ideological grounds (Schapiro, 1983: 29–34; Bracher, 1991: 243–52). Because of these laws Otto Klemperer and Bruno Walter fled Nazi Germany. Arnold Schoenberg resigned his teaching post. The violinists Jascha Heifetz and the young Yehudi Menuhin were not allowed to perform in Germany and all gramophone recordings by Jews were outlawed. With its highly developed bureaucratic structures, Germany found the task of excluding Jewish musicians a straightforward enterprise. Those Jews who did not leave Germany were forced to enrol in the *Judische Kulturbund* but were not allowed to teach or to perform in public. The membership list of the *Judische Kulturbund* was later used by SS officials in the Holocaust.

The more difficult task for Goebbels was that of ridding Germany of Jewish-influenced music. At first the works of prominent Jewish composers were censured. Kurt Weill and Arnold Schoenberg were especially marked out for attack, as was black jazz. Things were then expanded and before long Offenbach's operas were outlawed. In Leipzig, the Mayor ordered the removal of Felix Mendelssohn's statue from the town centre. The city of Leipzig was congratulated for this by the Ministry of Propaganda. Here again one detects a pattern. Firstly, the music of Jewish composers is censured; secondly, that music is marginalized and excluded from public performance; thirdly, the statues of Jewish composers, their musical scores and other artifacts are destroyed. It should be as if no Jew had ever produced music.

The Nazis in their onslaught against Jewish musical prowess had in mind certain long-term goals. The ideological machinery of Nazism wanted to expunge Jews from the consciousness of future generations. The thoroughness of the Nazi ideologists and their jack-booted helpers went well beyond a simple attempt to tarnish Jewish musical life. The notion was, surely, to annihilate all Jews from Europe, and as part of that process it was necessary to remove Jewish music and other Jewish cultural heritage from a Europe whose cultural heritage was, in large measure, formed by Jews. The entire point of all Nazi anti-Semitic policies after 1933 was logically to annihilate European Jewry. At the same time they instituted a new musical life to fill the gap left by Schoenberg *et al*. To this end the works of Beethoven and Mozart were esteemed, though the Nazis were not averse to tampering with the scores to make them more 'German'. The Nazis were largely successful in their attempts to purge Jewish elements from the music repertoire of the Third Reich, and a similar fate beset the modernists and socialists of the musical world.

The Nazis instituted new genres of music. The German folk song was esteemed as wholesome and honest. The march and the fanfare were great favourites at large-scale events such as the Nuremberg Rally. Music was integrated into the larger operation of the Ministry for Propaganda and with the long-term survival of Nazism in mind the Hitler Youth would sing hearty songs or listen to concerts of Beethoven's music. The Nazis having all but eliminated Jewish influence in German music began to effect profound changes on the musical life of the nation. A fierce campaign against Jews involved in Germany's musical life had left a considerable vacuum, to be filled by a musical/cultural policy that was more often characterized by confused prejudice than by clear stylistic goals but which, none-the-less, was designed to bolster the authority of the Party and to uphold Nazi ideology.

Nazi ideology dictated that a censorious policy of anti-Semitism be instituted. It dictated that Jewish contributions in the field of music be at first marginalized and then eliminated altogether. This basic methodology of censure, exclusion and annihilation is readily detected in all aspects of Nazi policy. It can be seen in the development of Nazi laws after 1933; in Nazi policy towards the arts; in the attitude of the Nazis to employment. It is readily detected in all Nazi policies aimed at German and European Jewry – policies which ultimately results in the deaths of millions of people. One must locate National Socialist policy towards the arts in the wider context of Nazi racial strategy. Culture was an important element in that strategy. It would be one thing to eliminate the Jews physically but quite another to eliminate their contribution to German life, especially German cultural life through history and their legacy in the arts. The long-term aim of Nazism was the annihilation of European Jewry. Anti-Semitism was merely part of an historical process; after the Jews had been destroyed in the Holocaust there would be no need of it. The Jews at first censured, then excluded would have disappeared. The only way of knowing what a Jew was at all would be through the eyes of the Nazi propagandist. The logic is clear: all Nazi policies were aimed at the man who, in several generations, his vision fashioned by Nazi ideology, would ask, 'What is a Jew?'. Of course the only answer he would receive would be given him by the propagandist. The reason why the arts were so important to the Nazis is two-fold. Firstly, the arts were used in a process of censuring the Jewish contribution to German civic life. The arts were involved in the contextualization of the Holocaust through their use by Nazi anti-Semitic policy-makers. Secondly, they were part of a longer term process which looked beyond the Holocaust and which was all about annihilating the Jew from history.

Conclusion

The elimination of Jews from German artistic life represented a fundamental racist violation of their human rights, but more than this, it prefigured an attempted annihilation of European Jewry in the Holocaust. Almost immediately after coming to power in 1933 the Nazis set about a well-planned and systematic attack on modern art, whose basis they conceived as degenerate, Jewish and Bolshevik. One of the first pieces of legislation passed by the Nazis was the notorious Civil Service Restoration Act, which though supposedly about restoring a tenured civil service was actually about creating a proper legal basis on which to dismiss teachers, museum curators and the like from employment on racial or political grounds. Jews and many others who did not find favour with the Third Reich were summarily dismissed from their posts. New directors, sympathetic to the cause of National Socialism, were installed in the museums, and exhibitions were organized to censure all forms of modernist art, to do down the Jews and to uphold the Aryan ideal. Art was not criticized as art but censured as 'degenerate'.

There was a vengeful aspect to the attack upon modern art. They saw modern art as both representative of those Jewish-Bolshevik elements which they believed had harmed Germany in the years after 1918, and also came to see in modern art a turning away from tradition. The attack on modern art was about stirring up anti-Semitic and to a lesser extent, anti-Bolshevik feelings. Works of art were attacked but so also were artists, dealers and collectors. Modern art was said to be degenerate; a term imported from biology and reserved for describing ill-health. In large measure such a censure as 'degenerate' was employed to undermine the intellectual basis of modern art – to juxtapose its supposed irrationality with the rationality of the classical Aryan artistic ideal. 'Irrationality' was to be replaced by Nazi order. Nazi health was to be preferred to the 'sickness' of modern art. The Jewish and Bolshevik elements which had come to pollute the German art of the post-1918 era were to be eliminated. This was the way in which the Nazis projected their attack on modern art. It was part of a larger attack upon the modernist movement and upon European Jewry.

The Nazis held to bizarre racist myths. These myths offered not merely an explanation of history but also a hope for the future. The Nazis used hideous stereotypes to convey their conception of the Jew. These stereotypes showed Jewish deceit, ugliness and avarice (Mosse, 1978: 34; Adam, 1992: 12). They exploited the fallacious notion that a person's external appearance was a good guide to personal nature. The Nazi stereotypes had a long lineage. The Aryan was strong, tall, blue-eyed and virile whereas the Jew was misshapen, dark-skinned and villainous. The Jew was not to be trusted (Sumner, 1994: 71). The Nazis offered a visual ideology which was more readily understood. When confronted with a Lombrosian Jew the only reaction was that of loathing. The Jew was sub-human and fit for experimentation upon by the scientists of eugenics or extermination.

The racism which the Nazis promoted fed off the Social Darwinist movement in an attempt to gain some respectability. It sought to blame the Jews and the Bolsheviks for all of Germany's ills. The racism of the Nazis was not pursued in order to explain German history but to escape from it. It is here that the role of art becomes important, since along with other aesthetic devices, it can so focus the mind over a period of time that persons come to see the world as it is presented to them rather than as it really is.

The Aryan was to become for the Nazis the ideal. Art under the Third Reich had to reflect that ideal. All forms of art which departed from the Aryan ideal were deemed degenerate. Adam quotes from a 1937 Ministry of Education pamphlet written by Dr Reinhold Krause in which he writes:

> *'Dadaism, Futurism, Cubism and other isms are the poisonous flower of a Jewish parasitical plant, grown on German soil. . . . Examples of these will be the strongest proof for the necessity of a radical solution to the Jewish question.'* (Adam, 1992: 12–15)

One detects in reasoning like this a desperate desire for racial purity. It was envisaged that if only Germany could develop an organic community, racially pure and in tune with nature, then all would, somehow, be well. The desire after inquiry was not encouraged. Yet such a vision, of gardens and of homogeneity, implies weeding out the unwanted and destroying the foreign, however novel. Nazism drew heavily upon biological and naturalistic imagery. The body of the Aryan nation was polluted and must be cleansed. Yet as Bracher notes, behind the Nazi attempt to build a racial science lay only the reality of myth. Nazi racial theory was merely the receptacle for a thousand thwarted hopes and desires and twisted emotions.

> The fact that the race concept was not spelled out made the race myth an ideal instrument of rule over a people designated as a race engaged in combat with the absolute enemy, and for the super moral justification of the subjugation and annihilation of undesirable groups, minorities, or even entire people: Jews, Poles, Russians – the subhumans. (Bracher, 1991: 320)

It is my contention that any proper attempt to understand the Nazi genocide of millions of men, women and children must engage in a cultural analysis of the inter-war period. Such an analysis would show up just what the Nazis censured and why. It would reveal the concept of beauty the Nazis were working with – a concept that was both restricted and classical. It would show up the censures of 'degeneracy' and insanity and reveal the preferred solution – annihilation – to these conditions. Any cultural analysis would be mindful of the way the Nazis gradually moved to exclude and then remove altogether the Jewish contribution. The fate of modern art in the inter-war period both gave a context for the Holocaust, as Nazi propaganda slandered the un-German elements of the modernist contribution, and prefigures the fate of those persons whom the Nazis sought to remove from the Aryan body-politic.

In the Nazi policy towards the arts one detects a greater goal in mind than simply the destruction of European Jewry's cultural accomplishments, vast though that enterprise was. What the Nazis envisaged was the total elimination of the Jews from history itself. In this regard the burning of books, the destruction of art, and the annihilation of persons were about the same thing.

The crime of the Holocaust encompasses both the annihilation of those Jews around during the period of the Third Reich, and the annihilation of all Jewish history and culture. The Holocaust was a project about the elimination of all Judaic history.

Notes

1   'The metropolis began its race-annihilating work. The coffee houses of the asphalt men became studios; theoretical, bastardized dialects became laws for ever-new directions. A race-chaos of Germans, Jews and anti-natural street races' (Rosenberg, 1970: 149).

2   This work describes the life of German Jesuits before the war and alludes to their fate.

3   Glaser's thesis makes much of the way Nazism adapted German literature, especially Schiller, in its attempt to portray a rural Aryan past which Nazi policy ought to reinstate. Schiller is actually a very accessible writer. A good basic work is: Schiller, F. (1967) *On the Aesthetic Education of Man in a Series of Letters*, tr. Wilkinson, E. and Willoughby, J., Oxford: Oxford University Press.

4   This is a very complex area of study. However some of Prinzhorn's work is available in English: Prinzhorn, H. (1932) *Psychotherapy*, tr. and Ed. Eiloart, A., London: Jonathan Cape.

5   Ironically, much of the *Entartete Kunst* exhibition went for sale after Hitler saw that it could generate income. Eventually the Galerie Fischer in Lucerne organized a sale after winning a tender from the London dealer Colnaghi and two Jewish gallery owners from Paris, Wildenstein and Seligmann (Adam, 1992: 127).

Chapter 5

Populism as Social Control in Latin America

Laurence Grant

For many years South America has appeared to be a forgotten continent as far as sociology has been concerned. For far too long it was perceived as being forever embroiled in, at first, epic battles for independence, and then later in the twentieth century as suffering from a succession of at best undemocratic, and at worst highly authoritarian regimes. The Southern Cone states, namely Chile, Uruguay, and Argentina, as well as Brazil, have long been the sites of radical social and political upheaval, particularly in the latter period of the twentieth century. Whilst much has been written of the authoritarian periods of these states and their anomalous position within the context of the polarized communist–fascist ideological dialectic evident in Europe at that time (1930s onwards), less attention seems to have been paid to the seemingly more interesting phenomenon that was populism. The political history of these countries – particularly that of Argentina and Brazil – has certainly been tainted by the detrimental effects of successive military juntas and heavily bureaucratic authoritarian systems of government, yet their populist experiences indicate just as much (if not more, as a result of their more democratic style) about the nature of their social, political, and economic character.

My aim in this chapter is to explore the populist experiences of Argentina during the period of the Perón administration and to try to establish a matrix of social, political, and economic relations in order to explain why it arose. Furthermore, having once established how and why Argentina and other Latin American countries[1] apparently chose to immerse themselves in systems of government that can be described in no other way than 'populist', I will attempt to illustrate with a variety of examples the way the populist years represented little more in terms of liberal democracy than the authoritarian regimes of the military kind. There are some difficulties posed by the use of the term populism. The term is valuable only through political and historical analysis and to talk about the aims of populism is somewhat misleading. This will be looked at a later stage. Essentially, the key question is: in what ways was populism appealing to the increasing hopes and aspirations of the people whose country had long suffered at the hands of tyranny, mass corruption, and economic minnowism, and subsequently, in what ways did populism take advantage of such popular optimism and manipulate it in order to sustain power for individual leaders?

My work will attempt to focus upon certain fundamentally characteristic features of the Perón era, referring to both the political tactics of the administration itself and to the social mobilization of the masses and the social conditions that led to the coming to power, the sustainment of, and eventually the downfall of what we now see as an archetypal populist experience.

The overt methods of social control that were so characteristic of the Perón regime, and other Latin American forms of populist political movements, must be seen as the epitome of the employment of violence – or more accurately the threat of violence – in order to erect a Leviathan of hegemony. Law and order, economic transition, social, scientific, and cultural homogeneity, were all goals of a movement that required the mass support of the electorate and the neutralization of the influence of potentially threatening, and supposedly subversive sectors of society. The nature of populism in Latin America is such that not only should one attempt to decipher the political and historical evolution of the ideological forms that were the catalyst for the emergence of such regimes, but equally as important is the issue of whom it was targeting its ideology at. Furthermore, who was it not targeting its ideology at? The populist propensity towards inclusion and exclusion is central to the wider discussion in this book and relates to the works of the other contributors, particularly Ethan Raup. The use of censures to create political demons and traitors to the national cause and 'destiny' was a method of establishing new political parameters within which it would be quite clear who is contributing to the cause and who is corrupting it. Populism is defined as much in its targeting as in its ideology; in fact the two dimensions are rather complementary features of the populist phenomena in Latin America. This chapter will, I hope, reveal something about the very nature of populist movements that illustrates the violence of censure and its inextricable links to the development and consolidation of such nationalist political movements. Just because there is no explicit expression of state violence and oppression does not exclude, firstly, the possible fact that it is occurring at a more sinister and covert level, or secondly, that the threat of violence is just as damaging to the freedom and liberty of the individuals and the psyche of the developing nation. Consent and democratic freedom, as has been all too clear in the twentieth century, are never absolute, never objective, never universal, never equal, and as a result are very much determined by extraneous variables such as the imposition of violence and indoctrination of the masses through propoganda and palatable ideology.

The importance of such an approach for criminology and, more specifically, the sociology of deviance, is clear. Not only will an exploration of a phenomenon like populism force one to examine issues around hegemony, ideology, authority, and mass society, but will I hope lend much academic support to the newly emerging school of critical criminology in Latin America. Latin American criminologists and academics of a variety of backgrounds showed in a meeting at the Instituto de Criminologia, Universidad del Zulia, Maracaibo, Venezuela (1986: *Hacia una Teoria*

Crítica del Social Control) how the study of social control is entering a new era. The development of 'critical criminology' by the organizer of the meeting, Lola Aniyar de Castro, was intended to 'direct its attention to the study of social control (formal as well as informal) rather than focus on the study of law as has traditionally been the case in Latin America'.[2]

The move away from specialization towards a broader, multi-disciplinarian, approach to issues of social control in Latin America resulted in the emergence of 'critical social control' instead of 'critical criminology'. The benefit of the adoption of such a paradigm is that one can introduce areas otherwise neglected, such as education, religion, economics, philosophy, history, politics, and various other disciplines, into a wider discourse. It would be simplistic and erroneous to assume that to cast a criminological eye over a phenomenon like populism would mean simply to assess the legal, criminal, and juridical corollaries of such political circumstances. Moreover, to extract any real theoretical understanding of the corollaries of populism for social control one must throw a wider contextual net over the area, and to include other disciplines within the discourse is, therefore, a necessary and highly illuminative strategy. However, I will limit myself to a series of examples of what I believe to be ways in which populism in Latin America attempted to create (and in some ways achieved) a mass society through the imposition of various methods of social control: a multi-class, urban-based, system of government that aimed to come to terms with the onset of modernity and inevitable phases of economic transition. Reference is made to the way in which populism as an anti status-quo method of social reform tempered the psyche of the masses and directed it towards a single (yet ideologically incoherent) national effort. As Hennessy (1969: 29) points out, 'populism in Latin America can be defined as an organisational weapon to synchronise divergent group interests and is applied to any movement not based in a specific social class'.

Whilst this is a wide definition that requires further qualification, it nevertheless indicates the way in which populism in Latin America was essentially a contrived and manipulative system of integrating marginal populations into the increasingly modern urban experience that was Buenos Aires, São Paulo, and Montevideo in the middle of the twentieth century. The economic arguments as to how and why populism emerged so strongly as a potential solution to the urbanization and modernization of these predominantly urban-based states are as complex as they are numerous; suffice to say that the emergence of populism was certainly more than a temporal coincidence. My analysis will attempt to show how the relationship between the masses and the rhetoric and symbolism of populist leaders necessitated certain methods of social control in order to sustain an administration that was stronger at a symbolic level than at a policy level (as was certainly the case in Argentina). Thus my discussion will be supra-economic, yet not avoiding certain economic factors.

Implicit in my conception of populism as a form of social control is the notion that populism is characterized by a series of overtly hegemonic policies and measures, so that whilst on the one hand it mobilized mass political participation and united various classes and cultural groups with traditional antagonisms underneath a strict hierarchy, it is on the other hand inherently authoritarian, as a result of its need to maintain a decent level of social order in a system that cannot possibly serve all the interests of its cross-sectional support. That is to say that the methods of social control were a way of hiding the corruptive and oligarchic elements of the Perónist government through reaffirming the more politically expedient calls to national social and political unity: a movement whose strength is its ability to sustain mass popular support by identifying with the base desires and anti-liberalist feelings of a large part of the electorate, yet concomitantly obstructing their ability to form an autonomous power group within that society.

Stuart Hall's (1979, 1983) concept of 'authoritarian populism' (AP) aims to interpret the rise of Thatcherism in Britain as a shift towards a hegemonic politics whereby a diverse cross-section of the population were mobilized behind a movement seeking to reaffirm the hegemonic position of state authority within society, whilst still retaining the democratic systems of political participation. A movement that he believes the Left in Britain have failed to match since. The definitive 'swing to the Right' witnessed in the early years of Thatcherism was much more than a delegitimization of traditional labour-based values, but was a result of a multiplicity of social and economic misfortunes and failures. However, he stresses that the popularity of the Right in Britain was significantly more than an ideological backlash. It was a result of a state in crisis; the recessionary period of the 1960s twinned with the increasing social and political significance of the law and order issue.[3] Heavily influenced by the works of Gramsci on hegemony, Hall sees AP in Thatcherite Britain as an attempt '[to] radically . . . deconstruct the social democratic framework involved in the post-war settlement and to construct a new "common sense" and a new "hegemonic project"' (Jessop *et al.*, 1984). In many ways the Thatcherite experience in Britain throws up some interesting and highly relevant illustrations of the way populism and the striving forward of the state for an amplified hegemony, behind (or underneath!) which the masses can come together and be unified, can be effected and sustained by, a consensus which favoured the ruling leaders (or populist hegemonic bloc if you will) more than it ever did the people. This new consensus was in effect a perfect representation of the inherent contradictions within the modern democratic state; the near oxymoron of 'authoritarian populism' captures well the passive revolutions that occurred in Thatcherite Britain, Perónist Argentina, and Getúlist Brazil – movements that were presented as the saviours of the state in crisis, but which were really conning the people into believing that these leaders had their best interests at heart – or which acted as a species of 'populist ventriloquism in which the power bloc speaks in the name of the people and dissimulates its own ideas as those of the people' (Jessop *et al.*, 1984: p. 36). Coercion and consent fused into a movement that promised to deliver exactly what the people wanted, presenting them with opportunities to buy their own houses, freeing them by freeing the market, and maintaining law and order by cracking down on those who dared to step out of line. Basically, in order to acquire and then secure power, the ruling bloc must be seen to represent the interests of a cross-section of class and status interests. Once this has been achieved – that is, once in government – the fight to stay there is so great and necessary that mobilization of popular support can only be effective through systematic hegemonic expression: new ideological forms that are transformed into apparently revolutionary policies that favour everybody, or more significantly favour the nation. In this sense they suppose the existence of a new and revolutionary agenda with solutions to old problems; what we really have is a bastardized form of democracy acting through overtly hegemonic forms of social control.

The Usefulness of the Term 'Populism'

Any discussion of populism in Latin America must be seen as distinctly different to other forms of populism in other regions. Whilst there are varying views of what populism in this region is, and whether or not it is a useful way of contextualizing the vast political, social, and economic upheavals that occurred in the periods of the Vargas and Perón administrations, there seems to be an academic consensus upon what the characteristic features of populism were at that time. The two main theoretical approaches are the classical approach and the discourse analysis approach.

The classical theorists' view is that populism is characterized by several distinguishing features. Firstly that populism was a 'loosely organised multiclass movement united by a charismatic leader behind an ideology and programme of social justice and nationalism' (Roxborough, 1987: p. 119). Secondly, there is an inherent link between 'ideology' and 'organization'. Thirdly there is a high level of political participation. The absence and/or weakness of an autonomous working class was also recognized as a distinct feature of populism. Finally, and probably most significantly to any discussion of social control and populism, the masses have little or no autonomy and subsequently follow the hegemonic strata of society.

The discourse analysis view on the other hand states that populism is purely an ideology (and nothing more) that implies some sort of political struggle between the masses and the imperialists or oligarchy. Such a view has been strongly supported by the work of Ernesto Laclau (particularly 1977).

One of the major problems with dealing with the concept of populism is that the distinction between the call to populist support, and a populist movement gravitating towards some sort of unifying, heteronomous force in politics is often not wholly clear. In this discussion one must be very careful to clarify what one means by the term 'populist' and what types of meaning are being attributed to the word. One does not necessarily flow from the other. Populism is a very confusing term in many ways. It is a generic term that is used to apply to a wide variety of political regimes or governments and is often applicable to cases identifiably diverse in social, economic, cultural, historical, and political circumstances. Inclusive definitions are not very useful and so there is a need to adopt a position whereby one can analyse the political and economic relations that are occurring, as well as the power relations of the individual–state kind. Nevertheless there are some useful features that one may look for when attempting to identify the true essence of the populist phenomenon:

1. Populist movements are generally urban in focus.

2. They are opposed to the status quo.

3. There is an orientation towards the acceleration of industrial development.

4. It is comprised of, and by, a construction of alliances across class boundaries.

5. It has a broadly nationalistic ideology (which may eclipse class antagonisms).

Stein (1987) takes a economic and Marxian view of populism when he suggests that populism can best be seen as a reaction to structural shifts in development, urbanization on a mass scale, industrialization, and the massifying nature of the rapidly developing economies. Oligarchies led to mass societies which in turn produced populist movements which constituted the principal form of social control in Latin America. The aim was to integrate the masses into a national entity without disrupting the existing system.

> In the very act of providing a form of structured participation to working-class people, populist movements have functioned as an institutional restraint to those sectors of society with the greatest potential for social explosion, converting them instead into a new base of support for an established system in crisis. (Stein, 1987: 128)

'Enforced stability' (Stein, 1987: 125) in Latin America, in the period of the Cuban revolution and the emergence of Castroism, confirmed a rightward trend in the continent. Even when authoritarianism has not been at the forefront of these societies, the expected build-up of revolutionary processes has not occurred. The lack of popular dissent in many of these states can be linked to the various mechanisms of social control that have helped to maintain the status quo. Stein believes that, 'For mass social control, the general climate of fear created in all societies where extensive repression has taken place has proven more important than isolated repressive acts' (1987: 126).[4] Furthermore, he identifies patrimonialist values as playing a significant role in the method of repression manifest in the framework of values which have supported, practically, the basic inequalities and worked to diffuse mass protest. Patrimonialism had its origins in the semi-feudal colonial systems of Spain and Portugal and official and folk Catholicism, and seemed to stress a society dictated by ideologies of hierarchy and organicism. Socially constructed channels of vertical kinship; a patron–client reciprocal network where the rich and the powerful elite charity the poor and the powerless, and they in return display gratitude and deference. Institutionally and politically speaking, this system of ideals has diminished, if not prevented, any ideas of the self- or class-consciousness to come between the rulers and the ruled. Yet again patrimonialism has encouraged the acceptance of 'elaborate patronage organs [having] exercised a seminal role in linking together the rulers and the ruled' (1987: 127). Stein then identifies certain features of populism in Latin America which correspond to his analysis. South American populist movements have been:

1. socially multi-class;

2. structurally hierarchical and authoritarian;

3. ideologically nationalistic and semi-corporatist;

4. characterized by a central dynamic that has personalistic and particularistic ties between the powerful leaders and the dependent followers;

5. appeared with large-scale social massification (brought on by rapid urbanization more often than not);

6. replaced traditional political elites whose ability to rule has been eroded by social discontinuities attendant to the massification process.

The primary impact then is vastly to increase the level of political participation whilst directing it into paternalistic forms serving to bolster an exploitative status quo. In this sense there is a definite element of conservatism here: despite the creation of new forms and a sense of popular mobilization as a reaction against the traditional oligarchic infrastructure, the creation of these forms as a vehicle to impede increasing levels of liberalization and what was seen as the dangerous corollaries of free-market capitalism and social democracy in a transitional era was implicit in populist ideology. Although Stein warns us of the immediate, wholesale adoption of the term 'populist' and its application, he recognizes three ways in which the term is rendered useful:

1. The term can be and has been used to refer to movements such as Getúlism and Perónism etc.

2. Many disparities are attributable to diverse and contrasting historical, socio-economic contexts.

3. Whilst not identical, many of the heralded models of populism display strong commonalties.

Laclau (1977) takes us through the various paradigms through which it is possible to see populism through theory. He identifies four basic approaches to a discourse on populism which fuse the ideology with the movement, and one which sees it merely as an ideological phenomenon.

Expression of a dominant class. In Latin America this is manifested in the political and ideological expression of petit-bourgeoisie; a national bourgeoisie seeking to mobilize the masses for a confrontation with the local oligarchies and imperialism (hence the opposition to liberalism and the propensity towards nationalism). The major problem with such a view is that it evades what it attempts to explain.

Theoretic nihilism. This view of populism suggests that the term be removed from the social sciences because it fails to make analyses of each divergent political structure or movement. The problem that arises with such a view however, is that 'We can even accept the argument that populism is insufficient to define the concrete specificity of a certain kind of political movement. But can we deny that it constitutes an abstract element of it?' (Laclau, 1977: 146).

Restriction of the term to an ideology only, with the application of the term to the movement itself omitted. The movement has certain relevant characteristics that must not be ignored here, such as the hostility to the status quo, mistrust of traditional politicians, appealing to the people and not the classes, and anti-intellectualism. This allows us room for application of the conceptualism of populism to historical retrospective analyses, where differing movements, from differing social, economic, political, and cultural bases, have been seen to adopt and adapt populism as such. For example, Perónism can be seen as a manifestation of the general distrust of the traditional politicians and the traditional oligarchic expressions and channels of political power. Furthermore the widespread corruptive elements were sewing the seeds of reaction and desire for an upheaval of these traditional political systems, the populist call for political and social unification managed effectively to mobilize across class and cultural boundaries because they recognized this single-consensus view of Argentine politics. The promulgation of the social and political censure of corruption into their ideological banner quite successfully attracted support by appearing to respond to the electorates' distrust and anger with corruption. There are two main problems here: firstly one is presented with a purely descriptive view of the features of populism, and secondly nothing is said of the 'populist element' at work.

The functionalist conception. In the previous approaches populism is seen as purely ideological. We shall now turn to the theoretical proponents of the functionalist analysis of the populist phenomenon. Two of the most significant contributors to contemporary functionalist thought of populism in Latin America are Gino Germani and Turcuato Di Tella. They both dismiss the simplistic Marxian analysis of class struggle and populism as an inevitable feature of societies attempting to come to terms with economic phases of transition, and instead focus upon a multiplicity of features which they see as contributing to the unique pattern of social change through nationalist ideology which is of a distinctive Latin American type.

Germani (1965) looks at the areas of economic development and how this has affected the circumstances through which the emergence of trends that are evident within Latin American populism have come about. The shift from traditional to industrial societies involves three fundamental changes:[5]

1. Passage from an institutionalization of tradition to that of change.

2. Evolution from relatively undifferentiated complex of institutions to an increasing modification of the type of social action.

3. Differentiation and specialization of them.

Germani uses this theoretical framework to illustrate how populist movements emerge, making a distinction between the two phases of the emergence of democracy in Western Europe and in Latin America. In the first phase the state was rational, bureaucratic and based upon a philosophy of individual liberty, yet there were no universal political rights – these were reserved for the bourgeoisie. In the second phase, as capital and the workers spread and became urbanized (and to an extent more organized), they became more a part of political life.[6] Latin America was different however, as a result of its differing degrees of integration of such processes and change, or as Germani puts it:

> The difference between the example of England and other Western countries and the case of Latin America lies, then, in the different degree of correspondence between the gradual mobilization of an increasing proportion of the population (and eventually all of it) and the emergence of multiple mechanisms of integration – and universities, education, social legislation, political parties, mass consumption – capable of absorbing these successive groups, providing them with means for adequate self-expression, both academically and lyrically, as well as other basic aspects of modern culture. (Germani, 1965: 157)

Consequently mobilization occurs in anti-institutional ways (quite different from European ways), and the impossibility of mobilization carried out through integration forms a matrix from which the national-popular movements emerge. Germani adds that premature incorporation of the masses into Latin American political life created unreasonable and unsustainable pressures of absorption and participation which the political structures were unable to provide for:

> Consequently, mass integration on the model of Nineteenth Century Europe could not be carried out, and various elites, influenced by the new historical climate of the Twentieth Century, manipulated the newly mobilized masses to service their own ends. The mentality of those masses, because of their insufficient integration, was characterized by the coexistence of traditional and modern features. Hence populist movements constitute a haphazard accumulation of fragments corresponding to the most dissimilar paradigms. (Laclau, 1977: 150–1)

Di Tella (1965) describes populism as 'a political movement which enjoys the support of the masses of the urban working-class and/or peasantry, but which does not result from the autonomous organizational power of either of those two sectors'. This is quite a functionalist description and recognizes that although classes are present within it, they are not operating upon class interests or through class consciousness. Like Germani, Di Tella notes that the divide between the classes and the non-class-based forms of expression can be traced to the asynchronism between processes of economic, social, and political development. But Di Tella seems to go somewhat further, and suggests that it is the 'revolution of rising expectations' and the demonstration effect that is responsible for this asynchronism. The explanation as to how this happened in Latin America is attributed to various contributory factors in society: the growth of the mass-media increases aspiration levels of the population; the proliferation of the arts, poetry, youth culture, and contemporary and folk-music played their part; and the dissemination of literature such as *The Rights of Man*. However, economic expansion was left sorely lagging behind, and the demographic explosion, reliance on foreign markets and capital, and the premature efforts of redistribution all contributed to the imbalance mentioned above, or as Laclau would call it 'a bottleneck' (1977: 152). These conditions then become established and the difficulties for traditional, Western-style democracies to have any real foundations or validity are enhanced – and so populism emerges. According to Di Tella the stage is reached whereby the conditions for populism are optimum, but how exactly are the masses mobilized into a coherent support-base for a populist regime? The explanation given is that the elite leads the potentially fractured disparate supporting groups, through an anti-status quo ideology. Emanating from this a mobilized mass is generated by a 'revolution of rising expectations' until finally there is an ideology with widespread appeal. It is important to note here that whilst Di Tella points out the *ad hoc* nature of such an ideology emanating from an asynchronistic limbo period during and between the periods of economic transition, he sees the adoption of populism as a positive and important instrument for reform and change.

Finally, as a general overview of populism we now turn to Wiles (1969: 166–8), who sets out a series of features that constitute populism, although it is important to note that not all are manifest in each case, and that because of this no case of populism is pure. Populism displays the following features:

It is moralistic rather than pragmatic (although the contrary could very easily be argued when looking at populism as a form of social control). Thus the leaders are important in their actions, image, and rhetoric. Populism therefore tends to throw up great leaders in 'mystical contact' with their masses. It is invariably a loosely organized and ill-disciplined movement rather than a party. Similarly its ideology is somewhat loose and incoherent and attempts to define it are deconstructive and cause hostility. Such populist movements are vehemently anti-intellectualist even to the extent of populist intellectuals following such a line. Hence the leaders are usually vicarious populists with self-denying ideologies. They also manifest highly anti-establishment tendencies and rhetoric – usually populist movements arise when a large group become, or feel, alienated from the centres of state power and as a result can adopt violence and conspiracy theories. This is very interesting for the discussion of Latin American populism, since when one looks at the large wave of new European immigrants in Brazil and Argentina at the turn of the century one can see how the urbanization of the labour force produced large numbers of people with a strong propensity towards bettering their lot, and the only way they could see themselves realizing greater aspirations was through the securing of greater political leverage. Certainly Latin American populist movements were innately violent, especially so in the case of *Perónismo*, but this was only sporadic, pragmatic and unglorified violence. There was rarely a struggle connected to any ideology as such – that is, it was hardly revolutionary violence.

Populism avoids class war in the Marxist sense, as in Marxism there was a greater leaning towards anti-intellectualism and anti-establishmentarianism than to class consciousness. This populism was typically anti-church, although often quite religious. There were tendencies towards ideological opposition to science and technocracy of course as a theoretical corollary of its heralding of tradition and simplicity, and as such populism is quite nostalgic. One must also recognize the integral role played by racialist tendencies within populism. This relates to the conservative nature of populism and the tendency toward the adoption of conspiracy theories as mentioned earlier. So we can see the prevalence of anti-Semitic and anti-native views attaching themselves to the populist movements in Argentina and Brazil, but only because they believe that such cultural differences of groups determine ulterior interests to that of 'the common man' and of the nation.

Now that we have seen some of the differing theoretical definitions of what populism is, and how the term can be interpreted in various ways, we can see how difficult it is to establish exactly what we mean by populism. Despite there being no single working definition of 'populism' I hope to have illustrated how populism as a set of social and political forms is inextricably linked to the political, the economic, and the cultural development of the countries we are concerned with. Furthermore, some of the features of populism in the states under scrutiny should now be clear. In the following pages I will attempt to display just how some of these features were manifest and in what ways the nationalistic tendencies, the role of the single charismatic leader, the anti-intellectualism, and the organization of labour, can be seen as aspects of a social system that was veering ever closer towards enslaving its people with false optimism, empty promises, and generally imposing strict social control over them by a carrot and stick method: the carrot being the promises of a new society free of corruption and free from a controlling oligarchy, and better opportunities and quality of life for the ever-growing urban masses; the stick being the threat of being ideologically isolated and being perceived as a traitor to the future of the nation.

The Rise of Perónism in Argentina

The rise of Perónism in Argentina after the military coup in 1943 was an inevitable watershed in Argentine politics. Not only did it represent a significant decline of deference from the masses to the politically and economically dominant oligarchic rulers, but it also heralded the initiation of a new form of democracy whereby the masses, or more specifically the *descamisados*,[7] were drawn into the political processes by the new leader, Juan Perón, and his wife Eva. No longer would the common man have to put up with the manipulation, economic betrayal, and the economic expropriation facilitated by the country being controlled by rich land-owners. In the new Argentina of Perón the oligarchy were the initial and primary enemy of the state. The evilness of this dominant class was explicitly expressed in speeches and public statements and was linked to its allies in the church, the military, and the rural masses as opposed to the urban population.

> To manage the economy of the country in such a manner that it may no longer be the privilege of a few, but the patrimony of all . . . ; to raise the economic standard of the citizens and to give all Argentines an opportunity to lead a worthier and better life. (Perón, 1950: 37)

Such an attack upon the oligarchy shows how they could act as a scape-goat, especially in economic terms, a symbol of the country bring held to ransom not too dissimilar to the Tory portrayal of the trade unions in the early and mid-term era of the Thatcher government in Britain. However, some theorists cast doubt upon the idea that the Perón government actually saw the oligarchy as a real threat to the future of the country. Blanksten (1953), for instance, notes that to actually attack the landowners' economic control through policies of a land reform kind was a step further than Perón was willing to go.

The diminished role of the oligarchy in political terms, vis-à-vis the power they wielded in the *Casa Rosada*, was certainly apparent after the *Perónistas* ascendance to power, yet if the oligarchy's economic dominance was truly to be challenged an economic revolution of mass land redistribution would have to take place. Not only was such a revolution unfeasible in the sense that it would destabilize any alliances that already existed between the *Perónistas* and the *estancieros*, but moreover it would effect such a rupture in the status and class position of the land-owning minority that it would threaten the whole legitimacy of the political arena within which the new administration was working. From such an analysis one could draw the conclusion that Perón was more committed to attacking the status position of the oligarchy and their historically unchallenged and undemocratic position at the apex of political power in Argentina, than their *actual* economic influence. That is to say that a *modus vivendi* was worked out between the land-owners and Perón, whereby any attacks upon them were restricted to verbal as-saults – 'buying thereby their acquiescence in his rule. This interpretation implies at least a tacit conspiracy between an individual (Perón) . . . and a class (*estancieros*) . . . to hoodwink another class (workers)' (Kirkpatrick, 1971: 35). Although an un-substantiated theory, such a view is the first of many examples of the way in which the Perónist government was seen to work on several political levels. It was sug-gested that the government's mandate was of a class-based nature, and that the interests of the urbanized labour of the cities were for once at the top of the political agenda thus drawing mass support from the traditionally disenfranchised and eco-nomically disempowered masses. Yet at the same time there was a strong relation-ship forming between the government and the supposed enemy of such interests; it was unwilling to follow through with action upon its anti-capitalist, anti-oligarchy rhetoric.

The *Perónistas* seemed to embody a philosophical opposition to the capitalist system of property ownership, which was seen by most as an undesirable remnant of the Spanish colonial system, and which fitted in nicely with the promise to push the Argentine economy into the direction of urban development and mass industrialization with a view to providing increased employment opportunities. The rhetoric was shrewdly pitched at one level, whilst the economic policy (or the lack of it) was clearly operating at another. Comprehensive land reform was absent, hence the suggestion that the Perónist hostility to the land-owners was more symbolic than real. This is certainly a bone of contention: is class struggle under a democratic system only real when it results in revolution, and is reform not possible in other ways? As mentioned above, the threat of revolutionary tendencies (or even undirected social disorder) from a class suddenly uprooted from its economic and geographical roots was all too real; a similar example would be the position of the formerly land-owning Afrikaners in the new multi-racial democratic Republic of South Africa.

Whether one believes that this whole process of failing to usurp the economic power-base and influence of the traditional elite was a result of the threat it may have posed to the wider restructuring plans that Perón had for the new Argentina, or whether one sees it as simply a two-faced political enterprise that would reap the benefits of economic support from both the oligarchs, and the masses who were being promised a state that served them, depends upon one basic question. That question is whether one really believes that Perón's aim was to act upon his promises and bring about a social and economic revolution that would take Argentina into a new era, or whether one believes that the Perónist movement was essentially dominated by an anti-liberal support for the status quo and that any elements of class consciousness were merely a cynical attempt to mobilize popular support from the masses.

Although the actions of the first Perónist government may not be reducible to such simple analysis, it is clear that the populist element of the administration was such that mobilization of mass popular support from the working class did not necessitate the political annihilation of the oligarchy. What is more relevant to the examination of the power of the oligarchy is their self-perception as having more status than actual power. Such feelings were not restricted to the large land-owning *estancieros*. The church too, in spite of its traditionally central position in a strongly Roman Catholic country, never believed that it actually exerted a significant amount of socio-economic or political leverage with any government.[8] This illustrates the perception by many of the *Perónista* supporters of the social elites as the enemy of the state. Kirkpatrick (1971) supports the theory that such propaganda from the Perónist administration was an extremely powerful and effective way of turning one sector of society upon another. It had as its central aim the portrayal of the social elites as being the stumbling block against the nation's facilitation of economic success and widespread social reform. Whilst class struggle was never a primary definer of the Peronist agenda, the suggestion that any revolution (whether democratic or otherwise!) would come from below, from the masses, was an explicit feature of the ideology of the movement. In this way one can recognize that the political identity and image of Perónism as a movement, was very different from its political agenda. Ideology was of paramount importance when talking about the mobilization of mass popular support, but as far as core Perónists were concerned the location of real power was never taken for granted; they knew that the power of the movement in Argentine society vastly exceeded its power in government. Here the dialectic of populism as a movement or an ideology raises its head once again – Perónism was an explicit attempt to put political power into the hands of a new hegemonic bloc by mobilizing mass opposition to a common political enemy. The irony was that the reason for such mass support for a strong national populist movement was the previous absence of any dominant source of political direction and power; the scape-goating of the social elites helped direct such populist support in the direction of a movement presenting a fallacious ideology.

Kirkpatrick notes, that like many other Latin American countries, Argentina's history since colonization is written with 'social aggregates as the principal actors' (1971: 121). This feature of Argentine history is such that he believes that the identity of certain social groupings became so strong through political commentary and journalism that they took on a political significance within social discourse that was often greater than in reality. The operation of Perónism as a populist ideological movement seemed to utilize this tendency to ascribe heavy political significance to the oligarchy and the *descamisados* alike, in order to paint a picture to the masses of a polarized political landscape that never really existed in that form. Not only did the Perónist manipulation of the Argentine propensity to view society through a collection of social aggregates (as opposed to individuals and organizations) attempt to mobilize a wide cross-section of support against a supposed enemy, it also attempted to portray the military and the professional politicians as running the country for their own benefit and lining their own pockets. On the one hand it was an attempt to encourage popular support for a movement that promised the removal from power of those whose personal interests were greater than the interests of the nation as a whole, and on the other hand, to portray the Perónist movement as the centre of the political universe.

Perónism: Allies, Enemies, and Populist Repression

Now we turn to the style of leadership that has often been described as overtly authoritarian in style, and not wholly democratic in policy terms either. The need to continuously mobilize support for the movement and maintain a high level of social unity requires the help of a little bit of populism taken from the European school. That is to say that although the unions and the church were linked to Perón he did not want them too close. The three appealing Perónist goals of economic independence, popular sovereignty, and social justice, were central to the popularity of the movement throughout the country and across the diverse spectrum of social aggregates, yet increasingly the politics of a populist movement began to resemble 'the politics of a dictatorship' (Alexander, 1951).

Although Perón achieved power through democratic means, he soon arrived at the point where he felt it unnecessary and irrelevant to continue operating in that mode. He never really valued the concept of political democracy and even suggested that:

> Whoever wishes to consider political questions without hypocrisy must acknowledge that all the democratic system was based upon hollow principles, because what really counted – and I have stated this on other occasions – was not the regime itself but its outward form. (Perón, *Political and Social Situation Prior to the Revolution of 1943*, pamphlet)

It seems that he had made a link between political democracy and capitalist economic exploitation. This was not unprecedented, yet it was unique in its sacrificing of democracy as a means to some end. The concept of having a leader who would operate through autocratic methods was increasingly becoming a reality.

Perón's drive to draft a new constitution through a constitutional convention in December 1948 was one that raised much opposition. The Argentine Bar Association and the socialist Radical Party, as well as other anti-Perónist groups voiced their opposition to any constitutional reform by the regime as they were beginning to see it as the thin end of the wedge. Perón had decided that the Argentine constitution of 1853 was very outdated and that 'it cannot serve a nation of 16,000,000 inhabitants already in the advanced stages of modern industry, with all the economic problems that the new situation proposes' (*La Prensa*, Buenos Aires, 4 September 1948). The following astute prediction was made in a Radical Party manifesto of the same year:

> The president has said . . . that the Argentine constitution is of the time of the horse and buggy and that today we live in the air age . . . the constitutions of the United States and England are also of the time of the horse and buggy in those countries. No jurist, no statesman, no thinker has yet confused mechanical progress with the stability of the cultural process reflected in political and social institutions. . . . The worst aspect of the reform with which we are menaced is its mystery. . . . Does anybody know what will happen to freedom of the press, to the federal system, to the judiciary? (*La Prensa*, Buenos Aires, 9 November 1948)

The Church and the State in Perón's Argentina

Prior to Perón, the church was slowly and carefully moving towards disestablishment. It was clear that religious liberty was freely granted in Argentina and that any constitutional links between the state and the church were unnecessary in terms of securing freedom of religious expression, and in terms of the Roman Catholic Church wielding any political power. In the 1943 revolution the issue of the church became somewhat of a political hot-potato. The church was however not a mono-lithic entity in Perónist Argentina – the split between the image of the church in the countryside and in the urban areas of Buenos Aires was a clear one that perhaps reflected the growing social cleavage within the Argentine populations.

In the interior of the country people tended to be more devout and pious, and the church certainly exerted significant political and social influence at the commu-nity and local government level. In the urban areas, and particularly in Buenos Aires, the people, although predominantly believing Catholics, were much less frequent church-goers as a result of the cultural context of a modern, industrialized, urban environment.

Any government supporting the church in Argentina would immediately com-mand support from a vast section of the population. Perón sought such support and was therefore expressing support himself for an institution that, while not com-manding much political influence at the national level, commanded a large sector of the population as its eternal ally. Perón attempted to stand astride this demo-graphic and cultural gap with a political foot in either camp. Propaganda in the interior portrayed him as the devout, religious man, a vast exaggeration of the true nature of the leader, whilst in Buenos Aires he was portrayed as the man of faith with a modernist perspective, sympathetic to the cosmopolitan intricacies of a city life that perhaps brought about a social dilution of traditional religious doctrine and Christian morality.

In the months following the 1943 revolution, several church leaders attempted to secure political access to the *Casa Rosada* and utilize the new government as a guarantor of the liberty of the people, but these leaders soon became enemies of the state when they questioned the issue of authoritarianism. The right-wing of the church however, led by Cardinal Santiago Luis Copello, the primate of Argentina, Monseñor Tranceschi, Padre Wilkinson Dirube, and later Padre Virgillio M. Filippo, became a strong ally of the regime. This wing of the church was strongly pro-authoritarian, anti-Semitic, and clearly anti-democratic and anti-liberal. To read this alliance as a matching of ideologies would not be difficult but above all it was much more of a political project, and an opportunist one at that, for both parties. To infer that Perón was an anti-Semite, a nationalist, and a devout Roman Catholic simply because of such a political alliance with the right-wing of the church is highly erroneous. Such moral and ideological issues were not dominant in his agenda and ultimately were far lower in the order of political merit than power and control – the retention of political power through authoritarian means was upper-most. The *Perónistas* who took power in 1943 were far from a homogeneous group of religious, conservative, anti-Semites; some were like that but generally power was the primary motive for the new hegemonic bloc. Furthermore, the parallel between the authoritarianism of the regime and certain religious figures and icons was one that reified the acceptability of certain measures of social control amongst the rank-and-file religious *descamisados* of the interior.

You must shut your mouth because Jesus Christ himself was a great dictator.
(Padre Filippo, quoted in Associated Press dispatch, 26 November 1945)

Perón soon realized the importance of an alliance between his regime and the clerics as another binding factor that could help to mobilize more support. Alexander suggests that Perón had 'attempted to lift *Peronismo* from the status of a political doctrine to an article of faith for all Argentines; the implication being that what Perón and the *Perónistas* [did] is not to be questioned, not even by the Church' (1951: 132). This is interesting because it can be seen as an attempt to create some sort of theological buttress between the ideology of *Perónismo* and the masses with two fundamental effects:

1. Greater legitimacy for the ideology itself by displaying an apparent interpolation of religious faith and national unity under the hegemonic bloc.

2. Consolidation of the already deeply entrenched channels of propaganda dissipation through the clerics and church.

God and Jesus were portrayed as the ultimate dictators, and so to portray Perón in a similar manner would strengthen the legitimacy given to his authoritarian style. Leadership, dictatorship, hegemony, direction and the quasi-divine fate of the nation strengthened the support base of the *Perónistas*. Anti-communist, anti-liberalist – the consolidation of all that was good – a conservative rhetoric, tradition and national pride tailor-made to whichever sector of the population he happened to be addressing at the time. A skilful adaptability of supporting, for example, anti-Semitism when profitable and switching the issue off when need be.

The imposition of religious instruction in schools in Decree No. 18,411 of 31 December 1943 represented not only a forging of the alliance between the regime and the conservative wings of the church, but also reflected the Perónist trump card: patriotism.

The transformation to the 'new Argentina' needed to include the church in some capacity in order not to risk the possibility of a religious backlash. Aligning himself with the church, Perón masterfully pulled off one of the major political confidence tricks (arguably there were many more to come!) of his times as leader of Argentina:

These [revival of compulsory religious instruction and redrafting of the constitution] and kindred measures were endorsed by the regime as vehicles for the transfer of some of the religious loyalty of the country's Catholics to the 'new Argentina'. (Blanksten, 1953: 235)

The mastery of this political manipulation of the church is seen in the way in which the church was never allowed to get in the way of the movement and the direction in which the country was being steered. Perón was the country's leader and that suggested that, whatever shreds of sincerity remained in his alliance with the church, it essentially played a sinecure role and this relationship was always subject to change. Perón was God in the realm of the 'new Argentina' and everything else was superfluous. As the regime continued, however, the trend towards totalitarianism accelerated and the church began to move away from Perónism as religion began to be subsumed under the dominant political doctrine.

Perónismo and the Media: Censorship or the Good of the Nation?

The *Perónistas* were not a party averse to gagging the media for their own political benefit. As we shall see, however, it was not simply a case of pure authoritarian control of sources of communication and information. As with the relationship with the church, alliances were made between certain groups and the regime whilst others were strictly controlled at best, banned or at worst physically destroyed. In 1947, following the 1946 election success and probably as part of the strategy of consolidating power, moves were made to close down some weekly newspapers under shallow and suspicious pretexts. Bribery and intimidation soon followed and control of the paper and print trades tightened the reins on a number of anti-Perónist publications. Furthermore several of the print unions, newspaper boy unions, and journalists' unions were smashed in response to their demands for improved pay and conditions. The anti-liberal element of the Perónist regime was beginning to show its true colours and more than piecemeal censorship became an integral part of the 'new Argentina'. The roots of censorship under Perón do however stretch back much earlier – to the hours following the success of the 1943 revolution. The view was expressed then that the installation of a new government representing a new future for the country could in no way be reconciled with journalism that may represent it in a negative light through 'abuse or calumny directed against representatives of authority' (Josephs, 1945: 77). It was not necessarily a manifestation of an anti-freedom of speech ideology but rather a tactic employed to warn those involved with the media that they were being watched and also to suggest that, as powerful and influential as they were, governmental and state interests would always take precedence. Various pieces of legislation were implemented in order legally to establish such controls; news in the provinces and news transmitted abroad were particularly closely observed by the authorities. Newspapers and journals had, for the most part, to rely upon official press releases for much of their information as all other copy that dealt with anything with more than a tenuous link to politics ran the risk of being used against them.[9]

More than just an arbitrary method of social control, the censorship and control of the press was a very effective way of reaffirming the ideological ground upon which the Perónists had laid out their political stall. If guidelines were transgressed then the government could easily portray the offending organizations and individuals as traitors to the national cause. Hence Decree No. 18,407[10] was promulgated stating that publications must not publish any items which were held by the regime to be contrary to:

1. the general interests of the nation or disturbing to public order;

2. Christian morals or good customs;

3. Argentina's relations with other states;

4. the reputation of government officials; or,

5. the truth.

One ingenious way that Perón manoeuvred the debate about press restrictions was to suggest to the people that these were basically capitalist enterprises that had little interest in real news and were merely concerned with profit, and consequently were committed to sabotaging any progress that the new regime, with its 'pseudo-socialist' leanings, might make. Many well-established newspapers with liberal leanings, most significantly *La Vanguardia* and *La Prensa*, were either forced out of business or were simply closed down through what was presented as a labour dispute between the workers and the government, although the government-affiliated unions often cancelled out any influence that could be derived from strike action. More common however was the defection of newspapers to the Perónist camp. To adhere to the new regime's guidelines basically meant to remain in operation, to do otherwise was to be a traitor to the national cause not to mention cutting off one's editorial nose to spite one's ideological face.

The war waged against the press was not only necessary to retain social and political cohesion amongst the populace, the consumers of these newspapers, but was more significantly a concerted effort by the government to flex its political muscles. It was consolidating its position as a regime with political and ideological direction and the control of the press was a primary step that it was required to take if it was going to do so.

Perónismo and Culture: the Universities and the Stage and Screen

Other areas of the media and arts were also strictly controlled by dictats from the *Casa Rosada*. The Perónist regime was, as mentioned earlier, attempting to position itself (or at least be perceived as being) at the centre of the political universe in Argentina. Censorship was a way of controlling the ideological forms that would either strengthen the rhetoric of the regime, or conversely threaten it. What I am suggesting is that because of the inherent weakness of the artificially manufactured ideological agenda that Perón had presented as the formulaic key to the 'new Argentina', extreme authoritarian methods of social control were required to eliminate confounding or adversary channels of ideological discourse. Alternative forms of political discourse posed a great threat to the success of the regime in selling their nationalistic agenda to the people. Dissident voices emanating from the media, student groups, or disenchanted union leaders needed to be appeased and their alternative political ideologies incorporated into the populist hegemony – social control through appearing to be the authentic origin of such popular political ideology.

The place of theatre and film in Argentina, even by the 1940s, was recognized as one of great wit, quality, self-reflection, and political importance. Self-reflection was (and to some extent still remains) a traditional feature of the arts in a culture riddled by a history of war, dictatorship, and mass political struggle and was perhaps reflected in the formulation of an artistic *zeitgeist* of melancholic, dark, sinister, yet essentially powerful and optimistic productions on both stage and screen. During the latter half of the twentieth century the city of Buenos Aires has provided the backdrop to some of the greatest cinematic pieces ever to have emerged from Latin America. Theatre too in Argentina has deep roots in the flamboyant diversity of the various immigrant communities that make up much of the population of this very European city. The role of theatre, art, and cinema has always been seen as an integral feature of the city's identity. Furthermore the huge impact that Tango made upon the city through the genius of one man, Carlos Gardel, suggests that Buenos Aires is a city that is not only steeped in culture and art, but more significantly is also a city whose artistic communities and thespian and cinematic networks are inextricably linked to its very identity as an urban concentration of liberal, politically active, and progressive *porteños*[11] within a European-style society.

On the other hand, Buenos Aires was rapidly becoming a sprawling metropolis of working-class migrants from the interior and from the indigenous communities of the north, whose interests lay only in labour, housing and the opportunity to extricate themselves from the entrenched poverty which they had left behind but was all too often was mirrored upon their arrival in the capital. Hence there was a split in the demographic composition of the dominant city of the Republic. Although Buenos Aires was a city that in no way represented the interior and the other states of the Republic, it had nevertheless become a microcosm of the polarization between the support for Perón and the pro-democratic sentiment that vociferously opposed any moves towards a single leader ruling by decree.

The revolution brought with it systematic censorship of radio as well as the press. The medium of radio in an era before television was one that had mass appeal. The country had over 31 radio stations of which 12 were established within the area of Buenos Aires. Hence, radio had great potential for manipulation by the regime. Not only was the medium censored but its programming was highly controlled; soap operas were prohibited along with contemporary interpretations of classical music. The nationalistic dimension of the 'new Argentina' was reflected in the obligation of stations to emphasize native folklore and concentrate upon Argentine musicians rather than foreign ones. In terms of news broadcasts – the place where most people got their information about the state of the nation and foreign affairs – news from a highly Argentine perspective was the norm and any short-wave foreign broadcasts were strictly forbidden.

Such a strategy is attributable not only to the desire to control the media and disseminate propaganda as news but also to the expression of support for the Axis war effort in Europe. The pro-fascist element in the military bloc that took power in the 1943 revolution was quite strong if not dominant, and the highly anti-Semitic sentiment which was part of the ideological populism leading to the take-over, and eventually Perón's coming to power in the 1946 elections, created much support amongst the *descamisados* for a fascist victory in Europe. A 1943 decree forced the country's radio stations to broadcast pro-Axis propaganda, and any British or North American broadcasts were banned (unless local censors had been allowed to edit them first) due to the obvious conflict of interests. The regime published, and distributed to those involved in the broadcasting industry, a booklet entitled 'Manual of Instructions for Radio Stations' on 14 May 1946, just preceding the elections of that year. It laid out the rules defining what was allowed to be broadcast: political speeches by non-Perónista politicians, for instance, were allowed but if there was a sudden departure from the previously approved/censored text then the plug was to be pulled immediately; political campaigns were not allowed to be broadcast over the air and so any misconceptions about the 1946 elections being the first 'democratic' elections in Argentina since the Castillo military dictatorship must be laid to rest.

The political importance of *porteño* theatre in the time of the populist phenomenon in Argentina was such that it was seen not only as subversive in content, but also as a manifestation of middle-class, liberal views and as such, as a direct attack upon the legitimacy and ideology of the regime. Political satire was prolific and, even when attacking political principles rather than Perón and Evita, was deemed unsuitable and tantamount to treason. By mid-1949, measures had been implemented to force theatres to put on at least two traditional native plays for each foreign one.

Cinema too was restricted in the number of foreign films and overseas production influences which were tolerated. The great proliferation of anti-Axis war films being produced at the time in Hollywood and Britain, such as *The Great Dictator* and *Edge of Darkness*, were restricted from being shown, and any other foreign films were preceded by heavily pro-Argentine newsreels. The formation of the General Directorate of Public Spectacles – a government agency whose job it was to ensure that the pictures produced in the Republic 'reflect faithfully the high culture, the customs, and the true ideology of the Argentine people' (*Democracia*, 12 July 1948), forced picture houses to direct at least 35 per cent of their earnings towards Argentine film-makers, thereby tightening the grip that the regime had upon the arts.

So the arts and the means of communication in Perónist Argentina were strictly censored, controlled, and strongly convinced into supporting the regime and its message by policy, by financial control, by threatening to close down businesses, and ultimately by the threat of violence. Argentina's means of communication and artistic world had been hijacked by the leader of the 'new Argentina' and was being used heavily in his favour. The *Casa Rosada* held the ultimate editorial veto on what people would see, hear, understand, enjoy, laugh at, cry at – the minds of the population were educated and informed by the highly partisan and nationalistic propaganda, disinformation and sterilized arts of the Perón manifestation of populist authoritarianism.

The education system under the control of the populist regime was such that the autonomy of the universities was usurped and the influence of the politically active student population was heavily attacked. Some of the greatest enemies of the regime (unsurprisingly considering its heavily anti-intellectual stance), were the university students, intellectuals, and the professional classes. The Argentine universities had traditionally been reactionary and were hotbeds of fervent opposition to the revolutionary take-over of power by the military caucus led by Perón in 1943, and the victory of Perón in the 1946 elections. At the time, five out of six universities were governed by representatives of the faculty and the student body. The mass student opposition to the pro-Axis support of the *Casa Rosada*, and to the regime's affiliation with anti-Semitism, and Perón's overt rhetoric, led to much conflict between the authorities and the students, culminating in the infamous riot-siege of the UBA (University of Buenos Aires) Faculty of the Exact Sciences in October 1945. This was mirrored in occupations of university buildings and campuses which expressed opposition to the way the country was being controlled and to the mass censorship, academic restructuring, and politically sanctioned violence that was being used against the traditional composition of the establishments of higher education in the middle classes.

Perón's responses to the students came thick and fast as soon as he won the elections of 1946. He effected severe reform of the university systems and thousands of staff were sacked at the slightest hint of any opposition to the regime. Bernado Houssay received the country's first Nobel Prize shortly after he was fired. Many of the teaching posts were filled by 'safe' *Perónistas*, and this led to a sudden deterioration in teaching standards. Perón was quoted as saying:

> Our universities merely served to give students a verbalist and hollow culture, without any real depth, in which theory was not supplemented by practice, and even less by scientific investigation. Up to the present our professionals and scientists have been obliged to teach themselves; they were formed, technically and scientifically, outside the halls of study. (Alexander, 1951)

He attributed such shortcomings in the education system to the supposed fact that professors neither lived with their students nor served as their guides and mentors. Generally they devoted the main part of their time to private work, which was economically more profitable, and only taught as a sideline. The post of professor – it is sad to acknowledge – was, with honourable exceptions, merely a means to defray expenses, a degree to dazzle society, and a bait to attract more private clientèle.

One of the major reasons why Perón attacked the students who mobilized against him and failed to fall in line behind the rest of the nationalist popular sentiment forming in the cities, was not only the political threat that their opposition posed to his position, but also the restructuring of the educational system that Perón wished to implement. Greater educational equity was one of the main policy drives that he was pushing for, although his motives for doing so were far from fuelled by any great educationalist philosophy but much more by the need to herald education and technical training as the avenue of success through which disaffected youth and the previously under-privileged families of the *descamisados* could foresee a better future for their children. The popular appeal was in the way he attempted to make degrees more accessible to people other than the middle classes, and to crush the esoteric nature and exclusivity of the university education in Argentina; Perón decided that to dismantle the existing structures would suggest that radical steps were being taken towards such a social shift. Furthermore, Perón saw the universities as a symbol of his ever-strengthening ideological message: the nation, the masses, opportunity, progress. It was an approach that worked effectively in tandem with the support he had created in the labour movement through the nationalization of public utilities and the championing of the poor against the rich.

The radical changes that were implemented in the structure of the education system were symbolic when set in their position in the ideological matrix that Perón was establishing, yet at the same time such changes acted as expedient proof that *Perónismo* represented popular changes in the social and economic infrastructure that had for too long been stacked against the vast majority of Argentines. Such a powerful symbol as the higher education system could not be besmirched by the existence of radical, reactionary opponents of the 'new Argentina', and so two birds were definitely being killed with one stone.

> The university must also affirm and encourage a national and historic conscience; organize scientific investigation in such a manner as to encourage those who have vocation and capacity to undertake it; compile, organize and disseminate learning and culture; stimulate the progress of applied science and technical creation; form a teaching staff exclusively devoted to university scientific life; promote and establish free tuition; create and keep up research institutes; publish scientific works, and encourage the development of scientific, social, juridical, economic, literary and artistic studies and activities. (Juan Domingo Perón). (Alexander, 1951)

Like many other governmental agencies the *Junta Nacional de Intelectuales* was established on behalf of the regime to keep a lid on areas of potential reaction to the revolutionary policy shift. Its brief was to oversee the world of academia and act as a watchdog that would detect any holes that needed to be filled in the education system. In fact it actually served as an organ of the state, conceived in the mould of the archetypal fascist/Stalinist 'thought-police'; rooting out the subversive element in the student bodies, and stifling any dissent to educational policy measures emanating from the university councils. The authoritarian nature of the regime, and more specifically of Perón himself, a military man with an almost inherent dislike of the world of academia, was severe, and university courses were radically changed to replicate the philosophy of Perón. The autonomy of the universities and of their individual faculties was lost and the regime established itself as the leading determinant of course content, style of teaching, and type of teachers. Philosophy and social and political science courses were redesigned to incorporate a strong reverence towards the leader and Evita: they were to be portrayed as national heroes in the same way that students were taught about San Martín.

Certainly under Perón the university system made significant advances and saw much modernization: many new buildings were built and more access to students from more diverse backgrounds had been effected – 68 460 students were enrolled on courses in Argentine institutions of higher education in 1945 and by 1955 that figure had more than doubled to 142 435.[12] But it must be recognized that the highly authoritarian repression of the students under the orders of Perón himself left the Argentine higher education system in such a state that it was almost as though the very heart had been torn from within it. Loss of autonomy, loss of its greatest academics, manipulation of the administration, and the manipulation of the system as a tool of indoctrination, or more simply, as Walter (1968: 149) puts it, 'Corruption, terrorism, and intellectual sterility were the characteristics of a university system that once had been the finest in Latin America'.

Despite imposing strict methods of social control upon students, the arts, political adversaries, and the media, Perón was growing in popularity by the time of his election and the church-*Perónista*-labour movement alliance had managed to mobilize mass support from the urban masses of Buenos Aires. The nationalistic, anti-Semitic elements of this movement were not merely explicit expressions of popular proletariat consciousness, but were fundamental expressions of the new hegemonic structure and forms of an Argentina that was going through an acutely significant phase of economic and political transition. The 'new Argentina' was a nation that was portrayed as one that signified the metamorphosis of a republic, and such a metamorphosis required an inspired and dedicated leader who was not afraid to lead from the top and whose convictions were an expression of the nationalism and patriotism that were to act as an example to all Argentines. Unfortunately, those who did not adhere to the new philosophy of *Perónismo* would be forced to do so by repression, violence, and authoritarian methods of coercion; significant illustrations of the fact that Perón's new brand of leadership was a highly undemocratic. Under Perón the state had become a vehicle for extreme social control and the extermination of any liberal conceptions of democracy and liberty, yet had found its way into the hearts, minds, and political favour of a mass of diverse social aggregates. Leadership had found its niche and dominant ideological forms had trickled down into the consciousness of a disenchanted population.

Conclusion

I hope to have indicated the way that this Latin American form of populism was a significant example of the way in which ideology and the creation of a wholly ideological polity can displace traditional authority and power with new forms of government. It is also apparent from the history books that it is certainly quite possible for such fundamental shifts of power to be instigated, if not effected, by a single charismatic leader whom the masses take to their hearts as symbolizing change, statehood, and the future. Although not adopting a Weberian paradigm for this overview of Latin American populism, I nevertheless believe that Weber's theory of the rationalization of the modern world provides us with a concise and accurate context for placing such a phenomenon as populism within:

> The probability that one actor . . . will be in a position to carry out his own will despite resistance, regardless of the basis on which this probability rests. (Weber, 1968: 53)

Weber pointed out that classes, status groups, parties, and other social groupings are all phenomena of the distribution of power – a complication of the Marxist analysis. This paradigm of the situation and sources of power is relevant to the discussion of populism as it picks up on the formation of parties (or for our purposes the populist 'movement') as the rational organization of the pursuit of certain goals. The state used as a tool of operation is the perfect manifestation of power over social groupings and ultimately the electorate. Perhaps this approach would help one to understand more fully the strength of populist movements *vis-à-vis* the manipulation of the psyche of the masses to consolidate and exercise hegemonic power. One must be careful not to interpret populism in Latin America as merely the grasp of inate power by one individual leader – as is too often the case in popular analyses of European fascism under Mussolini or Hitler, or even the reign of terror in Stalinist Russia. Moreover, my theory of populism in Latin America as a form of social control requires more than merely analysing the policy corollaries of populism as it inevitably careers towards authoritarianism. I would like to suggest that not only do these instances of Latin American populism illustrate that populism invariably works because it plays upon the aspirations of a disenchanted populace in calling for direction, modernization, and leadership, and because the phenomenon itself actually acts as a framework for a new hegemonic order to be established. That is, populism in this form not only inevitably leads to authoritarian social control and state violence, but is in essence a form of social control within itself as it subjects the masses to a new style of deference; it mobilizes them into a falsely contrived homogeneous bloc that acts as a buttress for the developing hegemony.

There are, as mentioned earlier, many parallels to be drawn between Latin American forms of populism and contemporary European examples of a new hegemony: Thatcherism is the clearest example, but traces of 'populist' tendencies and strategies have reared their head in Italy for instance where attempts to unify a modern industrialized mass through nationalist ideology can be seen in the rise of the Northern League. People want radical change and parties or movements offer it to them through a violent social control model presented in a politically ambivalent manner. Violence is not always apparent, and whilst it would be a simplistic assumption to equate ideological formations with violence, it is clear that a deconstruction of popular notions of violence would necessarily include a reassessment of the social control polity at the heart of the industrialized capitalist nation state. The problem of populism as a theory is that it is all too simple to interpret any political movement as populist, yet through the Latin American cases I hope to have shown how strong such movements can be in the future of developing societies, how in Africa populism is rife, and how even today we see a resurgence of populism in Argentina in the figure of one Carlos Menem.

This is still a highly important and relevant discourse in which to immerse ourselves because it reveals the relationships between power, statehood, economics, culture, law, and other conditions entering into the complex equation between ideology and social identity.

Notes

1 For a similar examination with reference to Brazil's experiences of populist social control see Grant (1995).

2 Quotation from the book review of Madriz (1986) in *Crime and Social Justice*, **30**, pp. 131–7.

3 The prevalence of 'moral panics' in the early 1970s; for example the mugging crisis in 1972–73 as represented in Hall *et al.* (1978).

4 Yet he still believes that physical repression *per se* has certainly played its role too; although one should not be misled by its prevalence.

5 All of these basic changes in the economic structure are accompanied by profound modifications in social relations.

6 This mobilization is ameliorated through 'integrative processes' whereby the masses are protected and society is protected from traumas, rupture and revolution.

7 The *descamisados*, or literally 'shirtless', were the natural enemy of the oligarchy in Argentina during this era as symbols of conflicting and contradictory social class, status, and political authority within Argentine society.

8 See De Imaz (1962: 55). The study was limited to a carefully selected group of the social elite. Asked how much importance the group had in the nation's political life, 70 per cent said they had no influence; 16 per cent said they had little influence; 16 per cent said they controlled it; 14 per cent said they did not know. Asked who did control political life, the responses of this group were as follows: 36 per cent, the middle class plus workers; 29 per cent, the middle class only; 18 per cent, the upper class only.

9 Some said that publishers were obliged to print these official press releases anyway.

10 Issued by the Subsecretariat of Information (*La Ley*, 31 December 1943).

11 The term *porteño* refers to an inhabitant of, or more accurately a person born in Buenos Aires. The character and image of the *porteño* is defined by the supposed cultural, intellectual, and economic superiority of their own self-image, over their respective partisan perception of non-*porteño* citizens (and in particular those from the extreme north, the extreme south, or those of indigenous extraction).

12 Statistics from República Argentina, Secretaría de Educación de la Nación, *Anuario estadístico, año* 1945 (Buenos Aires, 1948); and República Argentina, Ministerio de Educación y Justicia, 'Hojas de apéndice correspondiente al año 1955' (Buenos Aires, 1955).

Chapter 6

The American Prison Problem, Hegemonic Crisis, and the Censure of Inner-City Blacks

Ethan Raup

'Bastards stole the power from the victims of the us v. them'.

(Michael Stipe, R.E.M.)

As we look mournfully to Bosnia, Rwanda, Chechnya, we can hear the beat of their tribalism echoed over our own airwaves, in our political campaigns, on the nightly news, through the voices of televangelists, not fully recognizing that American society is in a similar process of disintegration, fragmenting into increasingly smaller and more insular blocs. As this social disorganization has combined with heightened political polarization and the collapse of social democracy, hegemonic majorities have developed around extremely repressive and divisive dominant ideologies. These ideologies have blatantly and defiantly spurned responsible, inclusive discourse. Instead, they have undermined our shared sense of common purpose and have exploited rising economic tensions with a divide and conquer strategy perpetrated through innuendo, accusation, and censure.

This epidemic of anger and intolerance is not limited to one side of the political spectrum, but is coming from all sides, with the axioms of those on the Right tending towards the Orwellian (Ignorance is Strength), and the axioms of those on the left tending towards the Stalinist (Politically Correct Intolerance). It is as if the worst of Machiavelli, Orwell, and Stalin have converged to feed off the emotionalism and ignorance of a body-politic too self-absorbed in its own hedonistic fantasies and self-pity to maintain its vigilance against these trends towards totalitarianism.

While the maintenance of power has always involved the reinvention and perpetration of images of immorality, popular legitimacy is increasingly dependent on portraying opposition groups as the enemy of the whole nation, not just as political rivals. Further, in the present social crisis, violence is playing an increasingly important role in establishing and mapping out these censures and systems of domination.

The politicality of definitions of violence has expanded, in part, through the over-use of violent imagery and language that has accompanied the increasingly common tendency to blame other individuals or groups for one's own perceived victimization. Abuse, rape, and discrimination, for example, no longer refer to traditionally defined and highly specific acts of violence, but can be applied to a permeable and amorphous category of behaviour. Thus, discrimination is tossed about recklessly by both genders and all ethnic groups, including white men, under-mining those claims that are legitimate and demand immediate action, while main-stream feminism has embraced the image of the woman as a helpless victim of male violence, and grown adults regularly accuse their parents of 'abuse' for past sins, real or imagined. These words, distorted in the heat of attack, have lost whatever stable meaning they once had.

In addition to the expanding lexicon of violence, dominant ideologies increas-ingly rely on violent acts to help construct a more coercive moral unity. The variations of the violent morality play that run through most movies and television programmes, where a simplified good is pitted against a clear-cut evil, also perme-ates our social and political arenas. Manifestations of this stretch from the banal (when Newt Gingrich blamed liberalism for the death of Susan Smith's children), to the sensational (the public infatuation with the O. J. Simpson trial), to the truly tragic (the Oklahoma City bombing).

The American Prison Crisis

Significantly, as violence is becoming more central to the politicality of censures, the censoriousness of politics is itself becoming more violent. Indeed the acceler-ating social crisis that has encouraged social censures, has also led to an increas-ingly intense form of carceral social control. The implications for subordinate social groups who have been the target of these dominant ideologies and increasingly repressive strategies of control have been profound, particularly when viewed in relation to developments within the US criminal justice system. Indeed, since the 1970s, when the US criminal justice system expanded and began to take on its present form, two primary trends have characterized the prison system: the dra-matic rise in the overall incarceration rate; and the disproportionate rise in the rate of black incarceration.

Through the 1970s and early 1980s, the rise in the black prison population mirrored the overall rise in the prison population. Thus, although black incarcera-tion rates were already higher than those for other groups, the two-fold expansion in the prison population between 1973 and 1982 led to a corresponding two-fold expansion in the black prison population. However, in the mid-1980s, increasingly punitive drug policies began to have a profound impact on the criminal justice system. In 1980, before Presidents Reagan and Bush declared their respective war(s) on drugs, drug offenders accounted for 27 per cent of the federal prison population. That percentage increased to 40 per cent following the 1986 Antidrug Abuse Act.

By 1990, 47 per cent of federal inmates were drug offenders, and the nationwide percentage of inmates incarcerated for drug offences soared to 54 per cent (Gilliard and Beck, 1993). State prison trends were equally bleak: from 1986 to 1991 drug-related sentences accounted for 44 per cent of the increase in the state prison population, which more than tripled during the same period. More importantly, as the general prison population expanded, the percentage of blacks incarcerated for drug-related offences made a dramatic 447 per cent increase between 1986 and 1991, while the percentage of whites incarcerated for similar offences increased by 115 per cent (McWilliams and Kramer, 1994: 28). As a result, while the rate of imprisonment per 100 000 for blacks increased from 368 in 1973 to 544 in 1979, it exploded during the mid- to late-1980s, reaching 1 860 by 1990 and 2 678 by 1992 (Gilliard, 1994: 9).

These imprisonment rates are far worse than those that existed in South Africa under apartheid, which begs the question: how did the United States, a society ostensibly committed to universal freedom and equality, reach a point where almost one in four black men between the ages of 20 and 29 were under some form of correctional supervision – with very few howls of protest from liberals, let alone moderates or conservatives? This chapter will attempt to account for this and at least partially explain the disproportionate rise in the black prison population by arguing essentially that several dominant ideologies have emerged from our worsening social crisis to dehumanize and subsequently criminalize inner-city blacks.

That a particular social group has been criminalized is not to suggest a conspiratorial use of the criminal justice apparatuses. Rather, the development and extension of the criminal sanction must be viewed as a sophisticated system of social regulation, developing out of complex, and often contradictory, moral and political discourses (Sumner, 1990a: 15). Indeed, the criminal justice system itself is a very active and effective ideological and political force whose language and procedures offer the most effective way to apply legitimate violence against those elements which fall outside the scope of public order. Because the parameters of public order are defined differently at different times and according to changing attitudes, changes in the type, nature and organization of crime, and changes in the differential application of the criminal category to include different groups and types of activity, the process of criminalization serves as a window through which we may view and reconstruct the complex development of power relations (economic, social, political), hegemonic discourses, and censures at a particular historical juncture. Viewed in this manner, we may begin to determine the role of criminalization in structuring popular morality and legitimating violence against a particular social group, in this case inner-city blacks.

Problems with 'Radical' Explanation

Because critical American criminologists have neither developed nor properly utilized a sophisticated theory of the capitalist state, they have been unable to offer a powerful explanation for either the prison crisis as a whole, or particular aspects of this crisis. Though the dogmatic instrumentalism common to American Marxist criminology in the 1970s (e.g., Quinney, 1974, 1977; Chambliss and Mankoff, 1976) has been abandoned, structuralist and post-structuralist efforts to develop a non-reductionist, non-determinist mode of analysing the American state and the criminal justice system have been wholly unsuccessful.

This is despite the fact that the move to structuralism was consciously motivated by the need to develop a systematic analysis that could account for structural limits on ruling groups, conflicts of interest within the state and between the state and the ruling class, and state activity that was not clearly manipulated by capital interests. Towards this end, structuralists argued that the state assumed a capitalist form not because of ruling-class individuals, as instrumentalists had claimed, but because, as part of the super-structure, the state itself reflected the economic base. Though this view correctly identified the essential class nature of the state, it fundamentally misrepresented the specific constitution of the capitalist state and its apparatuses, as well as the relationship between the state and the economy.

The topographical 'base/super-structure' representation, which views the state as a mechanistic reflection of the economic base, is ultimately as deterministic as instrumentalism: if the state functions according to the needs of the economy, then the state, its policies, and the criminal justice system must follow a path strictly determined by the productive forces. Moreover, that the economy is composed of elements that remain unchanged through various modes of production, suggests a trans-historical functioning of a self-regulating and rigidly demarcated space. This not only disregards the role of dynamic popular struggles, which are central to the constitution of the mode of production, but, when applied to the super-structure, it similarly reduces political and social institutions to autonomous theoretical objects that remain essentially unchanged over time.

Though unqualified structuralism remains vigorous within American Marxist criminology, some radical criminologists, realizing the limits of structural materialism, began to draw on more sophisticated European social theory to help account for the relationship between the economy, the state, and civil society. Gramsci's writings seem to have penetrated the American criminological consciousness in the early 1980s, followed closely by the related work of British social theorist Stuart Hall. However, post-structural criminologists (Spitzer, the Schwendingers, Greenberg, Humphries, Childs), while invoking the names and work of Gramsci, Hall, and Althusser, among others, failed to understand the intricacies and developments of modern European Marxist and post-Marxist theory. As a result, certain complex concepts, such as hegemony, the role of human agency, and the constitution of the state and its apparatuses, are simplified and transposed onto an essentially unchanged structural, materialist, body of social theory.

For example, in his article 'Towards a trans-communality, the highest stage of multiculturalism' (1993), Childs argues that many African-Americans have been confined to inner-city ghettos by increasingly heavy structures of repression because fundamental economic transformations severely constricted the 'hegemonic bloc'. According to Childs, the dominant group leads a larger bloc solely by granting subordinate social groups economic concessions – usually jobs. Thus, as the in-dustrial base has contracted, the ruling elites have been unable to concede jobs to the lower classes, typically minority groups, and have thus permanently institution-alized them in inner-city ghettos. Though the eroding manufacturing base has un-questionably taken its toll, particularly in the inner-city, Childs completely ignores the complex role of discourses and ideology in the constitution and maintenance of hegemony. Furthermore, Childs suggests that the hegemonic bloc exists and func-tions as an autonomous space, intervening in the economy and in civil society to maintain its dominance. However, the state, a hegemonic bloc, or a dominant group can neither exist exterior to the economy, nor to the totality of popular struggles, including the struggles of groups which are relatively exterior to the hegemonic bloc. Indeed, it is the totality of popular struggles which constitute the state's materiality.

In *Social Class and the Definition of Crime* (1981), the Schwendingers offer an equally reductionist abuse of Gramsci through his interpretation of the hegemonic domination of the ruling class. Throughout this work, they merely replace the term 'ideology' with 'hegemony', entirely avoiding an in-depth development of the concept of 'hegemony'. Because ideology, and therefore hegemony, is implicitly portrayed as part of the super-structure, it too is ultimately dependent on the eco-nomic base: hegemony, then, becomes a 'false consciousness' which is foisted upon the dominated by the dominant. This use of hegemony fails to incorporate its most significant aspect: that civil society plays an active role in developing and legitimating existing power relations.

Happily, Tony Platt has called on the Left to arm itself with a more sophis-ticated theory that charts a course 'between the extremes of heroic resilience [and] an overdetermined structuralism', and places culture in its rightful place as an agent for social change (Platt, 1993: i–v). Unfortunately, after this promising start, Platt has more recently attempted to account for the continuation of 'tough on crime' strategies through the Clinton administration by tossing in a selected sprinkling of Hall's concepts. Platt's use of these concepts suggest that politicians have secured increasingly repressive criminal justice measures by conspiring with the media to create a series of moral panics over crime. Stating that 'There is nothing particu-larly new about politicians and the media constructing moral panics to mobilize public opinion against illusory crime waves', Platt invokes Hall's 'populist moral-ism' without clarifying that it is not conspiratorially 'constructed' by politicians and the media (Platt, 1994: 5). As with hegemony, it is absolutely crucial to iden-tify civil society and social relations as very active variables in the authoritarian populist equation.

As Camille Paglia has said, 'All the P.R. in the world cannot make a hit movie or sitcom' (Paglia, 1992: ix). This one, seemingly obvious statement exposes the folly of critical American criminology. Paglia's argument that the purist strain within American Marxism has undermined its academic credibility and real-world relevance, would seem to be well placed. While Platt, Schwendinger and other critical American criminologists are clearly on the right path (i.e., struggling to account for the increasingly repressive American criminal justice system), they have continuously fallen short because they do not truly understand the intricacies of sophisticated critical European social theory. As a result, their best efforts – those that dress their work in ready-to-wear European concepts – are ultimately unable to develop links between social phenomena and the underlying theory that are strong enough to withstand critical scrutiny.

A Theoretical Framework

To understand the rising violence of the US criminal justice system, particularly in relation to inner-city blacks, it is helpful to begin with Poulantzas' view of the modern capitalist state, as expressed in his later writings. For Poulantzas, the state does not exist in a position of topographical exteriority to the economic and social spheres, for the economic and political are 'from the very beginning constituted by their mutual relation and articulation – a process that is effected in each mode of production through the determining role of the relations of production' (Poulantzas, 1978: 17). Super-structural causality, therefore, cannot be based on a mechanical reflection of the mode of production, for the mode of production is itself constituted by the totality of political, economic, and social relations and struggles.

Thus the state is not a monolithic bloc that confronts actors from above, but is the material condensation of a relationship of forces from below. As the site of intersecting power relations, the state is able to materialize power and popular struggles in a relationship of forces. Therefore, because the state is itself a collection of social and productive relations, its material framework cannot be reduced to mere political domination. Politicians, the media, and public-relations firms do not subvert the masses by creating and perpetrating a false consciousness. Rather, political domination, as constitutive of social and productive relations, is itself inscribed in the institutional materiality of the state.

Because the state intervenes in power relations and popular struggles – organizing, materializing, and reproducing the various forms of power in order to further consolidate the economic, political and ideological powers of the dominant groups – many apparatuses that Foucault, for example, believes lie outside the state, including private institutions, are essential to the state's strategic field, for they penetrate popular struggles and discourses, materializing their symbolic power within the dominant hegemonic ideology.

For example, the intense popular struggles that have mobilized around gun rights, have been channelled into, and materialized within, the institutional structure of the National Rifle Association (NRA), which began initially as a grass-roots organization dedicated to firearms safety programmes. The resulting impact on the state and the form of hegemony has been profound, for the intensity of the gun-rights movement, and the NRA's ability to raise money have significantly impacted American electoral politics, pushing the discourse on guns and crime far to the Right.

Poulantzas' argument that the state is an organic site that contains national and class contradictions emerging from apparatuses such as the NRA, as well as from divisions between levels of government and various agencies within government, is particularly helpful in the case of the United States, for this view is able to account for complex relations between federal, state, and local governments, geographic divisions, and inter- or intra-party divisions on specific issues. For example, because many Republicans, at the urging of the NRA, have steadfastly refused to support bans on assault weapons or 'cop-killer' bullets, they have alienated law-enforcement groups that would otherwise be a natural Republican constituency. This particular division has become crucial to partisan relations of power over crime and gun control.

However, this does not mean that a hegemonic consensus on overall crime strategies has been threatened, for through the process of division/unification, the state, at each level and through all of its apparatuses, condenses and materializes struggles and relations of power, moulding and organizing them into a conflictual unity. In this process, an alliance of dominant groups is organized in an unstable equilibrium of compromises. Thus, on the issue of crime, potential inter-party divisions over gun control have been mediated by the overwhelming bipartisan agreement on the overriding need to get tough on crime, which will be discussed in greater detail below.

Thus, through its institutional framework, and in the name of the general will, the state organizes hegemony and secures social cohesion and popular consent. This process is accomplished through more than one form: on the one hand cohesion depends on force and coercion; in a society of 'free individuals', people have to be disciplined to abide by the state's overarching framework (Hall *et al.*, 1978: 202). Social cohesion, however, is much stronger when discipline is the result of popular consent. Therefore, in its ideal form, hegemony occurs when a power bloc of leading groups has, on the basis of popular consent, extended the needs of capital, led in the social and ideological spheres, and assumed control of the state's coercive apparatuses.

America in the 1950s offers an appropriate example of this hegemonic ideal. This resulted, in part, from the phase of (organized) capitalism, and from the postwar economic boom. In addition, the Cold War not only provided a 'sustained defence of the fantasy of the American way through a constant ideological attack on anything that could be labelled communist' (Dionne, 1992: 51), but it also drove every major political movement towards the centre where political life stabilized around interventionist foreign policy, the welfare state, and Keynesian economics. Under these circumstances, it is easy to understand why Bell and other academics could plausibly proclaim 'the end of ideology'.

The Crisis of Hegemony in America

Because hegemony is never a static condition, it must be continuously mediated to unify ever-changing and developing economic, political, intellectual and moral struggles. Moreover, if these struggles intensify, it can be increasingly difficult for the power bloc to maintain the level of consent that had been established during an 'ideal' period of hegemony. For example, as economic conditions deteriorate and/ or as political struggles proliferate, the equilibrium of compromises between many of the dominant groups may be undermined and relations with dominated groups may become increasingly problematic, leading ultimately to a crisis of hegemony.

Thus, as the American welfare state expanded in the 1940s and 1950s, it became increasingly involved in regulating the economy, intervening more and more to maintain and reproduce the relations of production. By increasingly draw- ing economic and popular struggles onto its own terrain, the state was more vul- nerable to the disorganizing effects of economic change. Moreover, because economic change is the precondition of the disorganization of civil society, which, in turn, effects the form of the state, the deterioration of the American economy and the related rise in social and political tensions combined to tear apart the hegemonic consensus that had developed in the 1950s. Indeed, the fragmentation of the power bloc, or vital centre, occurred throughout the political spectrum, and is apparent in the rise of interest-group pluralism, which, by the end of the 1960s, included blacks, feminists, homosexuals, Native Americans, and consumer, environmental and religious groups. It also occurred within the Democratic party, as 'reform' Democrats gained more power at the expense of traditional, New Deal Democrats, as the 'New Left' formed as a grass-roots reaction against establishment liberalism, and as Neoconservatives defected to the Right.

Under these conditions, not only was the seeming universalization of the state to the 'general will' increasingly difficult, but conflicts more closely associated with the social sphere increasingly emerged as both the origin and effect of the rising politicization. As this trend worsened, the state moved increasingly towards crisis in the management of itself and of society. As the mode of hegemony shifted from its ideal pole towards crisis, the state moved increasingly towards the use and expansion of its more coercive apparatuses. This movement has not led to the collapse of the state, but, as the mode of hegemony has shifted towards crisis, those apparatuses and discourses inclined more towards fostering consent have been superseded by those more inclined towards coercion (Hall *et al.*, 1978: 217).

In this move, the criminal justice system, which even in the best of times plays a crucial role in materializing the hegemonic ideology and organizing consent, has played an increasingly important role in managing the crisis. As both a cause and effect of the modern American state and the current form of social relations, the criminal justice system occupies a strategic space that maps out the terrain of publicly accepted morality within which repressive social control is widely re- garded as legitimate. Thus, as both the state and the general public have called for increasingly tough law enforcement since the late 1960s, the criminal justice sys- tem has expanded, taking on an altogether new form.

After insignificant expansion in criminal justice expenditures in the 1950s and 1960s (0.5 to 1 per cent of GNP), spending increased 42 per cent between 1971 and 1974. Moreover, increasing federal expenditures to state and local authorities con- tributed to the proliferation of a 'police-industrial complex', which reorganized criminal justice apparatuses nationwide along the lines of a 'military corporate model' that emphasized technology, specialization, and managerial techniques of 'command and control'. In addition, several criminal justice apparatuses were created or enlarged under the guise of anti-drug policies. The Bureau of Narcotics and Dangerous Drugs was established within the Justice Department in 1968, and the Nixon administration established a series of federal agencies during the early 1970s, culminating in the Drug Enforcement Agency in 1973.

State disciplinary apparatuses have continued to grow throughout the Reagan, Bush, and Clinton administrations, albeit at a slower rate than in the 1970s. The 1986 Antidrug Abuse Act, for example, stiffened mandatory sentences and tripled the budget for the overall war on drugs, which targeted street drug-traffickers in disadvantaged urban minority communities. Moreover, the rate of expansion can be deceiving, for contractions in one part of the criminal justice system often merely reflected a reallocation of resources. Thus, although police spending peaked in 1977, its decline in the 1980s can be partially attributed to rising expenditures on prison construction.

The courts, too, contributed to greater disciplinary policies: the death penalty was reauthorized by the Supreme Court in 1976, and by 1979 there were 567 prisoners on death row. By 1988, well over half of the states had reinstituted the death penalty, and the death row population had swelled to 1 900, half of whom were black. In addition, through the 1980s, the courts implemented a conservative agenda regarding police powers, preventive detention, and defendants' rights. Under the cover of the drug war, the courts consistently eroded the *Miranda* ruling, and broadened the search and seizure law to permit 'good faith' exceptions to warrant procedures.

The Disorganization of Relations of Production

This rise in state discipline should not be overemphasized as a cause of the prison crisis or of the censure of inner-city blacks. In Hall's view of the crisis of hege-mony, for example, there is a tendency to over-emphasize the coercive pole of state power. Indeed, in *Policing the Crisis*, Hall admits that his account of the British crisis has a top-down bias (Hall *et al.*, 1978: 218). To avoid this, and to avoid slipping into pluralism, it is crucial that we first identify and explore the social and productive forces that have over-determined the particular form of the crisis in America. Having done this, we may then begin to make connections between immediate and deep structural levels of causality, specifying the precise impact this crisis and the fundamental shift towards increased state discipline has had on the criminal justice system and subordinate social groups.

In locating the present state of productive relations, I will draw on the work of Lash and Urry, who argue that the era of 'organized' monopoly capitalism, char-acterized by the concentration and centralization of capital and the development of the welfare state, has ended in the industrialized world in general and in America in particular, and has been displaced by an increasing trend towards 'disorganization', which has transformed spatial relations, the economy, culture, and general social relations throughout Western societies.

Disorganized capitalism partly refers to the deregulation of national markets by nationally based corporations, and a general decentralization of capitalism due to declining tariffs and the increased activity and independence of multinational corporations (Lash and Urry, 1987: 2). It also refers to the internationalization of industry and finance with separate and uncoordinated structures, the related development of structures increasingly removed from direct state regulation, and increasingly difficult monetary control. All of these factors have combined to make it more difficult for individual countries to regulate international trade and to organize their own economies.

Another essential aspect of the move towards disorganized social and productive relations has been the spatial organization of the social formation, which has been characterized by the deconcentration of population and industrial centres. In this regard, America has led the world in spatial decentralization: industrial cities have declined in size and regional significance, reflecting the flight from inner cities to smaller towns and suburban areas, where the 'facts of production' (i.e., pollution, noise, crime) could be banished from the landscape. For example, in 1950, one-quarter of Americans lived in the suburbs. By 1970 the number had increased to almost two-fifths, and by 1980 it had moved well beyond two-fifths (Lash and Urry, 1987: 116).

While spatial relations will be discussed in greater detail below, it is important to note here that spatial organization is essential to the way in which any society operates. It should be no surprise, then, that this exaggerated spatial dispersal has impacted American society at all levels, from the economic structure, to power relations and popular struggles, to the way in which individuals and groups relate to and perceive one another. In each case, spatial decentralization has effected the present form of the crisis of hegemony by reinforcing and accentuating the move towards social deconstruction, and the formation of ever smaller, more isolated, and mistrustful social groups.

The Changing Nature of the Middle Class

In addition to the flight to the suburbs, there have been two economic trends affecting the middle class that have led to a further disorganization of American society. The first is the development and perpetration of a new international division of labour. The growth of 'world market factories' in an increasing number of 'free production zones' in the Third World, as well as the generally lower cost of production in developing countries, has contributed to the expansion of this new division of labour, which has played a major role in the disorganization of American capitalism: the shift of manufacturing industries to the Third World, and the related restructuring of the American economy towards the service sector has led to a decline in the number of manufacturing jobs and, as the American economy has de-industrialized, a decline in the size and structure of the middle class.

The second trend affecting the middle class is the changing nature of the service class (white-collar, college-educated America). The complex managerial structures that developed in many American companies during the first half of this century led to the extensive growth of white-collar employment, which helped produce an inter-connected complex of institutional developments in universities, private foundations, professional occupations, and large corporate bureaucracies following the Second World War. This, in turn, led to a significant expansion of this class in the 1950s and 1960s.

The growth of these white-collar positions accounted, in part, for the productive relations unique to the United States; however, this class has also played an important role in the proliferation of new social and political movements that are not directly structured by the relations of production. As the service class grew and increasingly defined American politics, it facilitated the rise of new political forms, namely issue-based politics. Due, in part, to the steady decline of party loyalties since 1964 (Abramson and Aldrich, 1982: 502) issues and ideological disputes have emerged as the most important factor in shaping electoral outcomes. The slogans and campaign structure of the Democratic Party became increasingly in-effective because they were centred around the New Deal strategy of delivering large working-class voting blocs based on traditional group identities and loyalties. As these traditional affiliations have been replaced with more individualized and inde-pendent social ties, previous class loyalties to the welfare state in general, and the Democratic Party in particular, have been undermined. As a result, the electorate has fragmented into tiny groups, de-massifying society (Lash and Urry, 1987: 221), and increasingly focusing political forms on the individual and specific issues.

Postmodernism and Changing Political Forms

As the media have stepped into the vacuum left by traditional politics, arguably acting as a fourth branch of government, old affiliations and shared meaning re-garding the nature and function of social democracy have been replaced by a fragmented, image-based politics, where meaning and identities are built, broken down, and reconstructed at an unprecedented rate. This is not to suggest, as some postmodern theorists claim, that social relations and popular struggles have become meaningless or irrelevant, that they have been subsumed and dispersed within the myriad cultural forms, but rather that capitalist social relations have taken on a qualitatively different form, which has contributed to the crisis of hegemony and a permanent law and order society. Indeed, postmodernism is not only consistent with 'law and order' discourses, social censures, and the rise of 'authoritarian populism', but it has played an active role in the move towards increased state coercion.

Postmodern culture, which differs from previous dominant cultural forms, is based on mechanical reproduction, disputes the separation of art from life, is consumed (rather than contemplated), and affects the audience through its immediate emotional impact. Jean Baudrillard, the foremost figure to discuss post-industrialism in culture, traces the transition from 'industrial capitalism' to 'consumer capitalism', which is similar to Lash and Urry's view of disorganized capitalism. For Baudrillard, the most important change in contemporary consumer capitalism is that individuals now consume images rather than products. Thus, in recent decades, as consumer appeals have been based more on image and less on practical rationality, the utility and functionality of products have become irrelevant. The new 'semiotics of everyday life' has thus conditioned a widespread audience to the reception of postmodern culture, where the separation between culture and life, image and form, is increasingly indistinguishable (Lash and Urry, 1987: 287). As these boundaries have blurred, television, the movies, and other forms of mass culture have emerged as the primary means whereby dominant morality, disguised beneath the shiny veneer of entertainment, is disseminated throughout the social formation.

As disorganized social relations and postmodern culture have replaced older modes of collective identity, morality, and meaning with image-based representations of individual identity, new political forms of domination have developed. In this new, postmodern politics, voters are studied and appealed to as individuals, not as constituent elements of larger groups. This is both the cause and effect of the rise of increasingly sophisticated polling, 10- to 30-second television sound-bites, television advertising, and direct mailing. It also helps explain the increasing divisiveness of political campaigning. Whereas, previously, voter loyalties could be appealed to in a positive way, even in a 30-second television advertisement, it is now much more effective to give impressions, appeal to feelings, arouse emotions: wedged in the midst of advertisements for all types of products, the political spot must grab its audience. This tends to rule out even a substantive 30-second discussion of the issues.

New political forms have accentuated the drive to replace meaning with symbolism. For example, the focus group – an apparatus of Fifth Avenue and the postmodern American electoral process – is designed specifically to test the reactions of a specific demographic group to various themes and issues thought up by campaign professionals. To be as precise as possible, individuals are attached to computerized hand-held 'galvonic response meters' which test their reactions to various attack ads. Through this sophisticated apparatus, the state has become increasingly proficient at exploring particular emotional reactions to determine which (usually divisive) message will most affect a particular social group.

In this manner, postmodern social relations and political apparatuses have modified the terrain of political domination, transforming the way in which popular struggles and social relations are inscribed within the state. The state is now able to intervene in the relations of power not only at an individual level, but at a subindividual level, transcending individual rationality to enter, identify and exploit negative emotions, gut reactions, deep prejudices, divisive instincts. In this era of Pavlovian politics, new technology, such as the computerized galvonic response meter, physically (and metaphysically) connect the individual's emotional response to various stimuli directly to the material state.

Moreover the state is able to draw on this knowledge to construct the symbolism, regardless of the substantive consequences, necessary to maintain a more coercive form of hegemony. The postmodern political form has thus facilitated the organization of a more coercive mode of hegemony by providing a more effective means of disorganizing and dividing opposition groups and movements. As the state's control sites have become more flexible, extending to new levels throughout the social fabric, the power bloc has been able to draw on new powers to legitimate increased discipline, to further fuel authoritarian populism, and to accentuate the censure of social enemies.

The move towards more direct forms of state coercion is not carried out by the state alone, but is part of a deeper process which is justified, amplified, and often initiated by real anxieties within the populace concerning social change wrought by the recent stage of capitalism and related developments within the social formation. This is where the coercive noose between the structural level, the state, and civil society tightens, for as the crisis of hegemony worsens, the state, political leaders, the media, and individual citizens all begin to search for causes. The search rarely reaches the structural level, however, for many more superficial and politically expedient scape-goats exist. To deal with these 'social enemies', the state is called upon by social groups, the media, and political leaders to take stronger measures: to 'get tough'.

Not all of these causes are spurious, for as economic, political and social struggles become more intense, and as groups fight for increasingly scarce resources, the very nature of social relations becomes far more antagonistic. Because social censures are solidly rooted in these social relations, they develop as very complex cultural forms, combining hegemonic ideologies with the real anxieties, fears and mistrust generated by popular struggles, and are expressed and experienced in a wide variety of ways – from the brutal force of the criminal justice apparatuses to subtle looks of disapproval by passers-by on the streets. Regardless of their particular form, they are couched in the language of the general will and common morality, implicating them as a primary means through which the state and dominant groups can mediate the constant struggle for hegemony.

Hegemonic Discourses: Power–truth–knowledge

To understand how inner-city blacks came to play such an important (negative) role in mediating the worsening crisis of hegemony in America, we must first turn our attention to the development and perpetration of specific conservative discourses, which became so pervasive and so accepted, that by the 1980s they had attained a social existence akin to what Foucault described as a 'regime of truth'.

In this view, an absolute truth is non-existent; rather, as Nietzsche argued, truth has no meaning outside a given order of power. Power thus produces and sustains particular regimes of truth. Each society, then, has its regime of truth, its 'general politics' of truth; that is, the types of discourse which it accepts as true; the mechanisms and instances which enable one to distinguish true and false statements (Foucault, 1980b: 131). Moreover, as truth and falsity are identified and separated, the many specific effects of power are attached to what is held up as true and positioned opposite what is targeted as false.

Because power operates in a positive manner, producing forms of knowledge and related discourses, it is not simply exercised as a means of overt domination, but is an essential component in an individual's active participation in her/his own subjugation. This is a crucial feature of Foucault's formulation of hegemony and modern systems of control: the multiple effects of power transcend the level of ideology, as understood by traditional Marxism, extending with maximum intensity to bodies that have been individualized by power relations.

It follows that truth is essentially an illusion which disguises the reality of power and power relations. That power proceeds beneath and in conjunction with the illusion of truth suggests that hegemonic discourses reinforce social cohesion through 'practices, techniques and methods which infiltrate minds and bodies', and 'cultural practices which cultivate behviours and beliefs, tastes, desires, and needs as seemingly naturally occurring qualities and properties embodied in the psychic and physical reality (or "truth") of the human subject' (Hoy, 1986: 160).

Language plays a decisive role in the development of these hegemonic discourses, attracting, organizing, and ultimately expressing the complex of effects and relationships of power, truth, and knowledge. By legitimating particular actions and rejecting others, and by defining and integrating social (power) relations through its system of symbols, language is implicated as a primary means whereby the techniques of power cultivate widespread acceptance and commitment to a regime of truth.

This is not to suggest, as some post-structuralists do, that there is no experience outside of language. Rather, because language helps define the larger body of normative intuitions that attach very specific meanings to everyday life experiences, the network of linguistics creates a cohesive framework of shared meaning without which we could not 'exist socially and in a disciplined manner' (Nietzsche, 1983: 73). Language thus structures our experiences in ways that lead to effective action – in this particular case the censure of inner-city blacks.

Conservative Regimes of Truth

To begin to understand the censure of inner-city blacks, it is necessary to trace the development of conservative discourses which became, in effect, accepted 'truth' in the United States in the 1980s, paying careful attention to the relationship between language and co-ordinates of knowledge.

Much of the underlying cohesion and logic of the conservative discourses on crime begins with laissez-faire economic doctrine, which, drawing on academics such as Fredrick von Hayek and Ludwig von Mises, maintains that the aspects of the welfare state which undermined free-market capitalism in the 1960s and 1970s were also responsible for the 'permissive' attitudes that led to increasing crime rates during the same period. The potential contradiction between laissez-faire economic and social welfare policy on the one hand, and increased criminal justice intervention on the other is thus resolved: if the welfare state was responsible both for America's economic decline, and for rising crime rates, then the state should be interventionist only in the area of law and order; indeed, the maintenance of law and order is necessary for the proper functioning of the market.

The doctrine of economic individualism found its echo in conservative explanations of crime, which held that the causes of crime must be located not in social conditions but in individual characteristics: thus, the criminal, like the consumer, engages in an overly simplistic process of rational decision-making, weighing the potential costs and benefits before acting. From this it follows that, to deter crime, the state must toughen its criminal sanctions and tighten its mechanisms of carceral control.

As these conservative discourses on crime have gained credibility over the past three decades, there has been a corresponding loss of faith in the social democratic enterprise. No doubt the failures, both real and perceived, of the Great Society programmes, as well as the conspicuous bankruptcy in liberal ideas and policies over the past two decades, have contributed to the state's loss of legitimacy. However, the sometimes ambivalent, and often hostile view of social democracy also results from a deep and often unconscious belief that benign state social control has failed as an integrative mechanism, and has been unable to provide the glue with which to bind capitalist society together. If the state is unable to stabilize capitalist social relations through social welfare policies, then the obvious alternative is to accept the rapid transformations of the free market, while relying on the state to maintain social control through more coercive methods: by shifting to a permanent carceral position, locking up, instead of helping, those who 'threaten' the social fabric.

An academic cadre of 'new realist' criminologists offered a highly influential argument supporting increased carceral social control. In *Thinking About Crime* (1975), James Q. Wilson put forth a pragmatic, policy-oriented approach which focused on burglary, robbery, larceny and car theft, since these were the crimes which 'makes difficult or impossible the maintenance of meaningful human communities' (Wilson, 1975: xix). He might well have said 'profitable economic markets'. Regardless, the widespread appeal of Wilson's brand of right-wing criminology was based on its ostensible commitment to improving the lives of middle- and lower-class groups. Because it is rooted in the very real fears and anxieties of the public, its more nefarious function is obfuscated, while at the same time, the fires of authoritarian populism are further fuelled.

Wilson also derided the notion of progressive social change, promoting instead efforts which concentrated on the management, control, and surveillance of public places, and on raising the 'expected cost of crime'. Similarly, Ernest van den Haag, challenging strict libertarians who had not been persuaded by the laissez-faire/'law and order' justification, further rationalized the conservative impulse to expand the criminal justice system:

> Conservatives believe in limited government. But in some respects, state power might be extended. Most conservatives would strengthen the ability of the government to apprehend and punish criminals, to impose the death penalty, and to control pornography. (van den Haag, 1975)

Thus through the 1970s, the new realists articulated a coherent discourse which called for 'tougher control of working class crime, empirically tested methods of punishment, a revitalization of moral outrage about crime, and an expansion of state measures of control' (Platt, 1987: 58). Though these discourses played an integral and reflexive role in the proliferation of the criminal justice system during the 1970s, these aspects of the 'law and order' ideology attained the level of social 'truth' in the 1980s as the White House, Congress, the Supreme Court, state legislatures, academia, and the media all accepted them as the reigning conventional wisdom.

As law and order became a dominant hegemonic ideology, it had a profound impact on developments in the criminal justice system. For example, passage of the Antidrug Abuse Act of 1986, which marked the official beginning of Reagan's second 'national crusade' to eliminate drug use, ushered in the most comprehensive anti-drug legislation to pass through Congress, including amendments stiffening the penalties for manufacture, distribution and possession of illegal drugs. Persons convicted of major drug-trafficking offences, those involving at least 5 kilograms of cocaine or 1 kilogram of heroin, were subject to a mandatory minimum sentence of 10 years' incarceration – a sentence that was considerably longer than the average federal sentence for homicide. This penalty was doubled for a second conviction. Offences involving 100 grams of heroin, 500 grams of cocaine or 5 grams of crack were made punishable by a 5- to 40-year sentence, and a drug-related death or serious injury was made punishable by a minimum 20-year sentence (McWilliams and Kramer, 1994: 13). Also, during the mid- to late-1980s, almost every state toughened its sentencing codes in some manner: mandatory sentences and presumptive sentencing stipulations frequently replaced indeterminate sentences; probation was terminated for an increasing number of crimes; sentences mandating long prison terms were lengthened (Caringella-MacDonald, 1990: 102).

The strength of the law and order ideology and its multifaceted impact on the criminal justice system have continued unabated through the 1990s. In fact, the centre of the crime discourse has moved so far to the Right that the counter-discourses associated with 1960s liberalism have been marginalized and relegated to the fringe of American politics. In his 1992 Presidential campaign, candidate Clinton confirmed that the traditional liberal pole on crime had entirely collapsed. While Clinton paid lip-service to a few 'smart on crime' programmes like Midnight Basketball, he employed a campaign strategy which sought to portray him as being as tough on crime as any Republican. For example, he demonstrated vociferous support for the death penalty and focused repeatedly on his pledge to increase the number of police on America's streets by 100 000 and pass a 'three-strikes-and-you're-out' bill.

The law and order consensus was further evidenced in the congressional crime debate of 1993–94. In the end, both Democratic controlled houses of Congress passed crime bills that expanded the death penalty by more than 50 additional offences, funded 100 000 new police, made 'three-strikes' a federal law, and allocated $8.8 billion towards new prison construction. Indeed, one of the few contentious issues was just how difficult to make the death-row appeal process.

Former Surgeon General Jocelyn Elders demonstrated just how marginalized counter-discourses on crime and drugs were in the mid-1990s. Speaking before the National Press Club in 1993, Dr Elders merely suggested that the federal government should study the idea of legalizing drugs. The bipartisan outcry was swift and severe, with Republicans calling for her resignation and the White House publicly rebuking her. This left little doubt that such arguments were so opposed to the dominant crime–drug ideology, that they would be either silenced or ignored.

Hegemonic Discourses and the Censure of Inner-city Blacks

Regimes of truth not only serve to construct a particular version of reality, but they may also serve to construct and perpetrate dominant censures of particular social groups or types of behaviour. Because power is not simply normalized through its outward manifestation as truth, but is inscribed in the procedures of state discipline, it is also normalized through the techniques and practices of state apparatuses and institutions. In this process, social censures – as constitutive of the hegemonic ideology, and as normalized through power–truth–discipline – 'provide a passionate impetus for the daily detail of social regulation' (Gelsthorpe and Morris, 1990: 29). In this manner, a hegemonic censure, having dehumanized its target, is able to legitimate and mobilize political forces against that group. Thus, a regime of truth not only labels a group as 'deviant', but also identifies that group as the cause of certain social evils and legitimates state violence against them in the eyes of larger society: truth–power–language create a moral unity which places even an insignificant infraction of established codes of conduct within an undifferentiated category of moral deviation.

In this manner, conservative discourses not only signified a general shift to the Right and to increased discipline, but they also created an ideological framework which spawned the censure of specific social enemies deemed to be more or less responsible for the moral breakdown and ensuing rise in crime. Thus, for example, as conservatives captured the 'family values' and 'back to basics' themes in the late 1960s they not only succeeded in undermining the most powerful argument liberals used in support of the welfare state, but they also began to tie the apparent failures of the welfare state more closely with liberalism's connection with the civil rights movement. As a result, though the welfare state had initially been viewed as a family policy, by the 1960s it had been associated with the rise of single mothers, particularly inner-city black women who were on welfare. Suddenly the welfare state became the enemy of the family, promoting dependency, illegitimacy, and 'permissiveness'.

Thus, the Democratic Party, which had reluctantly tried to accommodate the growing Black Power movement in the late 1960s, not only alienated conservative southern Democrats, but also inadvertently angered lower-class whites by creating the perception that the welfare state was more committed to uplifting blacks than to easing the burdens of whites. These perceptions provided conservatives with the means of casting liberals as north-eastern, establishment 'elites' who were indifferent to the concerns of average (white) Americans. Paradoxically then, because the whites who were most exposed to the impact of liberal racial policies tended to be less affluent, divisive racial politics allowed Republicans to utilize the class inequalities that their laissez-faire economic policies accentuated: by attacking welfare expenditures, forced bussing, and affirmative action, conservatives were able to capture lower-class white votes by playing on subtle racial antagonisms, and in the process, to divert attention from the potentially harsh effects of their economic policies.

Ronald Reagan offered a fitting example of the way in which conservative discourses which attacked the welfare state carried inherent racial undertones. In his 1976 Presidential bid, Reagan, in the best tradition of Nixon's 'positive polarization', utilized the term 'welfare queen' as a racial code word, playing on white America's biggest concerns with liberalism, the welfare state, and civil rights. The term 'welfare queen' originated inauspiciously enough, as the result of headlines in the Chicago Tribune, which reported on a Chicago woman who had received yearly public assistance payments of $150 000 (Mills, 1993: 12).

However, in the hands of Reagan, who incorporated this into his standard stump speech, 'welfare queen' became the symbol for welfare's failures: the social welfare system, which was supported by the hard-earned tax dollars of white America, was responsible for the 'laziness' and 'idleness' of inner-city black women. This is precisely the work that hegemonic discourses can do to reality, for the 'truth' of a one-dimensional welfare cheat which Reagan helped construct entirely disregarded the reality of both inner-city black social relations, and the overall impact of particular social welfare policies.

The Black Underclass Ideology

'Welfare queen', however, represented only a fragment of the discourses which dehumanized inner-city blacks. Indeed, African Americans in general have long suffered beneath the weight of dehumanizing dominant ideologies. As Gunnar Myrdal pointed out in *An American Dilemma* in 1944, white Americans have dealt with the troubling discrepancy between the hallowed 'American creed' and the oppressive way they have treated African Americans by putting on ideological blinders and obstinately refusing to confront the issue head on.

However the term 'black underclass', which developed as a highly targeted means of categorizing inner-city blacks as an autonomous social group sharing similar characteristics from city to city, did much more than past ideologies to dehumanize this particular group of African Americans. In 'the black "underclass" ideology in race relations analysis', Innis and Feagin (1988) trace the development of this term, suggesting that it has been highly political – representing a way of defining the problems of poor minorities in terms of a pathologically deviant sub-culture, rather than as the result of the flight of capital from inner-city areas, the effects of poor education, latent or overt racism, or lack of opportunity.

The concept of an 'underclass', a 'dangerous class' or a 'lumpenproletariat' has a long history in Western thought in general, and in American sociology in particular. For example, American sociologists such as Park in the 1920s and 1930s, and Parsons in the 1950s, drew on Durkheim to develop the notion that a socially deviant sub-culture was inherent to the development of the social system. For both Park and Parsons, the tendency towards deviant behaviour was continuously mediated and controlled by the social system's organic ability to re-establish and maintain equilibrium. Essential to this notion of equilibrium was the benign function of the state to help integrate social deviants into larger society. However, beginning with Myrdal's *Challenge to America*, published in 1963, the socially deviant 'underclass' began to describe a population 'of unemployed and gradually unemployable persons and families at the bottom of society' (Innis and Feagin, 1988: 15). The notion that this group was permanently 'unemployable', despite the best efforts of social democracy, was a significant step in the intellectual attack on the state's efforts towards integrative social regulation. The next step, linking this description with inner-city blacks, was made in the popular press towards the end of the 1960s (e.g., the *Observer*, and *New Statesman*). Moreover, through the late 1960s American academics increasingly accepted the concept and existence of a permanent black underclass and began producing a significant amount of literature on the subject. These academic discourses overwhelmingly supported the view that poor black inner-city communities created and accentuated pathological traits which became 'a way of life which is passed down from generation to generation' (Innis and Feagin, 1988: 16).

This continued and intensified in the 1970s as media commentators, politicians, and social scientists (e.g., Murray, Loury, Lemann, Glazer, Moynihan) further legitimated and consolidated the belief that the black ghetto was mired in a 'tangle of pathology'. For example, in 1977 *Time* magazine published an article on blacks in New York, stating that: 'The underclass has been left behind. . . . Its members are victims and victimizers in the culture of the street hustle, the quick fix, the rip-off, and, not least, violent crime' (*Time*, 29 August, 1977). Similar articles began to appear in such prominent magazines as *The New Yorker* and *The New York Times Magazine*, all of which reinforced the idea of a pathological inner-city black culture:

> What primarily defines [the minority underclass] is not so much their poverty or race as their behaviour – their chronic lawlessness, drug use, out-of-wedlock births, welfare dependency, and school failure. 'Underclass' describes a state of mind and a way of life. It is at least as much a cultural as an economic condition. (Innis and Feagin, 1988: 130)

This quote is significant, for although it defines the underclass in cultural terms, explicitly rejecting the notion of a racial categorization, it implicitly links the given cultural traits to inner-city minority groups. This link was also made, either implicitly or explicitly, by the rest of the popular media, politicians, academia, and the general public.

The power and widespread acceptance of this ideology in the media and popular culture has continued into the 1990s. Significantly, it also continues to be legitimized by American academics. For example, in 1987, William Julius Wilson published *The Truly Disadvantaged*, which quickly became the academic departure point for those concerned with the state of inner-city blacks. There was very little new or revolutionary about this work however. Indeed, while Wilson sought to emphasize the role of joblessness, he also reinforced the most damning aspects of the black underclass ideology; namely, the socially separate and internally reproducing deviant values of this group (Wilson, 1987).

As Innis and Feagin point out, by moving the discussion away from decent-paying jobs, capital flight, and racism, many of these 'underclass' discourses have played an important role in legitimating existing racial inequalities. But more importantly, by moving the public discussion towards the issues of crime, welfare dependency, illegitimacy, and self-contained and automatically reproducing ghetto pathologies, the black underclass discourses have become a negative ideological category, not only identifying and dehumanizing inner-city blacks, but also pointing to them as the cause of many of the social evils that were associated with liberalism, but that were, in reality, the product of the deep shift towards economic, political, and social crisis. In this manner, though the underclass discourse echoed Park's description of social deviants in the 1920s, this version has differed in one important respect: by suggesting that the black underclass was a culturally deviant, self-reproducing social group, this discourse created an artificial separation between inner-city blacks and the rest of society. Thus, because this was both a permanent black underclass, and a social group that was entirely separate from the rest of the social formation, there was little the larger social formation or the state could do to integrate inner-city blacks into the social system, thereby re-establishing equilibrium. Instead, the only possible response was to police the deviant behaviour in the inner city, and ensure that their behaviour had the least possible impact on the rest of society.

Perhaps realizing the implications of this argument, Wilson has urged scholars to consider rejecting the 'black underclass' concept. Citing widespread journalistic usage of the concept to describe inner-city behaviour, Wilson believes it has become too ideologically loaded to be of academic use. While Wilson's conversion is encouraging, it has had little impact on academic, let alone popular, usage of the term.

It is also important to note that the widespread acceptance of this version of the black underclass ideology has been encouraged by the decentralization of spatial relations, which is an essential aspect of the move towards disorganized capitalism. A more particular trend in America's spatial organization has been the dramatic degree of segregation of racial groups. Though there is overwhelming evidence of continuing residential segregation at every level, the most significant distinction is between the (generally) black inner-city and (generally) white suburbia. While white America has continued to flee from the inner city, black suburbanization has remained low. For example, in 1988, only one-tenth of black Americans lived in the suburbs; indeed, housing segregation data suggests that even middle-income black families have not moved far from ghetto areas, choosing to live instead on the fringe of the ghetto (Innis and Feagin, 1988: 30). As a result, by 1992, 86 per cent of white suburban Americans lived in neighbourhoods that were less than 1 per cent black (West, 1993).

Because most white people do not live near a black family, let alone the black inner city, white America's perceptions of inner-city black life has been increasingly dependent on media interpretations, which have further perpetrated the 'black underclass' ideology and all of its pathological associations (drugs, violence, poor education, laziness, lack of 'proper' values). This was evident as early as 1968, when Richard Nixon used race and crime to great effect in areas such as New Hampshire, which were overwhelmingly white and experienced relatively low crime rates. In a letter to Eisenhower, Nixon wrote: 'I have found great audience for this theme in all parts of the country, including areas like New Hampshire, where there is no race problem and very little crime' (quoted in Dionne, 1992: 19). Though this touches essentially on new forms of 'disorganized politics', it is also important to note that crime was not only a code word for race. The public had become sensitized to increasing crime rates and was generally less concerned with aspects of the accused and structural causes than with finding a quick solution.

Anti-drug Discourses: the Inner-city and 'Crack' Cocaine

If the black underclass discourse dehumanized inner-city blacks and pointed to them as the cause of certain social evils, then the anti-drug discourses took the censure of inner-city blacks a step further, actively mobilizing and legitimating political action against them. Though there were many drug discourses targeted at many different types of behaviour which were clearly not limited to the ghetto, there developed, particularly in the 1980s, a highly targeted discourse which linked 'crack' cocaine with 'underclass' pathologies, particularly violent crime.

In the 1950s drugs did not have the same politico-economic significance as they did in the 1980s, nor had drug consumption increased significantly, and as a result, drugs were not perceived as such a threat to the social fabric (del Olmo, 1990: 15). However, as drug use in the 1960s expanded and came to be associated with the youth rebellion, the counter-culture, 'mystic' searches, Black Power, and political protest, drugs came to be viewed increasingly as a social 'problem' – as a struggle between 'good and evil' with the drug consumer portrayed as a demon incarnate. It is no surprise, then, that Nixon, responding to widespread moral concern, proclaimed drugs 'the enemy within', stating that 'Drug abuse has taken on dimensions of a national emergency' (del Olmo, 1990: 19).

Whereas for Nixon the drug problem had been associated with LSD and heroin – the drugs of choice for the anti-war movement – the anti-drug discourses of the 1970s began to shift towards cocaine. Though initially portrayed in the media as a glamorous, trendy drug, the cocaine discourse transformed between 1978 and 1982, increasingly dramatizing cocaine as the drug problem. This transformation was made all the more significant by the emergence of crack cocaine in the mid-1980s. Crack, a cheaper and highly addictive form of cocaine, came to be the most visible symbol of pathological inner-city drug abuse, as well as the most important perceived cause of crime in the inner city. The link between drugs and crime was a necessary aspect of mobilizing political forces against inner-city blacks, for if the real problem in the inner city was drug-related crime, then the answer was increased law enforcement, not social programmes.

These discourses had the effect of creating popular assumptions about the nature and persuasiveness of drug consumption and drug-related crime. Though there is much debate over the rise in crime rates over the past three decades, partially because crime statistics are inherently problematic, there seems to be a general consensus, that with the notable exception of black-on-black violence, crime (robbery, assault, burglary, auto theft) has declined marginally since 1970 (Caringella-MacDonald, 1990; Blonston, 1993). Thus the (white) public perception of crime in general and drug-related violence in particular is not justified by comparable increases in official crime rates.

To explain these inflated public perceptions, we must first turn to the media. As Stuart Hall has argued, the media relies heavily on official 'claims-makers' from academia and the government who have a built-in bias towards supporting hegemonic discourses, and thus reinforcing state policies. In this manner, the media have been a primary vehicle through which crack came to be viewed as a pandemic inner-city problem. For example, as James Orcutt and Blake Turner have documented, public concern about drugs in general, and crack in particular, reached their highest points (1981, 1986 and 1988) during the 'feeding frenzy' of media drug coverage corresponding to the President, Congress, and other claims-makers who were, at those times, calling for renewed drug wars (Orcutt and Turner, 1993).

Concerning the mobilization of political forces against inner-city blacks, the media not only played a vital catalytic role in defining inner-city drug abuse as a cause of crime and as a pandemic problem, but also in shaping the public's view of random drug violence. Though the cases of random violence are a real social tragedy and are not in any sense fabrications, the media have focused disproportionate attention on drug-related random violence, particularly black-on-white crime, such as car-jackings and drive-by shootings, which has helped perpetrate the image of a drug-infested black inner city that is a pervasive threat to white middle-class suburbia.

This should not in any way suggest a conspiratorial construction of a moral panic between the state and the media. The media have no conscious interest in fuelling authoritarian fires. Like any business, the media are motivated in large part by the need to maximize profits. And crime clearly sells. That is why crime, fire, war and similar dramas invariably lead on the local and national news, and why 'virtual reality' crime shows such as 'COPS' and 'Emergency 911' have proliferated so dramatically. This is not to excuse the media from culpability. Through their irresponsible sensationalism, the shadowy figures of the Central Park jogger and the Long Island Commuter Train gunman, among other notable examples of random violence, have been firmly embedded in America's collective social conscience.

This image of widespread random drug violence has helped to mobilize an even more repressive response from middle-class America towards the 'tangle of pathology' in the ghetto. In the National Drug Control Strategy, published in September 1989 as a blue print for Bush's drug war, William Bennett, the national 'Drug Czar', provided a suitable example of the way in which the state was able to organize and target rising social concerns over crime and drugs in order to legitimate increasing state coercion. According to Bennett, 'the intensifying drug-related chaos' may be predominantly attributed to crack: 'Our most intense and immediate problem is inner-city crack use', which 'is spreading like a plague' (Bennett, 1989: 3–5). Moreover, 'anyone who sells drugs and anyone who uses them – is involved in an international criminal enterprise that is killing thousands of Americans each year' (Bennett, 1989: 4). The logical response, according to Bennett, is not to try a new approach, such as focusing on demand (education, treatment) rather than supply, but is to be 'tough on drugs – much tougher than we are now'. Towards this end, Bennett suggested that 'we should be extremely reluctant to restrict [drug enforcement officers] within formal and arbitrary lines' (Bennett, 1989: 7, 8). In other words, since, as everyone can see in the press, the drug problem has become a crisis which is threatening to 'spiral out of control', the government must respond by redoubling its regulatory efforts, even if those efforts have to overlook certain inconvenient constitutional guarantees.

Finally, in its discussion of drugs, particularly crack, Bennett's report characterized the effort to control drugs as essentially a struggle between good and evil: not only is drug use defined as a moral problem, but the populace is divided between the morally righteous majority of honest, hard-working Americans who abstain from drug use, and the drug-users, who represent the forces of evil. However, the executive branch was not alone in offering a discourse which characterized drug consumers as tangible examples of moral depravity: the courts and Congress also reinforced this discourse, and more importantly, acted on Bennett's suggestion to get 'tougher' – thus mobilizing the full political force of the state against that type of behaviour most associated with inner-city blacks.

Moreover, because the criminal justice system was incorporated into this censure, increasing state coercion was even further legitimated, for the criminal justice system, as the symbolic sphere where good is distinguished from evil, plays a central role in normalizing hegemonic censures throughout the social formation

(Sumner, 1990a: 47). Thus, the criminalization of certain drugs legitimated the distinction between good and evil by declaring illegal that behaviour and those individuals associated with a specific illegal drug. The censure of drugs thus worked towards unifying the conservative version of morality at the expense of criminalizing the perceived behaviour of a specific social group.

Because the juridical discourse, which emphasized the criminal stereotype of drug-users, particularly blacks, was congruent with both the black underclass discourse and the inner-city drug/random violence discourse, the 'black underclass' was criminalized with the active support of the general public. Thus, the social censure of inner-city blacks, who existed well outside the hegemonic bloc, served an important purpose in uniting the hegemonic bloc behind an increasingly repressive state. In this manner, popular moral pressure based on the very real fears of many Americans combined with the trend towards increased state discipline to mobilize civil society and the state against a specific social enemy, leading to ever greater legitimate social discipline, increasingly strict anti-drug laws, expanding criminal justice budgets and apparatuses, billions of dollars of new prison space, and an exploding (black) prison population.

Conclusion

Rooted solidly in the accelerating disorganization of American society that has defined the present crisis of hegemony, repressive hegemonic ideologies have so marginalized inner-city blacks that this group has been abandoned by a state and society that views them as so fundamentally and permanently deviant that there is little that can or should be done to integrate them within 'respectable' society. Indeed, as the crisis of hegemony has deepened, this group has not only been 'left to rot', but in the narrow search for causes of the crisis, inner-city blacks have also been implicated as a social evil, as a root cause of the crisis, and have thus felt the full force of the state's coercive apparatuses.

In this process, not only did the state's overt mechanisms of coercion target street drug traffickers in disadvantaged urban minority communities, but the state's more subtle apparatuses of coercion, most notably the law and the criminal justice system, served to legitimate and implement a shifting and expanding criminal category. As a result, not only have economic conditions for inner-city blacks degenerated into conditions worse than those which existed under eighteenth- and nineteenth-century colonial occupation, but ghetto life has also become considerably more repressive than life for South African blacks under apartheid (Kramer and Steffensmeir, 1993).

Although individual human agency may be little able to immediately affect the deep trends towards disorganized social and productive relations, there are many ways to alter the more superficial manifestations of the move towards coercive hegemony. To effect positive change in the form of the crisis, we must engage in a dispassionate analysis of crime-reduction proposals that unequivocally rejects quick, easy, tough 'solutions', seeking instead substantive policies which account for deep structural trends, as well as for the more superficial manifestations. This should include a re-examination of conservative discourses, ideologies, and policies regarding law and order, the 'black underclass', and drug prohibition. Because the inner city is the one area where crime, particularly violent crime, has increased significantly in the past 25 years (Blonston, 1993), this re-examination must begin by uncategorically rejecting the notion that increased law enforcement and carceral social control will somehow solve the problems associated with the 'tangle of ghetto pathology' (*ibid*).

Similarly, a renewed discussion of, and commitment to, social democracy must also develop within social, political, and intellectual movements. To revitalize itself, and to chip away at what appears to be a coercive hegemonic bloc, a renewed social democratic enterprise must abandon the tired, rigid liberal ideology of the past, and develop new principles, imaginative ideas, and creative policies, while retaining a commitment to integrative social regulation. Newt Gingrich's argument, that in the information age we no longer need the state to bolster and reinforce social ties, is ludicrous. Because social breakdown is, if anything, occurring at a faster rate now than during industrialism, there is as much need as ever for the stabilizing influence of social democracy.

I have no intention of sugar-coating this conclusion, however. The prospects for a wide-ranging discourse that could reverse this deleterious downward spiral are not good. How can a society steeped in naive political cynicism and utterly committed to postmodern social relations produce the kind of leadership that will begin to take on these issues in a responsible manner? While people lash out and point fingers at the most obvious symbols of political and social decay, too few are willing to admit that much of the fault ultimately lies within themselves. Direct personal ties between the electorate and public officials will never be re-established so long as our sickening addiction to television continues unabated. For this is ultimately the driving-force behind divisive media-driven campaigns and the tremendous amount of money they demand. How else, but through 30-second ads, can politicians reach 'the people?'.

Nevertheless, if the conservative impulse to entirely abandon social democracy and integrative social regulation in favour of increased carceral control continues, the quality of life, even for upper-class whites who have previously remained aloof from the destructive effects of their social and economic policies, their views of social reality obscured by the evil of suburbia, will so degenerate that the crisis of hegemony may well come to a violent conclusion. While law and order and carceral social control is already immoral and ineffective, ultimately it may become impossible to maintain.

Chapter 7

Natural Born Killers:
Violence, Film and Anxiety

Victoria Harbord

Expression of fear about filmic nihilism is explored in this chapter to arm with insight those who dislike the censure of violent film as a form of social control which legitimates censorship. *Natural Born Killers* (Warner Brothers, 1994) and movies like it are focused on because they seem to represent a growing tendency in mainstream film to depict violence in a certain way. The first section outlines how uses of film narrative and characterization may serve to deepen anxiety about violent movies and consequently about aggression. The chapter also looks at Hollywood's *modus operandi* – its financial, rating, and technical imperatives – to reveal their impact on the amount and type of violence depicted. Lacanian film theory is used to consider cinema-goers' relationships to the nihilistic image. Not considered here is whether films influence people's attitudes: instead, the piece reassesses and refutes the claim that they incite viewers to violence. Discourse about violent imagery is thus opened up to its distortions. My aim is to expose its paralogic and misinformed nature.

The media linked ten murders to Oliver Stone's film, *Natural Born Killers*. Speculation arose, and became assertion, that criminals had copied the screen scenario that depicts a couple on a killing spree across America. Headlines like this appeared: 'Two young men have murdered four people – including three pensioners – in a *real-life imitation* of a brutal, new Hollywood blockbuster' (*Sunday Mirror*, 11 September 1994). Such assertions should not have been taken seriously. However, they fed into public discourse and had important results.

The censors, the Board of British Film Classification (BBFC), were prompted to withhold the film's certificate, to investigate allegations of causal links, and to reassure the public with research showing the *similarities* between viewing habits of aggressive and non-aggressive children (Hagell and Newburn, 1994). The government also became involved, especially as Judge Morland had alluded to violent video films in his summing-up of the James Bulger murder trial.[1] Violent crime was again symbolically linked to film (as it had been in the 1983 Conservative Manifesto, which claimed that the spread of violent and obscene video cassettes was dangerous, quoted in Barker, 1984: 10). Subsequent to the judge's comments, legislation in the 1994 Criminal Justice Act imposed a formula that the BBFC (currently an independent body), must apply when awarding a certificate. The legislation allows their decisions to be challenged in the courts for the first time, giving potential for state censorship.

The BBFC investigation into 'links' confirmed what anyone conversant with the issues would have predicted about *Natural Born Killers*:

> In all but one of the cases linked by the press with the title of the film, the accused or dominant member of an accused pair had been in prison and, in one case, also in a mental hospital, for serious acts of violence, including in three cases murder. In the remaining case, an intention to commit the offence had been stated to a friend many months before the killing and access to guns established. In the two cases where a series of killings was attributed to an accused pair, the first killing had been committed before the film opened and there was no evidence that the accused had ever seen the film. On the other hand, drugs seem to have been involved in all the American cases. The one case in France is now known to have been politically motivated, the killers having formed their own anarchist group well in advance of the crime and having been supplied with a pump action shot gun by two other anarchists who have been imprisoned for complicity in the offence. There is no evidence in this case that either of the accused ' had ever seen the film in question. (BBFC Press Statement, 12 December 1994)

There were no headlines admitting 'Sorry, we were wrong!'.

Concern was assuaged, but reassurances seem incapable of calming the issue for very long. This is one of the ways in which the violence/film debate no longer conforms easily to Pearson's assertion (1983) that it is part of a moral crisis that has surfaced without alteration every 20 or 30 years for the last 200 years, when Britain goes through a panic about the family, loss of parental control, and the impending breakdown of law and order. The crisis seems recently to have become fastened to expressions of fear about the impact of violent images on viewers, rendering the BBFC, the media, and thus people, in a state of perpetual anxiety.

Outbreak of that crisis coincides regularly with the release of each controversial or violent film. Several months after the *Natural Born Killers* uproar, the BBFC was refusing to give a certificate to young film-maker Ray Brady's film *Boy Meets Girl*, on the grounds of its aggressive content. One former BBFC examiner complained that the classification system should guide and educate the public, rather than bowing to public pressures (*The Times*, 30 May 1995). However, the BBFC was confronted from every side by strong displays of emotion over its role. From the Left (anti-censorship lobby) it was criticized for 'protecting people from art' and for imposing its middle-class sensibilities on the working and under classes (of which it is thought to be doggedly mistrustful). On the Right (church leaders, moralists and politicians), it was seen as the impotent friend of increasingly exploitative and unruly film-makers (*Empire of the Censors*, BBC2, 28 May 1995).

Empirical studies seeking to find a link between viewing material and aggressive behaviour have, for a long time, also been conducive to the confusion which stokes such strong feeling. Academia and the media (mis)inform each other, spurring themselves on to suggest or assert a causal link between film and aggression which can never be proved. It is an angels-on-pinhead approach. Between 1972 and 1982 Pearl *et al.* (1982) counted 2 500 academic contributions to the study of screen violence. For 30 years these have been either flawed, or at best inconclusive (Barker, 1995). Such studies are often premised on contentious grounds, especially in their assumptions about how (and at what age) violent tendencies are formed. Furthermore, the complexities of interpretation are not considered, or not integrated within inferences. Violent images are presented as having an effect on behaviour to a greater or lesser extent, but the possibility that the receiving sensibility of the individual will be conditioned elsewhere, away from the screen, cannot inform searches for causal links. It simply undermines them. For example, Singer and Singer concluded that their data 'seem to suggest that we cannot rule out the possible causal link between TV-viewing and subsequent aggression' (1981: 114.) However, this conclusion is contradicted by their previous statement that 'it might be argued just as well that children who are inherently aggressive might simply prefer to watch aggressive material' (1981: 111).[2] A causal approach to the issue fuels a discourse which is often repetitive and intellectually stagnant, one which stubbornly refuses to die (Sparks, 1992: 20). To connect aggressive behaviour to screen stimulation trivializes the issue of violence and its complex determinants. Such research tends to generate fear and waste money. Large-scale studies of convicted violent offenders reveal that most have histories of mental health and social problems, of physical and sexual abuse (Toch and Adams, 1989).

The early 1980s report, *Video Violence and Children* (Hall, 1983) is probably largely responsible for shaping the cause/effect mentality which is widespread in Britain and which allowed *Natural Born Killers* to be linked to ten murders. It claimed that 40 per cent of Britain's under 16s, and 37 per cent of the under 7s had seen a video nasty. In *Video Nasties – Freedom and Censorship in the Media* (1984) academic Brian Brown details how he presided over the report, only to see it hijacked by moralists intent on proving a causal link between viewing violence and violent crime. The figures which came from it were culled from 46 completed questionnaires. Of those returns, only three children had seen a so-called video nasty. The report claimed that working-class children were having their social values moulded by obscene films. It was given to the press at the Fleet Street journalists' church in the presence of the Archbishop of Canterbury. It was seen as accurate and important, and rightly so. The document was endorsed by parliament, the church and academia.[3]

Legislation against the distribution of video nasties followed. No doubt genuine concern was manifest in the decision to legislate, however the suggestion that media outcry was used as a vehicle for political point-scoring (Barker, 1984) rings true. Nothing could have been more fortuitous to the government at that time than a document negating the notion that aggression (like that which erupted into inner-city riots) is a display of despair by people on the scrap heap, without work or the hope of finding it. Violence could subtly be equated with the watching of *Driller Killer* on the video, rather than with the human malaise at the core of Britain's decimated manufacturing base.

Sensibilities were perhaps conditioned by the video nasty outcry. However Barker's claim that it gave right-wing moralism a tremendous boost is harder to concede. Moral panics may serve political purposes in the short term. In the long run they seem ineffective. More than anything they are expressive. Cohen writes:

> The Mods and Rockers symbolized something far more important than what they actually did. They touched the delicate and ambivalent nerves through which post-war social change in Britain was experienced . . . one does not have to make any conspiratorial assumptions about deviants being deliberately picked out to clarify normative contours at times of cultural strain and ambiguity, to detect in the response to them declarations about moral boundaries, about how much diversity can be tolerated. (1980: 192–3)

The 1984 video nasty outcry came and went, again sewing seeds of misinformation in the popular imagination. A decade later technology had made it possible to watch a banned film on the Internet, or on satellite television, beamed in from some remote country. The free market opened up more channels of information resulting in even less control over what people view. Perhaps the 1994 moral panic over films like *Child's Play 3* and *Natural Born Killers* expresses anxiety about the violent movie because it would be hopeless to rally against the large and uncontrollable new mediums. Cinema is one of the last legitimate targets left for enforceable legislation.

Anxiety and Moral Panic

'Art unrelated to the objective spirit of its time is equally as unimaginable as art without the moment which transcends it'.

(Theodor Adorno)

Sparks (1983, 1992) advanced our understanding of the continued portrayal of crime fiction (which is invariably violent) by arguing that it relates to the audience on a deep level, both in terms of reassurance and in terms of our symbolic relationship to retribution and punishment. Here, I intend to extend his conclusions to film, to highlight why recent changes in the crime drama genre have the potential to provoke deep anxiety amongst sections of cinema audiences.

An understanding of the conclusions of research into the screen representation of crime and violence leads to elucidation of what the extensive showing of aggression reflects culturally and artistically. Analysis of crime and violence in television drama concluded that attention should steer away from empirical work (on supposed effects), and should instead investigate the 'kind of institutions, market forces, technical constraints', and more importantly fictional conventions, which shape our visual diets (Sparks, 1983: 8).

For years the detective story was seen (by some cultural theorists) as a mere vehicle for didactic messages, for teaching preferred notions of right and wrong. That is, the criminal embodies the bad, and the detective the good. Sparks revealed that the perennial formula of crime drama is not just related to desires to instil certain moral values into audiences' minds, but is the product, *inter alia*, of fictional imperatives vital to the story-teller:

> Since narrative classically demands a consecutive sequence of events unfolding in time, some kind of transgressive act is necessary to initiate the story. An analogy which is commonly drawn from this between modern popular culture and myth tends to be pushed too far and too literally. Nevertheless it may be reasonable to see in the crime drama an opening through which the mythic intrudes upon the everyday, at least in the sense that it draws upon topics and structures which are both widespread and venerable. (Sparks, 1992: 37)

Transgression fulfils three tasks for the crime story-teller. Most obviously it provides an impetus for the story. (A crime or wrong-doing is vital for a tale to develop, hence its continued screen depiction.) It also introduces a 'hero as problem solver', usually in the shape of a detective, and it allows the 'good/bad twinning metaphor' to emotionally underpin events (i.e., the audience knows whose side to be on). Thus, poetic justice can be seen to be done.

Just as the incorporation of retribution and mercy in fairy tales seems to 'strike some inner chord, to resonate with something fundamental in our inarticulate understanding of the world' (Slattery, 1990: 29), so too does the form and content of the detective story. Sparks (1992: 43) combines Gouldner's notion (1976) of the paleo-symbolic, the visceral ability of murder mysteries' formulaic components to please audiences, with Garland's claim (1990) that punishment is more than just a form of social control.[4] Garland argues that punishment is rich in symbolic meaning and deeply rooted in the emotional needs and desires of ordinary people (1990: 11). Sparks rightly marries these two ideas together to conclude that crime fiction taps into not only what an audience thinks, but also into what it feels. Narrative conventions are shown to be the servants of ontological fears and desires. Through this insight law and order centred fiction, which comprises so much film and television content, comes to be understood not just in terms of the audience's relationship to power or ideology, but also in terms of its human needs. Many of Sparks' conclusions about television apply to film, even though there are subtle differences between them, and measurable disparities between the art house and mainstream movie.

In his work on violence, Twitchell also examines the idea that film narrative and characterization reflect human uncertainties and needs. He believes that modern horror films outline *communal dreams* by showing the big monster attacking *little us*, the abnormal *it* threatening normal *us* (1989: 207). The hero as an agent of retribution or a tool of revenge brings about a return to the former state of things. From Sherlock Holmes to James Bond, a capable individual is the one able to save us from the 'big monster', the one able to restore order. In the formulaic narrative, as in the Manichean struggle, good always wins.

Conflict once acted within the work of art as a means of overcoming time through 'sustaining intra-temporal tension' (Adorno, 1991: 63). Its function when applied to 'popular' or 'low' art then served in film and television to assist in the playing-out of moral tales, to confirm 'shared' values and to allow the narrative to unfold. The violence depicted could worry audiences, but as Sparks notes: 'The debate about whether or not television causes fear of crime suffers from a failure to recognise that the narrative is directed towards precisely the area of tension between anxiety and resolution. This is what Adorno has in mind when he remarks that detective fictions *charm away* the challenge of disorder' (1992: 25).

Sparks chose to concentrate on television images because it has long been the case that the uses of crime and punishment in the cinema have been more various and complex than on the television. I have chosen to focus on films because recently there has been a tendency for movies which are marketed at mainstream audiences to take on art-house film characteristics. Naturally, not all films conform to the narrative developments outlined below. However, the cross-over of post-modern, nihilistic themes and motifs to the mass market is a tendency which seems capable of increasing anxiety about violent images. Below it will be shown that the films which provoke the most censure are often not the most violent, but the most perverse.

New Hollywood Narratives

Like tyres, narrative genres seem to have only a certain mileage. Ways of presenting the same scenario need to be found, as in the case of the western which changed and developed from its early white/black hat theme in order to retain its audience's interest. A re-tread is necessary, rather than a new radial, because the crime fiction genre has been shown to be perennially popular. As already stated, the writer needs a transgression to allow fictional events to unfold. For that reason, when new forms of the same theme are developed they inevitably involve the depiction of violence.

Content analysis of recent popular film releases[5] reveals that more and more Hollywood movie directors are doing without the detective figure. The detective–criminal binary opposition seems to have become exhausted and replaced by conflict and violence which forms part of a bad–bad equation as opposed to the good–bad equation described by Sparks. The mainstream audience may have seen screen sadism, stabbing, shootings, rapes, all before, but nearly always within a particular (and often simplistic) moral framework. Film director Quentin Tarantino has been described in the press as the high priest of moral vacuity. The violence in his films *is* often sadistic. However, what feels more unsettling about his work is that there is no longer the comforting presence of a detective figure, or knowing individual, behind the bloody scenes, to restore order and to dish out poetic justice. Films like this, which provoke much anxiety and outcry, have become crime centred rather than law and order centred. In his popular film, *Pulp Fiction* (Miramax, 1994), there is transgression after transgression. Nobody calls the police. No detective is on the wrongdoers' trail, who by default (narratively) are the heroes.

In Tarantino's sophisticated, bloody (and moral) film, *Reservoir Dogs* (Miramax, 1992) the price of violence is destruction. The censor writes eloquently in the *BBFC 1992 Annual Report*: 'The falling-out of thieves in *Reservoir Dogs* left the final scene littered with corpses, as in *Hamlet*'. Two police officers (one undercover and shot in the belly, the other captured and tied to a chair) are together in a warehouse after a failed heist. The captured policeman is tortured, loses his ear, is soaked in petrol. A 'gangster' is about to set light to him. We wait for the police to burst through the warehouse doors, the way they normally do in films. However, the cops do not arrive until the very last frame. By that time it is too late for a resolution, a return to order. The forces of law and order are portrayed as powerless. They have no central role to play. The distortion of expectation increases the viewer's anticipation. It is also potentially disturbing.

The BBFC choice to hold back this film's video release was based on 16 letters and 'many phone calls' (*Annual Report, 1993*). The decision to deny the movie *Bad Lieutenant* (Aries Films, 1992) (about an errant cop) video release was prompted by only five letters. Given that the BBFC's postbag does not reflect a great public outcry over these films, it is tempting to surmise that those decisions were somehow founded on the Board's own (perhaps unacknowledged) dislike of the new use of transgression – transgression for its own sake – in mainstream films. The children's film *Jurassic Park* (Universal, 1993) provoked 44 letters of complaint. Admittedly, a children's film would also be watched by protective parents, so a greater response could be expected. However, the BBFC had test-screened it before release to see if it was too frightening for children (showing that the Board was already unsure about its levels of violence). The subsequent influx of letters did not cause its video certification to be re-questioned. This decision then is perhaps taken on the grounds that *Jurassic Park*'s violence develops within a clear moral framework, one which conforms to normal expectations. The violence of *Reservoir Dogs* and *Bad Lieutenant* does not.

It is telling that the censor allowed the extremely violent film *Man Bites Dog* (Roxie Releasing, 1993),[6] which contains an 'appallingly brutal gang rape', to be certified without too many qualms. 'It was a decision to trust the audience, in the knowledge that, as a black and white sub-titled film, it would reach a very limited audience, most of whom would be familiar with the black comedy genre and its underlying moral agenda' (*BBFC, 1992 Annual Report*). This attitude seems to indicate that films which pervert moral norms are acceptable as long as they are not mainstream. By the same logic, popular films with lots of violence are screenable to children, provided the violence conforms to the 'good–bad', 'right–wrong' binary oppositions. The above report describes them approvingly as 'compensating frameworks of moral values'.

For some years now, the film hero or protagonist often no longer fits the Hollywood good-guy stereotype. For example, consider the character Hannibal Lector in *Silence of the Lambs* (Orion, 1991) – cannibalistic serial killer. Heroes can now be murderers, vampires or bad cops. They can be handsome, charismatic, knowing, like the detective figure. The audience is thrown into a new situation where it is forced to identify with protagonists who transcend their once rigid stereotypes. These bad-guy figures often hurt others, cheat, rape, kill. In the esoteric offering, *Man Bites Dog*, we are cast into the world of a charismatic serial killer, and we find ourselves laughing at both his jokes and his murders. This is disconcerting for sections of an audience which have grown up on a visual diet of good guys, particularly when there is a popular perception that film heroes can, or should be, role models for viewers. The next section of this essay explains how this disconcerting new aspect of mainstream film is intensified for the viewer, following technological innovations in filming.

Fiske and Hartley stated that screen violence enacts social, rather than personal relations; it takes place between personalized moralities (good versus bad, efficient versus inefficient, culturally esteemed versus culturally deviant) rather than between individuals per se (1978: 179). In relation to much mainstream cinema, this statement rarely applies in the 1990s. The apple-cart of symbolic meaning is regularly upset. The aggression and the transgression remain, but the moral narrative has, in many films, gone or changed into a shadow of its former self. This change induces anxiety about the representation of violence in sectors of the audience for two reasons, outlined below.

Possible Reactions to Characterization and Narrative Developments

Firstly, the reassuring aspect of popular film is undermined by these new fictional modes. Sparks related the symbolic power of crime drama to Bourdieu's concept (1977) of 'doxa', that is the familiar, or everything which can be taken for granted. Doxa describes what is thought to be a security-inducing element of traditional, non-differentiated society. In viewing crime fiction there is believed to be a 'doxic' effect, whereby diversity and antagonism can be overcome by a sort of 'underlying complicity' or 'consensus within dissensus' (Sparks, 1992: 51). The crime fiction narrative acted as a 'consolation against anxiety and dread'. Security induction is rarely a component of recent mainstream crime movies, not because directors wish to deprive their viewers of this, but because their way of story-telling is changing, as perhaps is the idea of consensus in postmodernity or radically modernized society (an issue which is explored later when this chapter considers questions of morality in relation to film).

Secondly, with the loss of expected reassurance comes loss of the film viewer's symbolic relationship to retribution and punishment. Sparks claimed that part of the inability of other commentators to provide an adequate critical language to address audience attachment to crime drama is also a failure to understand the level at which people demand retribution, if only on the screen. The perennial interest in fictional crime and punishment is thought to lie in 'primordial, less discursively available moral categories' (1992: 52).

Between 14 January 1994 and 1 January 1995 there were 255 newspaper articles in 20 newspapers on the subject of *Natural Born Killers'* postponed screening in Britain. Even though the articles tended not to allude directly to the narrative changes outlined in the argument above, the columns resonate a concern that the moral framework of much mainstream film has drastically altered. Concern can be detected in the following quotes:

'The nineties have seen cartoon violence, in which style and humour have displaced motive and consequence, fare increasingly well at the box-office' (*The Independent*, 27 October 1994);

'The films of John Ford . . . were as violent as anything Quentin Tarantino can offer. But you still left feeling that there was hope for the human race' (*Evening Standard*, 27 October 1994);

'The violence of NBK is nastier, sicker, scarier than other films, altogether weird' (*Herald Tribune*, 29 October 1994);

'The teenage audience is simply applauding a pair of happy butchers getting away with murder' (*The Times*, 28 October 1994);

'NBK is likely to encourage morally deadened young people to commit vicious crimes rather than produce any reform in society' (*Dallas Morning News*, 28 October 1994);

'Take away the cartoon satire and the parody of pop television, and all that remains in the eye of the beholder is highly stylised violence inflicted by sexy young renegades' (*The Independent*, 27 October 1994).

These quotes, and others like them, convey an anxiety which it appears is not just concerned with the (preposterous) violence of films like *Natural Born Killers*, but rather with its missing moral context and missing detective figure. When considering whether the film should be shown in Britain, the Liberal Democrat MP for Liverpool, David Alton (who successfully campaigned for new curbs on videos in the 1994 Criminal Justice Act), commented: 'I accept that violence has always existed. I am not talking about sanitising that. What I am saying is that it should be put in a moral setting' (*Today*, 10 November 1994.) Press concern is also directed at a particular scene in Tarantino's *Pulp Fiction*. An innocent character has his head shot-off in the back of a car as it drives over a bump and accidentally triggers the protagonist's gun. Brains and blood explode onto the car's upholstery, and yet, because the shooting was an accident, it is very funny. We laugh at a screen death for which there will be no revenge. No one will pay any price for it. No detective will track down the killers who are autonomous, stylish, funny, and untouched by the law. There is often analysis in the quality press about the urge to scape-goat film for society's shortcomings. At the same time, an unacknowledged sense of unease can be gleamed about the way transgressions are now depicted.

When asked by Melvyn Bragg, 'Why the controversy over your film?' Oliver Stone replied: 'The characters kill without remorse. They get away with it. The prisons, the media, the police are presented as being as bad as the killers, or even worse, in the sense that they don't improve whilst the murderers do' (*Start The Week*, BBC Radio 4, 20 February 1995).

Hollywood

'I went into the business for money and art grew out of it. If people are disillusioned by that remark, I can't help it. It's the truth'.
(Charlie Chaplin, 1972, after accepting an honorary Academy Award)

Analysis of mass communication systems is not reducible to literary theory. They have a material base. So too does the depiction of aggression. Finance bears a significant relationship to the amount and type of violence shown in films. The audience to be targeted dictates the sort of movie to be made. Concern about violent images is logically intensified by their proliferation. This section examines the production of those images in Hollywood, drawing heavily on Wasko's work, *Hollywood in the Information Age* (1994). The aim is to reassess the violence/film question in the light not only of social and narrative developments, but also in terms of financial, rating and technological changes. These technical changes are analysed with respect to psychoanalytic cinema theory, to suggest how audiences' reaction to screen-depicted violence could be heightened by them.

How the Target-audience Determines Levels of Screen Violence

Both Twitchell (1989) and Hutchings (1993) claim that Hollywood's preferred audience is the affluent (male) teenager. According to box office statistics, the average American visits the cinema 4.6 times per year. By contrast, the US teenager goes once a month. In Europe, 50 per cent of box office admissions are to people aged 15 to 24 years of age (Tydeman and Jakes Kelm, 1986: 69).

The relative tameness of postwar films is ascribed to the fact that they were produced for the middle-aged market. In the 1960s, television came along and robbed cinemas of their lucrative audience. 'Films could only be successful by showing what could not be shown on the living room screen. Essentially, the movies had to tell stories which were too big, too sexy, or too violent for television'

(Twitchell, 1989: 189). With strong competition from the tube, Hollywood had to adapt or die.

In a newly competitive marketplace, effective (i.e., popular) Hollywood film formulae dictated what followed. Violence appeared to work, so its levels were continually raised. Hammer House horror films seem tame now, in comparison to their successors which became progressively gorier. Teenage audiences wanted something more than television could offer. They also wanted special effects. Whereas a generation ago matinee audiences were eager to follow the adventures of Flash Gordon, Tarzan or Hopalong Cassidy, they now follow the repeated adventures of villains and heroes like Michael Myers in *Halloween* (Compass International), or Freddie in *Nightmare On Elm Street* (New Line Cinema).

This depiction of 'bad' or aggressive characters enhances action, by raising the audience's emotional stake in viewing it. Violence also crosses state and national boundaries. It is the much-derided lowest common denominator.

Sex, of course, is the other potent universal – whose depiction has not developed on the silver screen in the same way as violence for reasons beyond the fact that, as earlier postulated, transgression plays an important role in story-telling. The US film industry's self-regulatory body, set up in 1968, stipulates that scenes of sex and of drug use should not be shown to adolescents. Prior to that there had been a more rigid coded authority governing film. Its president proposed abandonment of the old code to woo people back into the cinemas. (A shrewd move at the time, because television was regulated by the strict 1934 Communications Act).

One journalist complains: 'America is a violent and puritan country. It loves guns and is afraid of sex. The movie-rating system lets the most frightful violence through but rejects nudity. The British costume drama, *The Advocate* (Miramax, 1994) was banned until its makers trimmed a rather mild sex-scene but there was no objection to hanging people' (*Herald Tribune*, 29 October 1994). The BBFC is particularly concerned about the violent images Hollywood produces. Ironically, this concern is not premised on a notion of causal links of film to violent crime. The Board's own research[7] shows that there are no significant disparities between the viewing habits of young violent offenders and non-offenders. On a mundane level the BBFC will edit out scenes which show explicitly how to complete criminal tasks, like hot-wiring a car. Beyond this, its role transcends logic, working almost (in my opinion) from the gut. There is a feeling that certain images are not healthy, but it cannot be explained why. Its function seems symbolic but necessary. Film-maker Bernardo Bertolucci describes the BBFC's role as one of 'Showing that someone takes images seriously, that someone cares' (*Empire Of The Censors*, BBC2, 28 May 1995). In the same programme, director Roman Polanski speculated on whether the examiners themselves become depraved from their continual exposure to violent and perverted images!

The regulation of violent scenes is an expression of the desire to control the out-pourings of America's growing video market, which the Board claims has provided a spur for the production of low-budget 'shockers': the Vietnam War is being repeatedly re-fought (and sometimes won) in the jungles of Taiwan and the Philippines, with righteous heroes inflicting ever more crushing revenge on wrongdoers, while unseen psychopaths wreak equally bloody havoc on student campuses, as they have done for more than a decade. The temptation to enliven mediocre scripts with lashings of gore is ever present (*BBFC Annual Report*, 1988). It is acknowledged that '. . . there is far more violence in the USA, and American society is evidently prepared to accept more violence in its media' (BBFC's *Student Guide to Film Classification and Censorship in Britain*).

The kind of rating a film receives is important to Hollywood's accountants. For this reason, directors are thought to be proactive, producing material to guarantee a certain certificate. In the United States, the parental guidance (PG) rating is suggested for under 13 year olds. An R-rated film allows children of any age to watch it, provided they are accompanied by a person over 17 years of age. The most desirable certificate is the PG-13 which captures the age group 13 to 17: a big, affluent, and largely uncritical, audience. In that category scenes of sex and drug use are prohibited, violence is not. This system influences enormously the amount of violence shown. The X-rating, was once used for violence – *Midnight Cowboy* (United Artists, 1969) and *A Clockwork Orange* (Warner Bros., 1971) both had Xs. This rating is now only synonymous with pornography (Twitchell, 1989: 186).

Natural Born Killers received an American R-rating. Children of any age could see it, accompanied by someone of 17 years or over. This was a decision which surprised many. Concern was aired by the BBFC and the press that the film's satirical message, whose conveyance entails a body count of over 100 people, may be lost on younger members of an audience. The US regulator had suggested an N-17 rating, which would have banned the under 17s from seeing it. The film's director went before the ratings board five times to defend his work against a proposed certificate which would have 'severely limited advertising' (*The Times*, 28 October 1994). He agreed to cut 150 of the most violent scenes to obtain a less restrictive, more financially viable, rating.

The drive towards more profit has been accelerated recently, following changes in the ownership of Hollywood film companies. A brief overview of the industry indicates the kind of financial interests involved and their relationship to the production of violent images. Hollywood has always been about making money. However, the increased involvement of major corporations is thought to have a significant impact on the violent nature of mainstream Hollywood films.

Columbia Pictures, previously owned by Coca Cola, was bought out by Sony for $3.46 billion in 1989. MGM was acquired by Matsushita in 1990. Twentieth Century Fox was bought by Rupert Murdoch's News International Corporation. During the 1990s, the mega-companies diversified into money-making schemes involving new technology, like cable and satellite channels, video games and CD-Rom production. They have also been buying up smaller, independent film companies: DEG, Embassy and Allied Artists were all bought out by corporations. These big companies are involved in cultural production, from audio-visual products, to publishing enterprises, to theme park operations.

News International's publishing arm, Harper Collins, published Michael Medved's critique of Hollywood's excesses (1992). Not surprisingly, this work of little scholarly value was serialized in the *Sunday Times*, one of News International's newspapers. The paper claimed that Medved had 'effected a sea change in the way we think about the influence of film violence in society'. In fact, the book added misinformation to the debate. *Hollywood Versus America* claims that violent television programmes produce 'ten thousand extra murders every year in the US'; that they are 'a causal factor in some 70,000 annual rapes and 700,000 injurious assaults' (1992: 248).[8]

Twentieth Century Fox gave the world such films as *The Exorcist III* (1990), *Marked For Death* (1993) and *The Vanishing* (1993). One part of Murdoch's corporation is willing to deride another part, to criticize Hollywood, even though it is part of it. (Medved himself was paid $8 000 by Paramount to be an expert witness against screenwriter Art Buchwald, who accused the company of stealing his ideas (*Guardian*, 15 March 1993).)

Corporate involvement in Hollywood means that the film companies no longer depend on movies as their only source of income (Wasko, 1994: 69). This may have given directors some limited financial breathing space – perhaps to experiment with narrative and characterization changes like those outlined above. However, given Hollywood's increasing corporate domination, this experimentation need not be about better exciting the audience for its own sake, but rather about investigating new avenues towards increased revenue.

A symptom of this intensified drive towards profit is the activity of product placement. In 1945 Joan Crawford was seen drinking Jack Daniels whisky in the film *Mildred Pierce*. In return the whisky company sent a couple of crates to the director, as a thank you. Today, placements cost between $5 000 and $250 000. Companies pay for their goods to be shown in a film. It does not matter what a movie's content is, so long as it can draw a large audience. Screen violence is effective in that task, hence its continued and maximized depiction. In the US there are 30 companies working exclusively to find film scenes suitable for their clients' merchandise. They receive scripts, and plough through them, looking for the best moments to (subliminally) advertise things. Already it is thought that fewer historical films are being made, as they lessen scope for product placement (Wasko, 1994: 214–15).

The growth of product placement coincides with developments in television. Digital and compression technology allows more information and channels than ever before to be squeezed onto coaxial cable wires, or fibre-optic lines. Because of these developments television audiences have the potential to be dispersed, and their sizes reduced.

For that reason, celluloid is now an important vehicle for advertising. A film which grosses $50m is thought to be seen by 13.7 million people at the public showing. It can sell 200 000 to 300 000 video cassettes. The video is then rented out. One film can give advertisers access to between 25 and 30 million viewers.

The BBFC could not have anticipated the significance technology changes would have on the film industry. With cable companies offering up to 500 television channels, more films are needed. Those films have increasingly violent contents and this is not likely to change so long as this is a money-making formula. Hollywood's corporate priorities appear to mirror those of the smaller 'exploitative' companies they recently swallowed.

Victoria Harbord

The Role of Special Effects in Heightening Anxiety about Violent Film Images

During the 1983 panic over video nasties voices could be heard claiming that the capacity to re-watch video cassettes would actually dilute films' supposed nefarious effects (Andrews, 1984: 47). However, this assertion was undermined at the time of 1994's panic by the sleek, no seams, special effects, which even a video cassette player would fail to reveal. The most important contribution to special effects is the Steadicam, a portable camera which sits on the operator's body and moves perfectly with it. This gives the impression that images are coming from eye level. The unit is balanced and carried in such a way that the resulting footage seems to be shot from the viewpoint of a moving human being. 'Whether in the novel or on film, point of view has a most powerful effect on interpretation. We are by nature sympathetic with a first person narrator. We see the experience through his eyes. Since the audience provides the visual field, the audience is perpetually in sync with the monster' (Twitchell, 1989: 208).

An audience's relationship to the cinematic image is believed by Lacanian psychoanalysts to involve complex emotional processes (Metz, 1990; Sarup, 1993). These theories are applied here to the violence/film question to show how anxiety may extend beyond surface fear of copycat crime, to deeper feelings. I will argue that an innovation like the Steadicam could have a significant impact on the viewer's perception of screen violence.

The Lacanian theorist, Metz, claimed that whilst watching a film the spectator is suspended in a state of disavowal. S/he may hold two incompatible positions at the same time, may be incredulous (disavowing what's happening on the screen as reality), and simultaneously credulous (believing depicted events to be real) (Sarup, 1993: 150).

If we give credence to the argument above (and one can be both credulous and incredulous of Lacanian theory!) then, given technical advances in film lighting and camera work, the reality conveyed on the screen must make disavowal harder. If blood no longer looks like tomato ketchup, if the vision of the criminal or monster is synchronized perfectly with bodily movements, then disconnecting oneself from the filmic depiction of violence must be increasingly difficult. This is not to claim that viewers are more likely to copy what they see. Violent behaviour has complex determinants. If, however audiences are prone to believe what they see as reality, they are also more likely to fear that what happens on the screen could happen to them. Even if special effects become a substitute for good writing and characterization (which are instrumental in allowing the viewer to empathize and identify with a film's protagonist), they probably also serve to heighten tension and fear.

How audiences relate to a screen subject is said to be determined by how a film is shot, and by the way in which 'cinematic texts' confer subjectivity upon viewers (suture). 'Some theorists argue that shot relationships are the equivalent of syntactic ones in linguistic discourse', explains Sarup (1993: 50). It is through them that meaning emerges and a subject position is constructed for the viewer. The way a viewer relates to the screen subject must influence the effect a film can have.

Film viewing can be compared to the mirror stage – the secondary identification with a unified subject (as Other) which is objectified and distanced. It is claimed that the cinematic convention of shot/reverse shot formation has a profound effect upon the viewer. This shot convention first shows a scene, the second shot depicts the field from which the first shot is assumed to have been taken, locating the spectator in the other 180 degrees of the same circular field. This,

> fosters the illusion that what is shown has an autonomous independent existence . . . the viewing subject perceives that s/he is lacking something. It is then realised that the camera is hiding things. The viewer therefore feels distrust. Psychoanalytic film theory claims that there then follows a realisation that s/he is only allowed to see what happens in the axis of the gaze of another spectator, who is ghostly or absent. This spectator has the attributes of what Lacan calls the symbolic father: potency, knowledge, self-sufficiency, transcendental vision, and discursive power. This sense of lack inspires the viewer to see more. (Sarup, 1993: 154)

The relevance of these theories in relation to innovations in film technology (like the Steadicam), is that the cinematic illusion seems to have become so well crafted that its ability to touch people on a deep emotional level must have been heightened. This argument is important to our understanding, even if all manifestations of fear about the violent image cannot be adequately explained in psychoanalytic terms. Where there is more identification with the first person narrator, then this coincides with the portrayal (in mainstream film) of the bad-guy hero. If we accept the notion of the symbolic father, then it must be disconcerting for viewers to see themselves guided (in places) through the action by a figure with whom identification has been discouraged in traditional formulaic narratives.

Disavowal may be harder, given advances in film technique, but there is no reason to believe that difficulties in discerning screen irreality are permanent. The first people to see the Lumière brothers' film of a moving train ducked under their seats to avoid being mowed down. It may be possible that the moral panics in which anxiety about violent film images are manifest may eventually abate. This, of course, would be a good thing, given the amount of misinformation which accompanies them.

Society and Film Violence

> 'When you're doing violence in movies, there's going to be a lot of people who aren't going to like it, because it's a mountain they can't climb. And they're not jerks. They're just not into that'.
>
> (Quentin Tarantino, 1995)

This final section of the chapter is perhaps more speculative than the others – not inferring from a body of evidence or content analysis, but marrying concepts of social theory to the violence/film debate, to suggest other factors which may account for the depth of anxiety aroused by the issue.

Morality in Modernity

In Barker's account of the video nasties scandal much fear centred on class. The 1983 influential and dubious report evoked an image of thousands (if not millions) of working-class children sitting on sofas up and down the country, tingling with pleasure at screen sadism, mutilation and rape. Barker wrote: 'And it is not only children who need the moral guardianship of the State to secure their childhood against rape and penetration [by images]. It is those adults who, in terms of this model, have never really escaped childhood' (1984: 32). This view is probably not just based on class prejudice as Barker suggests. It is more likely to be founded on fear. Fear of the unknown.

Adults who lack maturity or moral guidance, who are isolated from their families, who have no work, no partner, and no stake in society might exist. People do not know with certainty 'anymore' whether, or how, a stranger has acquired knowledge about how to behave. In modernity, we can speak on the computer Internet to a colleague or a friend thousands of miles away. Yet, at the same time we may not know anything about the people who live on the other side of the partition which divides our home from theirs. Historically, if people were fearful of someone from another class, then they could call upon the stereotype of that class mentality to reassure (or warn) them of the stranger's value system.

Today, the so-called underclass, a disparate group which seems to have been unsuccessful in attaining the relative prosperity of the working classes, does not have a 'mentality' inscribed for it in culture. As yet it is an unknown quantity. Its very emergence as a class is denied traditional justification. The poverty and powerlessness its 'members' experience 'in the metaphysics of the postmodern condition', means that

> contingency impacts as a criminogenic factor. . . . The experience of deep inequalities, bereft of the security of naturalness and cast in the light of contingency, create not alienation (for what is there to be alienated from?) but resentment. As Nietzsche warned, the emotion of the repressed in the post-modern condition cannot be seen in the rationality of meaningful dialectical engagement, but as an absence of meaningfulness. (Morrison, 1994: 148)

When moral institutions had authority and different classes had fixed identities, even if we did not know our neighbour, it could be assumed that s/he would conform to, or share, certain societal values. Not through choice, but through tradition.

Tradition is an orientation to the past, such that the past has a heavy influence over the present. In a sense, tradition is also about the future, since established practices are used as a way of organizing future time (Giddens, 1994: 62). From Wittgenstein's assertion that there can be no private language, Giddens derives that there can be no such thing as private tradition, and that it is therefore an organizing medium of collective memory. 'There are ordinarily deep emotional investments in tradition, although these are indirect rather than direct, they come from mechanisms of anxiety-control that traditional modes of action and belief provide' (Giddens, 1994: 63). When tradition's ritual and formulaic truth lapses into custom or habit, certainties about behaviour are lifted.

From this, the idea of reflexivity has been developed which (put simply) asserts that if people no longer draw on the past (tradition) to guide them through life, then they become reflexive on the information which surrounds them. Giddens' argument takes us nearer to a factor which could be central to the anxiety manifest in the violence/film debate: the uncertainty of morality in reflexively informed society.

If some adult members of cinema audiences find themselves relying in part upon tradition, and partly on constantly up-dated information (like statistics, magazine articles, etc.), then they must fear that others who seem less reliant on the traditional are learning to behave via the (magnificently crafted, high tech, hyperreal) images Hollywood sells to them. If this fear exists, it is based on a potent mixture of paralogism and misinformation, and does not take into account at what age, or how, we learn about morality and gentleness. Nor does it differentiate between making choices reflexively (which is what statistics might be used for) and the fundamentally different variables such as psychosis, bad and abusive parenting, or sexual abuse which determine whether a person will be violent towards others.

Postmodern Influences in Mainstream Film and Society

Changing social relationships may significantly condition the way in which filmgoers receive and respond to films. Beck *et al.* (1994) construct an image of Western society experiencing a period of transition, from the traditional to the detraditionalized, with some people buying into past values, and others relying more reflexively on the shifting information of the moment. Giddens (1990) used the term 'radicalized modernity' to describe mixed societies which are influenced by both – preferring it to the term postmodern (Lyotard, 1985; Hebdidge, 1988), which seems to underplay the influence and importance of the traditional.

In radically modernizing society it would seem that high or avant garde art embraces aspects of depiction which can be identified as postmodern. It is often associated with a revolt against authority and signification, and a tendency towards pastiche, parody, quotation, self-referentiality, and eclecticism (Bradbury, 1990: 671). The postmodern seems to have seeped into popular, mainstream Hollywood art. Films like *Natural Born Killers* and *Pulp Fiction* appear to use playfulness and irony to oppose the moral seriousness of modernity.

Director Tarantino's view on violence in film coincides with Adorno and Horkheimer's description (1973) of the cultural logic of postmodernism carried to its furthest reaches: the celebration of the self ends in extolling intellectual impulse, sensual immediacy, and eroticism. Its endless rages against order, limits, and boundaries end in nihilism. For example, Tarantino claims:

> I don't take violence very seriously. I find violence funny, especially in the stories I've been telling recently. Violence is part of this world and I am drawn to the outrageousness of real-life violence. It isn't about lowering people from helicopters on to speeding trains, or about terrorists hijacking something or other. Real life violence is, you're in a restaurant and a man and his wife are having an argument and all of a sudden that guy gets so mad at her, he picks up a fork and stabs her in the face. That's really crazy and comic bookish – but it also happens. . . . To me, violence is a totally aesthetic subject. (1995: ix)

It gets shown in his films without a formulaic moral framework. If the stabbing situation described above were a scene in a Tarantino movie, there would probably be no explanation as to why the man did it or what the consequences of his actions were. Tarantino's artistic approach to screen violence is not formed in a cultural vacuum (just as neither is violent behaviour). It too has complex determinants, some of which are alluded to below.

Tarantino's lack of concern for the suffering of characters can be seen in two ways as a product, or a reflection, of postmodernism. Firstly, it may relate to the way in which people formulate the subjectivity of others in radical modernity. In the anomic atmosphere of large conurbations strangers are continually encountered. Bech (1992) sums up the superficiality of much human interaction in large urban spaces:

> In the crowds of the city, human beings become surfaces to one another – for the simple reason that this is the only thing a person can notice in the urban space of lots of strangers. The others turn into surfaces for theirs, which one cannot escape being aware of. Thus, the surface becomes the object of the form of evaluation which can be performed by gaze – that is, an aesthetic evaluation, according to criteria such as beautiful or disgusting, boring or fascinating. (Quoted in Bauman, 1993: 173)

For Tarantino violence is a 'totally aesthetic subject'. The character then is no more than a surface. The boy whose head is blown-off in *Pulp Fiction* is portrayed as a mere surface. Or rather, the nature of his death lets us see him in that way. The film presents us with a meta-reality, it shows the logical extremes of the sort of society in which we live. This must be disconcerting for sections of an audience, who on top of coping with increased, and more skilfully depicted violence, in an unexpected moral framework, must also try to assimilate the postmodern expressions which have crept into mainstream film.

Another suggested reason for the increased depiction of cartoonic style violence can be constructed from Baudrillard's critique of consumerism (1970), which claims that in affluent consumer society, individuals are no longer surrounded by other human beings as they were in the past, but by objects.

> Just as the wolf-child becomes a wolf by living amongst them, so we are ourselves becoming functional objects. We are living the period of objects: that is, we live by their rhythm, according to their incessant succession. Today, it is we who are observing their birth, fulfilment and death; whereas in all previous civilizations, it was the object, instrument and perennial monument that survived the generations of men. . . . In this way a washing machine serves as an element of comfort, or of prestige and so on. It is the latter that is specifically the field of consumption. . . . A need is not a need for a particular object as much as it is a need for difference. (Baudrillard, 1970: 106–7, quoted in Kellner, 1989)

To be integrated within consumer society one must buy certain goods. Yet because these are prestige goods, they involve differentiation from other human beings, and therefore distanciation. To be part of that society one is distanced from other people, either because we have these goods, or because we are ashamed or jealous not to own them.[9] Thus, the process of integration actually requires distancing.

Baudrillard's theory is painted in broad brush strokes. As ever, it is trying to be more provocative than truthful. The argument made is refined by Kellner (1989) who claims that a better approach to the issue of consumerism is to look at advertising (which Baudrillard's early work posits as the propaganda of consumer society) using Barthes' semiological theory of interpretation (as expounded in *S/Z*, 1970). It is an approach upon which Hall and others developed their theoretical standpoints. Media messages comprise multifarious codes of which meaning[10] is always 'overdetermined, open to a multiplicity of readings and constantly changing' (Kellner, 1989: 20). If Kellner's interpretative approach (when applied to Baudrillard's theory) is valid, then in a society which often privileges objects over human beings, it is inevitable that some film-makers will reflect this in their work, consciously or not. Certain directors are influenced by the codes which determine objectification, whilst others aren't. Violence is a good vehicle for its reflection.

A further argument can be distilled from Baudrillard's work to suggest why a director like Tarantino might not want to convey meaning to explain the violent acts he depicts. A postmodern theorist would probably argue that this is because meaning is defunct in the late twentieth century, given that the grand narratives of Enlightenment reason have failed. From the 1960s onwards, the thorough-going analysis of ideology undermined theoretical and moral truth claims. Argument or explanation, in these terms can at best only be persuasive, never true. Why show resolution in crime fiction, or give a fixed sense to violent acts in an age of complexity and uncertainty? Baudrillard (1983a) extends this notion by saying that it is not the case that desire for meaning has diminished, but rather that too much has been produced. In the media meaning is everywhere. One explanation supplants another, but not in some dialectical succession, unfolding gently in time, but rather as an entropic mixture of claims and counter-claims.

A kind of cultural lethargy results from this constant overdose of meaning. It gives rise to an 'overwhelming desire for spectacle' which has also been heightened by reporting imperatives. Baudrillard claims that the style of reporting, say of a futile terrorist act, reduces that act to spectacle. It is not important whether a hostage or a terrorist dies. What matters most to the journalists, is that something sensational happens. This is one of *Natural Born Killers'* attempted messages against the media's insistence on providing spectacle as entertainment, and indirectly cashing in on people's fears. Director Stone's sentiment echoes in Baudrillard's words (perhaps more than it does in the film):

> The media are terrorists in their own fashion, working continually to produce (good) sense, but at the same time, violently defeating it by arousing everywhere a fascination without scruples, that is to say, a paralysis of meaning, to the profit of a single scenario. (1983a: 113)

The Oklahoma bombing, or the Sarin gas attack (ironically in a city's central nervous system) on Tokyo's underground, seem like meaningless acts, spectacle for spectacle's sake: a trend of radically modernized culture which is increasingly reflected in films portraying transgression for transgression's sake.

Conclusion

The main point of sketching these arguments and of reassessing why certain images upset or frighten some people, is to put the issue of violent crime and screen violence into some sort of intelligent perspective. The areas explored all have potential to deepen anxiety concerning the question of film, though none of them are posited as truths. They all rely on audience interpretation and sensibility. The main points of this chapter can be summarized as follows:

- Mainstream Hollywood crime film narrative conforms less and less to a simple moral framework, and can therefore be disconcerting or frightening for audiences. This (unacknowledged) disconcertion may underlie some of the panic expressed about violent films.

- Popular discourse is misinformed by the media and academia (e.g., in the linking of 10 murders to *Natural Born Killers*), and by reports like *Video Violence and Children* (1983).

- The amount and type of violence shown in film has been increased and changed by financial imperatives and technological advances, thus deepening concern about nihilistic images.

- The myth of conformity to class distinctions no longer determines how the behaviour of others is perceived. Fear fills the ensuing vacuum of lost expectation.

- Transition from the moral constraints and comforts of traditional, to radically modern, society, is ontologically disconcerting. Laments for the passing of tradition manifest themselves in attempts to regain moral surety through censorship.

- Avant garde, or postmodern artistic influences, have seeped into some mainstream films, and consequently, film-makers like Tarantino treat violence as a totally aesthetic subject.

- The cartoonic depiction of violence seems aided by the attachment to objects entailed by consumer society.

- The loss or over-production of meaning in the media abets the cinematic depiction of violence out of formulaic moral context.

These issues (and no doubt, many more) need to be taken into account when screen violence is debated. As we have seen, the depiction of aggression has concrete, artistic, financial and societal roots. These will not be dug out and banished by fervent editorials or dubious research findings, no matter how distressing it can be to watch sadistic and aggressive film images. Hopefully this work will re-inform the issue, and open it up to its distortions and its complexities. For it seems that the violence/film debate reflects more about the fears we as an audience have – both with artistic developments in film and the society we live in.

Notes

General content analysis of the press reaction to the *Natural Born Killers* controversy was done, using Cambridge University's Periodical On-line facility to scan 255 newspaper articles published on the subject between 14 January 1994 and 1 January 1995, prior to and after the period the BBFC refused to release the film in Britain. This allowed me to examine the speculations, distortions and analysis of 20 tabloid/broadsheet publications before and following the refusal. These newspapers were scanned: *The Financial Times, The Independent, The Guardian, Today, The Daily Telegraph, The Sunday Telegraph, The Times* and *Sunday Times, The Observer, Lloyd's List, The European, The Scotsman, The Northern Echo, The Herald, The Daily Mail,* and *The Mail On Sunday, The Irish Times, Daily Mirror* and *Sunday Mirror*. The films were chosen for content analysis, through repeated viewing, either for their lack of conformity to traditional formulaic narratives; their exaggerated violent content, or their unconventional characterization: *Natural Born Killers, Pulp Fiction, Reservoir Dogs, Bad Lieutenant, Jurassic Park, Man Bites Dog, Silence of the Lambs.*

1   In summing up at the Bulger trial (18 February 1993) Judge Morland speculated: 'It is not for me to pass judgment on the boys' upbringings, but I suspect that exposure to violent video films may in part be an explanation'.

2   Again, press coverage of empirical findings can distort public perceptions by not being able to explain the study in depth. One of Singer and Singer's criteria for detecting 'signs of violence in the home' was to ask interviewers to note down 'the relative orderliness or disorderliness of the house – were toys left lying around, were dirty dishes piled-up in the sink?' (1981: 121). There were no questions on the amount of love parents and children show to each other, or attempts to gain information on histories of physical brutalities or incest within the family.

3   Brown remarked how it was ironic that Mary Whitehouse, long-time campaigner against the on-screen depiction of sex, violence and 'bad language', embraced the report with open arms, claiming it to be 'neutral, objective and scientific'. Previously she had set her face firmly 'against research of any kind'.

4   It is on this point that Garland critiques Foucault's theory (in terms of power) of punishment by claiming that it fails to acknowledge the deeply entrenched relationship ordinary people have to retribution and notions of justice.

5   See note above for selection criteria of newspapers and films for content analysis.

6   This film is actually highly didactic, using violence which is so disgusting to shock viewers from any pleasure they may feel for it.

7   Sponsored in conjunction with the BBC, the British Standards Council and the Independent Television Commission.

8   This claim is based on an article by Dr Brandon Centerwall, in the *Journal of the American Medical Association*, June 1992. In it he compares societies before and after they have access to television. Medved does not question the assertions, but accepts them without considering to what extent other variables in those societies could be connected to increased crime rates.

9   Increases in borrowing and spending during the 1980s indicate that more and more people were encouraged and willing to buy into the value system of consumer society. In the same work, Baudrillard prophetically remarks that this form of society has negative effects such as anomie, cultural and criminal violence and fatigue with the demands of labour, leisure and consumption.

10   Theorist Sreberny Mohammadi (1992) argues that it is not so much American values which Hollywood exports, but rather generalized capitalist consumption values. However, Liebes and Katz (1990) maintain that meaning is not exported, but created by different cultural sectors of the audience in relation to their already-formed cultural attitudes and political perceptions.

Chapter 8

Nihilism and the Philosophy of Violence

Steve Goodman

Surveying the literature and the contemporary socio-political climate, it is not necessarily unreasonable to bin the etymology of the term 'violence' and despair that there are 'no facts, only interpretations'. Yet the power of feminisms and multiculturalisms, in problematizing previously unpoliticized zones, in de-centering purely class-based critique and hence rendering 'violence', as a censure, as a site of increased contestation,[1] means that the reaction of nostalgia for some mythic age of conceptual stability can be resisted. Whatever violence signifies – and the reader will ideally share some uncertainty after reading this volume as a whole – all I hope to illustrate is the need for a greater ethical sensitivity in writing violence and opposing its multifarious instances. At the close of a particularly nasty century and with 'progress' in the style of the dominant philosophical currents of the last 2 000 years smelling particularly unsavoury, perhaps receiving the sediment of *victimage* is all that remains. Alternatively, now could be viewed as the time for a creative harnessing of a new set of rhythms. For this task, philosophy attains a nomadic, lateral mode, more akin to literature in its chaotic choreography. But must this dancing stop? If one ignores the rhythms of decomposition dancing stops with death. There is no greater shackle than that which destroys or stratifies to 'death', not just music, but life itself. And while writing about music rarely avoids the banal, writing politically about violence is intended to spoil the flow.

The problem that this chapter addresses is that of nihilism and violence. Particularly, I will be interested in the various modem configurations of the movement from the statement that 'if nothing is true, all is permitted' to revolutionary doctrines which celebrate destruction for its own sake.[2] In what will be for some many words worthy of infinite deferral,[3] I hope to convey an intuition that the philosophical desire to move 'beyond nihilism' – to reconstruct after deconstruction – is not, in itself, unproblematic.

Violence is a metaphor that reverberates within a plurality of discourses: theology, anthropology, philosophy, sociology, psychology, ethology, psychiatry, medicine, law, international relations, history. The more one thinks about 'violence' the more it means – it lends itself to dissertation because it is so firmly embedded in such a vast academic and cultural corpus (Barthes, 1985: 307). Yet despite the truth of its multifarious inscription on, in and around bodies (see Kafka, 1961; Foucault, 1977a; Scarry, 1985), discussions of violence usually remain on the plateau of a legitimatory or normalizing mode of reasoning. Commonly, violence points to that site which a disciplinary society has not succeeded in completely colonizing. Discursively, this metaphoric locale can set in motion chains of signification that intimate a pre-social barbarity, escalations of vengeance or in more radical theories, a kind of *mythology of catharsis* (Burton, 1980).

And it is this grounding in 'state philosophy', or the representational thinking that has characterized the hegemonic canons of Western metaphysics since Plato, that has suffered an at least momentary setback during the last quarter century at the hands of a variety of post-structuralist thinkers. My focus will fall on twentieth-century cathartic conceptualizations of violence, a divination emphasizing expiation, purity and bloodlessness. This topic is worthy of exposition because, as its most extreme manifestation testifies clearly, it reveals disturbing complicities between discourses of 'liberation' and 'the final solution'.

> When one thinks of the gas chambers and the crematorion ovens, this allusion to an extermination that would be expiatory because bloodless must cause one to shudder. One is terrified at the idea of an interpretation that would make of the holocaust an expiation and an indecipherable signature of the just and violent anger of God. (Derrida, 1992: 62)

Zygmunt Bauman's recent reflections on modern violence are helpful here. For Bauman, it is a distinctly modern ambivalence about might, force and coercion that makes violence the slippery concept alluded to above. Crudely, the project of modernity has been concerned with amassing power. Through this accumulation, Western civilization intrinsically needs to provoke and transgress its own boundaries. As it transgresses it has to order and shape beyond its frontiers, smoothing over difference and simultaneously creating new ones. Modernity, for Bauman sees the West as a self-perpetuating frontier civilization (Bauman, 1991: 143–4). Modernity's ambivalence towards violence has legitimated itself as a civilizing process: 'Like most legitimations, however, this one is more an advertising copy than an account of reality' (Bauman, 1994: 144). Rather than an uprooting of violence, all that occurs is a redistribution. In Max Weber's classic formulation, 'a compulsory political organization with continuous operations will be called a 'state' insofar as its administrative staff successfully upholds the claim to the monopoly of the legitimate use of force' (Weber, 1968: 54). Two kinds of violence are thus distinguished using dichotomies such as public–private, legal–illegal, legitimate–illegitimate, useful–harmful etc. These are only distinguishable by the partisan justification given to one. In fact, one is termed positively – for example punishment or the enforcement of law and order – while the other is *censured* as violence. While evolving from social reaction theory and the sociology of deviance, Sumner's concept of censure is a useful unmasking tool here, in that it directs us to distinct power differentials. It begs the following questions: who censures? In what cultural form does the censure crystallize? and who is the target? Bauman notes that what this linguistic opposition conceals 'is that the condemned "violence" is also about a certain ordering, certain laws to be enforced – only those are not the laws which the makers of the distinction had in mind' (Bauman, 1991: 145).

The distinction therefore conveys the difference between the designed order and all the rest: between controlled and uncontrolled, regular and erratic, foreseeable and unexpected, grounded and contingent. Bauman cites Jan Philipp Reemtsma who captures the flavour of modern violence in terms of shock: 'reaction to the unexpected, unheard of events which reveal the habitual forms of truth and information processing as inadequate' (Reemtsma in Bauman, 1991: 146).

Modern violence, is then for Bauman:

> the productive waste of the order factory; something that cannot be re-cycled into something useful, handled with available tools. . . . If order-making means coercing things into *regularity*, 'violence' stands for *irregular* coercion, such as saps the regularity here and now, that regularity which is synonimical with order. Such coercion is violence . . . no order is ever exactly like it wants itself to be, and since one man's order is another man's disorder, and since the visions of order keep changing, as [do] the order-keepers themselves . . . (1991: xxx)

This chapter attempts to steer through the wasteland of the collapsed hierarchies and distinctions of modern philosophies of violence in an attempt to show that the standard complaint of 'moral ambivalence' or even nihilism made against recent 'post-structuralist' and 'postmodernist' theories is perhaps misguided. Why is this necessary? Because in the 'empty space' of the post-Cold War 1990s, nihilism is not obviously something to be avoided.

Maurice Blanchot makes the case for relativism in a nihilist period:

> Here, then is a first approach to nihilism: it is not an individual experience or a philosophical doctrine, nor is it a fatal light cast over human nature, eternally vowed to nothingness. Rather, nihilism is an event achieved in history, and yet it is like a shedding off of history, a moulting period, when history changes its direction and is indicated by a negative trait: that values no longer have value by themselves. There is also a positive trait: for the first time the horizon is infinitely opened to knowledge – 'all is permitted'. (Blanchot, 1977: 122)

More politically incisive, William Connolly points out that:

> nor is relativism the consummate danger in the late-modern world, where every culture intersects with most other in economies of interdependence, exchange, and competition. Relativism is an invention of academics who yearn for a type of unity that probably never existed, who worry about an alienation from established culture that seldom finds sufficient opportunity

> to get off the ground, and who insist that ethical discourse cannot proceed unless it locates its authority in a transcendental command. (Connolly, 1991: 174)

Moreover,

> the political task, in a time of closure and danger, is to try to open up what is enclosed, to try to think thoughts that stretch and extend fixed patterns of insistence. That is why Nietzsche, Foucault, and Heidegger do not worry too much about the ethico-political problematic of 'relativism' – partly because we are already located on a field of discourse that is so difficult to stretch and revise in any event and partly because we live in an age in which so many areas of the world are being drawn into the orbit of late modern life. The relativist worry is untimely. (1991: 59)

Sliding between concepts such as relativism, nihilism, perspectivism, textualism etc. should certainly not be done uncritically. But it is my purpose in this discussion to at least bring into contact with such positive appraisals of nihilism, the problem of violence.

It is misguided, however to see this climate of nihilism, whereby 'anything goes', as just confined to the academy. What John Carroll has described recently as 'the wreck of Western culture (Carroll, 1993) is what recent 'post-structuralist' and 'postmodernist' philosophy is most successful in representing:

> It is the contemporary human situation of living at the violent edge of primitivism and simulation, of an indefinite reversibility in the order of things wherein only the excessive cancellation of difference through violence reenergizes the process. (Kroker, 1992: 18)

The late twentieth century, confirming Heidegger, sees technology as the latest, if not the final stage of nihilism – the historical process of the loss of Being (Fandozzi, 1982: 117). The nineteenth century, especially in the ideal of the 'rule of law', represented the most self-conscious, if naive and unsuccessful, repudiation of violence as the destiny of man. By contrast, this century, with its chaos of human relations, the separation, isolation and artificialization of urban life sees what Cotta describes as a 'recourse' to violence consisting of the re-emergence of war violence and the recrudescence of revolutionary violence (Cotta, 1985). The prefixing of the word 'course' by 're-' does not imply that the apocalyptic flavour of violence this century represents some kind aberration or reversal against the flow of some teleological, linear historical process of civilization, rather – as my discussion of nihilism will hopefully show – modernization merely signifies certain historically specific re-configurations. What is the novelty of today's violence? Some have suggested that it lies most significantly in the contemporary subjective sensibility to the spatio-temporality of existence – the complicity of the philosophical and the political (well captured in the term 'state philosophy') means that an implosion of established conceptions of living space is the political complement of the implosion of established conceptions of thinking space; the fiction of an outside is dispelled by the simultaneous experience of living space and spatialized thought which are both equally global. Moreover, while speed and acceleration transform everyday life, the philosophical conception of temporality in relation to the 'beyond' of Western metaphysics has been thrown into crisis. As Caygill puts it:

> With world society, the potential for violence displaced to the periphery returns to the centre with increasing speed, or more properly, periphery and centre collapse into each other. Instead of the uniform space of reason becoming sustained by the violence of its expansion, violence recoils, and the shock of its return warps the space of reason making it complex, characterised by unfamiliar and inexplicable folds, gaps, and tears. The predicament of reason itself has changed. (Caygill, 1993: 12)

This situation in which the perception of 'violence' becomes increasingly contingent on perspective is only comprehensible against the back-drop of a discussion of nihilism and the recent history of philosophical discussions of violence. The demand to engage philosophy, as one of several sites of political practice, with violence continues to echo in the hollowness which accompanies Occidental civilization's acquired capability for total self-annihilation. On this back-drop, Friedrich Nietzsche, 'the perfect nihilist' glows; the following chapter will I hope serve as some kind of Geiger counter, helping us to survive and gauge the radioactivity of his prophetic writings on power, violence and morality which illuminate much of the horror of the twentieth century.

Nihilism, Modernity, Violence

The 'Recourse' to Violence

As Sergio Cotta has argued, in the recent history of Western violence, two philosophical approaches can be separated out: firstly, a position which presupposes a traditional negative judgment and sees the progress of history in terms of a restraining or overcoming of violence – this he terms the (slow) course of violence. On the other hand, Cotta identifies a (rapid) recourse whereby violence is if anything appreciated, glorified as purifying and interpreted as capable of reclaiming both theoretically and practically the territory from which it was thought to have been forced to withdraw – violence is *deliberately* invited to return.

For Cotta, this recourse swept away the course (and its disciplining of violence by means of law) at the turn of this century. In this picture, the nineteenth century is seen as the great period of juridical construction. Earlier, the formation of the modern nation state, and the overcoming of disorder and violence through culture becomes a crucial juncture. From the early modern thought of Hobbes, Spinoza and

Descartes to the Enlightenment, the seeds for not just the state, but also the realm of the social were cast. The civilization and organization of the city were to replace the ignorance and brutality of peasant society.

But it is in the nineteenth century that the course of, or what was sold as being the triumph over violence takes on its specific characteristics in the form of, for example, the theories of war of Clausewitz and Hegel, theories of revolution of Mazzini, Marx and Bakunin and the power politics of Treitschke. Although pacifist movements were subordinated to these theories of violence, these non-violent aims were actually subsumed; so although theorists of violence, these writers on war and revolution should not be described as advocates of it.

> The fact is that the nineteenth century draws its optimistic and confident perspective precisely from its own realistic-activistic currents of thought. Its great secular faiths – historicism, positivism, Marxism, evolutionism – find inspiration, in various ways, in the idea of progress (be it gradual or in fits and starts) and in its pacifying capability, and they come to the final conclusion that violence will be overcome. (Cotta, 1985: 21)

In this dominant cultural climate of fetishized rule, law, measure and form etc. where the natural appears comprehensible and the human world interpretable, the marketing ploy told tales of the minimization or overcoming of violence and un-ruliness. Capturing this spirit, in his concept of *anomie*, Emile Durkheim described the dissolving power which would accompany the loss of this sense of order and result in suicide.

For Sergio Cotta, the recourse to violence represents a twentieth-century projection of this cultural tendency. How did this occur? In 1918, after World War I, Simmel, in his *Philosophy of Life* described how the coercive imposition of form upon life, encouraged life to struggle against form. Simmel took his cue from the expressionist movement in art; a rejection of form followed by a rejection of values from which life could receive directive and formative criteria of manifestation. And 'it is not surprising, therefore, if this vitalism implies not only the negation of the products of history (institutional forms, traditions and habits) but also the negation of every element of objectivity, which is dissolved into a limitless pragmatic subjectivism' (Cotta, 1985: 21). The transition into the twentieth century therefore led Simmel, following Dostoevsky and preceding Heidegger, to point to Friedrich Nietzsche as the key thinker of the modern age. With the assistance of Schopenhauer, Nietzsche's thought destabilizes Kant, Hegel, Comte and Marx, four canonic nineteenth-century thinkers. But in addition, and more than any other thinker, brought about a crisis, and through his extremity, clarified its essential terms.

Nihilism, Nietzsche, Violence

'For some time now, our whole European culture has been moving as toward a catastrophe, with a tension that is growing from decade to decade: restlessly, violently, headlong, like a river that wants to reach the end, that no longer reflects, that is afraid to reflect' (Nietzsche, 1967: 3). So wrote the 'perfect nihilist', Friedrich Nietzsche between November 1887 and March 1888. Globally, there is no shortage of violent catastrophes imprinted on Western civilizations conscience of the twentieth century. The prophetic power of Nietzsche demands he be heard, whether one is repulsed or fascinated by his teachings. Through an examination of Nietzsche's conception of nihilism, it is my aim in this section to embark on the discussion and tracing of this recourse to violence up to the contemporary, the task which will form the torso of this essay.

For Nietzsche, nihilism means 'That the highest values devaluate themselves'. The crisis of Western culture that Nietzsche identifies entails the undermining of the religious and moral bases of society. After the death of the Judeo-Christian god, post-Enlightenment culture must see the collapse of everything which was constructed around this belief. Without this unifying foundation for Western values, Nietzsche argues, the advent of nihilism is inevitable. Nihilism, therefore is a historical phenomenon, characterized by the inability to comprehend its own nature. Nietzsche demands that we must be able to reflect; we must experience nihilism before we can find out the value our values really had – we need to re-evaluate and create new values.

The historical context is the Christian moral world view and philosophy since Plato. What both had in common was the belief in 'another world', which transcended human experience but became standard for our conception of truth. This belief in another, metaphysical world persuaded man to need an overarching purpose of human existence, a need met in concepts such as 'aim', 'unity' and 'truth'. These categories 'which we used to project some value into the world – we *pull out* again so the world looks *valueless*' (Nietzsche, 1967: 3). In particular, it was in the pursuit of natural science, that our concepts of 'purpose' and 'totality' revealed themselves as merely subjective values. The Enlightenment legacy of the objective pursuit of truth undermined the veracity of such other-worldly doctrines.

Nietzsche's onslaught on the descent of Western culture into nihilism is matched up with three stages and their corresponding psychological states: firstly, one tries and fails to find meaning in events; secondly, one tries and fails to impose a totality or unity to events to create a whole; finally, man passes sentence on the world of becoming as deception and invents a true world beyond it.

> But as soon as man finds out how that world is fabricated solely from psychological needs, and how he has absolutely no right to it, the last form of nihilism comes into being: it includes disbelief in any metaphysical world and forbids itself any belief in a *true* world. Having reached this standpoint, one grants the reality of becoming as the *only* reality. (Nietzsche, 1967: 13)

The ambivalence of the world is then clear – one cannot endure this world though one does not want to deny it. Nietzsche concludes that it is the modern faith in the categories of reason, referring to a purely fictitious world, that is the cause of nihilism.

For Nietzsche, all attempts to salvage 'value' to overcome nihilism arise from utilitarian considerations on the maintenance and increase of human constructs of domination – these values have been falsely projected into the essence of things. Value here is seen as relative to valuators and hence does not escape nihilism since value merely reflects the strength of value positors. Nietzsche then describes the most extreme form of nihilism in terms of the doctrine of perspectivism (see Bergoffen, 1990 for a good demarcation between nihilism, perspectivism and relativism). Seeing reality as a matter of perspective is described as a 'test of strength' and perhaps a 'divine way of thinking'. It is important here to comment on the ambiguity of nihilism – is it the highest state of man or something beyond the human? He distinguishes two kinds of nihilism: active nihilism he describes 'as a sign of increased power of the spirit' which 'reaches its maximum of relative strength as a violent force of destruction'.[4] Passive nihilism on the other hand is described 'as decline and recession of the power of the spirit' (Nietzsche 1967: 17–18). What distinguishes these two varieties of nihilism is then strength of will; the advent of nihilism is then a critical point in the history of the *will to power*, which is for Nietzsche the key to history. In order to connect this history of the will to power to the role of violence in the history of social, political, legal and moral institutions it is useful to turn to perhaps the most fashionable Nietzschean text of the late twentieth century, *The Genealogy of Morality*.

Nietzsche's *Genealogy* is a history of active and reactive, affirmative and negative forces, a history of masters and slaves. As an unmasking of desire, it traces the sublimation of the will to power, a will that turns inward to vent its energy on the self, creating the moral conscience of Judeo-Christian and ultimately, the modern style. For Nietzsche, this tradition corresponds to a slave, reactive morality – a secondary instantiation of value which expresses *ressentiment* towards subordination.

Nietzsche's analysis is of specific interest here because of the way it deconstructs the difference between the morally legitimated violence of punishment and its excluded/subsumed double, transgression. Describing the 'primitive' response to law-breaking, Nietzsche contends that 'Punishment' at this level of civilization is simply a copy, a *mimus*, of normal behaviour towards a hated, disarmed enemy who has been defeated, and who has not only forfeited all rights and safeguards, but all mercy as well – in fact, the rules of war and the victory celebration of *vae victis*! in all their mercilessness and cruelty. This explains the fact that war itself (including the war-like cult of the sacrificial victim) has given us all *forms* in which punishment manifests itself in history (Nietzsche, 1994: 50–1).

The genealogical method attempts to avoid the paralogism of conflating the origin of punishment with its historically specific purpose:

So people think punishment has evolved for the purpose of punishing. But every purpose and use is just a sign that the will to power has achieved mastery over something less powerful, and has impressed upon its own idea of a use function; and the whole history of a 'thing', an organ, a tradition can to this extent be a continuous chain of signs, continually revealing new interpretations and adaptions, the causes of which need not be connected even amongst themselves, but rather sometimes just follow and replace one another at random. The 'development' of a thing, a tradition, an organ is therefore certainly not its *progressus* towards a goal, still less is it a logical progress, taking the shortest route with least expenditure of energy and cost, – instead it is a succession of more or less profound, more or less mutually independent processes of subjugation exacted on the thing, added to this the resistances encountered every time, the attempted transformations for the purpose of defence and reaction, and the results, too, of successful countermeasures. The form is fluid, the 'meaning' even more so . . . (Nietzsche, 1994: 55)

This approach celebrated in recent French theory leads Nietzsche to the following provocative conclusions:

To talk of 'just' and 'unjust' as such is meaningless, an act of injury, violence, exploitation or destruction cannot be 'unjust' as such, because life functions essentially in an injurious, violent, exploitative and destruc- tive manner, or at least these are its fundamental processes and it cannot be thought of without these characteristics. (Nietzsche, 1994: 54)

In a similar way, Michel Foucault's genealogy of punishment in *Discipline and Punish* is understandably, if wrongly indicted for its apparent ambivalence to cruelty; the moralistic critique monotonously complains that the disappearance of torture as a public spectacle, contra Nietzsche's and Foucault's celebrations of cruelty, is attributable to a process of humanization that has softened the often savage violence of premodern societies (for an interesting discussion of such ambivalences, see Miller, 1990).

Nietzsche, Nazism

Because of his historical malleability and appropriation, it is almost impossible to think of the name of Nietzsche without some association between the violent 'excesses' of his philosophy and the content of discourses of Nazism and fascism. In his later thought, he indicts liberal egalitarianism for the threat it poses to aristocratic values, for the war it wages on 'everything rare, strange, privileged, the higher man, the higher soul, the higher duty, the higher responsibility, creative fullness of power and mastery' (Nietzsche, 1973: 144). As Ansell-Pearson (1994) points out, this critique of liberalism resembles that which was made by Hitler and the Nazis in order to champion German greatness and sacrifice. But the greatness Nietzsche had in mind was that of culture, not a nationalism and a militarism inspired by *ressentiment*. In a discussion of Nietzsche and violence, it is however most important to draw out some of the issues raised by contemporary theorists such as Derrida, who asks how a 'reactive' culture like Nazism could exploit the same language and rallying cries as the 'active' culture Nietzsche sought to promote (Derrida, 1987: 126).

From the discussion so far, it is obvious that the seeds of such an association are there, if totally misguided. How did the connection of Nietzsche with Nazism come about? As Ansell-Pearson points out,

> the dissemination and reception of Nietzsche's philosophy after his mental collapse in 1889 was very varied. His work did not immediately appeal to the right, as one might expect given its aristocratic pretensions and distaste for socialism. On the contrary, in the two decades following his breakdown, it was taken up with interest and imagination by socialist, anarchists, and feminists, all of whom saw Nietzsche's work as preoccupied with the quest for individual self-realisation. (Ansell-Pearson, 1994: 29)

This is despite there being little sympathy in his writings for political radicalism and socialism.

Equally important, his writing conveyed little sense of allegiance with German nationalism, and his atheism distanced him from German conservatism. It seems reasonable therefore, agreeing with historian Ernst Nolte, to view the name of Nietzsche at this time as a battlefield (Ansell-Pearson, 1994: 29). But it was the popularity of Nietzsche's writings in Germany during the First World War which facilitated the Nazis ideologically appropriating his work in the inter-war period.[5] His celebrity had risen to a level where his philosophy could provide justification and legitimacy to the Nazi movement. Here, the role of Nietzsche's anti-Semitic sister Elizabeth is crucial; Ansell-Pearson relates how she both suppressed the publication of certain manuscripts, for example *Ecce Homo*, but also interfered with texts and forged letters she claimed to have been produced by Nietzsche himself. With her assistance, the Nazis transformed Nietzsche's popularity both at home and abroad. Suspect, but highly successful methods were used in the Nazification of Nietzsche; typically, small anthologies containing his essential 'Nazi sayings' were published under his name, but with no acknowledgement of their edited nature. A good example was the collection entitled *Judaism, Christianity, Germanity* which contained passages on the Jews as well as the infamous section on the 'blond beast' from the *Genealogy of Morals*. Such passages are emphasized, while Nietzsche's admiration for Latin culture and distaste for German nationalism are suppressed. Hence, a misreading of Nietzsche's argument was encouraged. As Ansell-Pearson illustrates, the 'blond beast' is not a Nazi concept, but specifically includes Arabs and Japanese. Moreover, Nietzsche always classified individuals in terms of culture and not biology or race (Ansell-Pearson, 1994: 31). If anything, Nazi ideology, embodied most despicably in the figure of Adolf Hitler, seems more suitably a correlate to what Nietzsche terms the slave morality, whereby the attribution of what is 'good' is reactive, premised not on self-affirmation, but on the negation of others.

However, there are obviously traits of his writing which at least make him 'easy-meat' for such appropriations. For my concerns, his advocacy of élitism, violence and cruelty can perhaps easily slip into a fascist reading; however when situated next to his anti-nationalism, his pan-Europeanism, his commitment to culture over politics and his onslaught on the modern bureaucratic state for its constraints on creativity and individuality, then it is obvious that the complexity of his position(s) evades simple attachment to any conventional political perspective.

> A rejection of classical morality is common to Marxism, Nietzscheanism, and National Socialism. The only essential is the value in whose name life asserts these higher rights. Once this principle of judgement is established, Nietzschean values are seen as opposing racist values within a context of the whole. . . . In Nietzsche's mind everything is subordinated to culture. While in the Third Reich, a reduced culture has only military might as its end. (Bataille, 1985)

If anything, Nietzsche is somewhat nostalgic for a Greek conception of politics, which as Ansell-Pearson suggests, has more in common with Hannah Arendt's philosophy of action. I will now turn to an examination of violence in fascist discourses in order more clearly to demarcate the apparent ambivalence to violence of active nihilism, and its threat to culminate as 'a violent force of destruction'.

Fascism, Violence: the Mythology of Catharsis

'The discourse of Fascism is full of imagined acts of violence which heal and restore order where there had been a perceived state of disease and disorder' (Forgacs, 1994: 5). Here, Forgacs identifies what I shall be discussing in the next few sections in relation to both Left and Right, that is, violence discussed in terms of the mythology of catharsis. Writing violence in terms of its cleansing/purging/purifying/releasing effect seems to be one of the key features to what Cotta termed the 'recourse' to violence.

In his essay, 'Fascism, violence and modernity', Forgacs seeks to show,

> first, that all manifestations of this imaginary have a displacement in common, through a sort of inversion or negation of the violent act from a hurting one to a healing one, and, second, that this displacement, whether in aesthetics, social theory or poetical discourse, has real effect and therefore needs to be identified and challenged. (1994: 5)

Fascism (re)presented itself as a modern form of heroism, justifying its violence in terms of correcting a social or political wrong – in particular, the rhetoric of just violence can be seen as converging on the notion of Fascist violence as therapy, as designed to heal and make whole the imagined body of society and the state (Forgacs, 1994: 9).

Take, for example, the following statement by Mussolini reported in Margherita Sarfaratti's early biography, *Dux*:

> However much one might deplore violence, it is clear that, in order to impose our ideas on people's brains we had to use the cudgel to touch refractory skulls. The expeditions must always have the character of a just retaliation and a legitimate reprisal. We do not make violence into a school, a system or, worse still an aesthetic. Violence must be generous, chivalric and surgical. (quoted in Forgacs, 1994: 6)

The use of metaphors of the body in political discourse was not new to fascism. But they were particularly important to the discourse of mature fascism post-1925 in Italy, and accompanied other methods of 'traditional legitimation' such as the use of ancient Roman myth and symbolism, the rejection of political modernity (democracy and parliamentary systems) and a return to the 'corporate state' as an organic ideal. Most interesting are the distinctively modern ills of the social body, for example,

> The body of the state administration is bloated with bureaucracy, infested with parasites which must be cut out . . . modern society is sick and appropriate forms of political intervention – by state, the party, the movement – can make it well. Such forms will be made clean, in operations carried out with sterile instruments: the scalpel, the drip and needle, the cauterising iron. These are the commonplaces of a medicalising rhetoric of violence which will be found also in Nazism. (Forgacs, 1994: 7)

Moreover, the elements of retaliation and lesson-teaching in Mussolini's statement are also in a sense traditional; Forgacs points out that the transmission of blame to the victims as initiators of violence, and hence deserving of retribution, is a typical mode of justifying aggression, particularly in crimes such as rape.

The revolutionary syndicalism of Georges Sorel, particularly his *Reflections on Violence* which first surfaced in 1906, is often cited as a major precursor of this fascist cult of violence. Sorel rejoices in the spontaneous violence which will inscribe the proletarian epic. This violence restores to a decadent bourgeoisie its formerly entrepreneurial vigour and aggressiveness. Sorel's syndicalism claims to be the energizing mythology motivating the proletariat into a pure and brutal class war in which the two great classes, restored as class-conscious entities, act out their sublime, immortal struggle. The same violence creates an ethic of the producer, a soldier-worker eager to make a new civilization. Violence is a value, an *elan vital*, purging the proletariat of parliamentary cretinism and dispelling the prejudices of philosophy which equate force with barbarism. Parliamentary socialism, he argues, is incapable of overthrowing the bourgeois status quo because it is willing to negotiate with the bourgeoisie, hence blurring the class demarcations required for revolutionary dynamics. The mythology of the general strike activates worker solidarity; a gelling through the experience of collective violence. Mythology, for Sorel collective 'idea-forces', frees the imagination in a way rationalist transitions through discipline and democracy cannot. Sorel's *Iliad* draws on Nietzsche's master values, Bergson's integral experience and romantic, utopianized Marxism. Violence is a salvation, a purgative, a source of creative energy which has been denigrated by the cleverness of social science which associates violence with barbarity. Sorel's syntax of discursive violence signifies catharsis, bonding and transcendence.

As the above illustrates, real acts of violence are less important than the imaginary violence which serves to create cohesion and collective identity in the minds of the workers. Violence, can for Sorel be both moral and civilized because it can facilitate the transition to a higher, socialist, form of civilization;

> Proletarian violence, exercised as a pure and simple manifestation of the feelings of class struggle, thus appears as something very beautiful and grandly heroic; it is at the service of the primordial interests of civilisation; it may not be, perhaps, the best way of obtaining immediate material advantages, but it is a way of escaping from the world of barbarity. (Sorel, 1961)

In the name of the free development of the social ownership of the means of production, Sorelian violence can be distinguished from the fascistic violence which resonated in the passage quoted above by Mussolini. As Forgacs concludes,

> Sorelian violence would seem to be, then, more spiritual than material, more image than reality; with a minimum of bloodshed it crystallises the class-consciousness of the proletariat, allows it to break away from the domination of the bourgeoisie and effect the passage to a higher level of civilisation. (Forgacs, 1994: 10)

However, the mythology of catharsis is at work in Sorel as it was in Mussolini; in both, violence can make society whole again, as healing and restoring order where their disruption has occurred. And notably in both, the representing of violence involves a series of displacements of effects. For Sorel the transfiguration occurs on the subject of violence, the proletariat, and the victims remain relatively invisible: 'In Sorel's conception of violence there need to be few real heads broken because violence will have done the major part of its work in creating proletarian class-consciousness' (Forgacs, 1994: 11).

In the case of nationalism and futurism the links with the fascist imaginary of violence are more direct. With syndicalism, they provided fascism with aspects of its early ideology (Forgacs, 1994: 11; see also Sternell, 1994). The glorifications of war in Marinetti's *Manifesto of Futurism* resembles Sorel in that violence is again seen as on the side of civilization against barbarism. The therapy of warfare in futurist and nationalist discourse, acts primarily not on the body of the enemy nation, but on that of the nation at home. 'Infected' nations, those affected with internal disorders, must go to war, let blood, in order that those disorders may be cured and their health restored. Texts such as Marinetti's, Forgacs argues, raise the question of the relationship between violence as fantasy, as aesthetic violence, and real acts of violence. Despite his actual participation in the Italian wars against Turkey in 1911–12 and the First World War, Marinetti's representations of violence involve 'increasingly wide analogies . . . [the] yoking together [of] terms belonging to distant semantic sets: for example the sight–sound analogy . . . "machine guns = pebbles + ebb tide + frogs." This is a poetry of cool detachment, a reworking of a battle into a series of technical innovations' (Forgacs, 1994: 13). Marinetti's aetheticization of violence, his displacements through techniques of removal into symbol, analogy and fantasies of detachment, provides him with a way of imagining it, and probably experiencing it, as something other than itself: as glorious, joyous, modern, heroic, life-affirming. His use of

> imaginary categories in which he framed and made sense of reality . . . his readers . . . are free to object that real violence is never like this for those who have it inflicted upon them: it hurts, it wounds or it kills. They can also say that to represent it as heroic, as life-affirming, indeed as anything other than itself is to play a dangerous game in which sympathy with other human beings becomes suspended and different sentiments get in the way. The myth of war as hygiene . . . [is] deeply dangerous, inhumane and anti-human, and it is not surprising that various forms of Fascism developed their own versions of the same divisive, 'eugenic' rhetoric.

And yet as Forgacs continues: 'There was nothing inevitable, in this period, about an equation of this kind between violence, modernisation and civilisation. It was a position like any other and an opposite view was possible' (Forgacs, 1994: 14–15).

This mythology blatantly pervaded Nazi anti-Semitic discourse as well. The metaphor of infestation of the body, of disease, is pivotal to the imagery of the Jews as parasite or inferior race, for example in Hitler's *Mein Kampf*. Such medical metaphors had real effect in that they helped the Nazi leadership legitimate genocide to itself, and helped its followers to carry it out:

> the racialist imaginary of a hierarchical separation of bodies and the pre-servation of the purity of the 'superior race' were placed in the service of violence of an historically unprecedented type and magnitude . . . however . . . [again] the imaginary of this violence worked by displacement and non-recognition, by turning violence into something other than itself. Mass murder became 'healing.' It was carried out not in the heat of passion but according to a cool, systematic 'medical' rationale. (Forgacs, 1994: 18)[6]

What do these displacements of violence illustrate about the relation between fascism and modernity? As Forgacs (1994) and Bauman (1989) point out, the view of fascism, Nazism and the Holocaust as an aberration of modernity, a regression against processes of civilization and the progress of Enlightenment, while possessing some rhetorical value in terms of opposition to such phenomenon, cannot provide us with an historically adequate account of, for example, 'the mentality of people who represented violence and killing, to themselves and to others, in civilising, modernising terms as a way forward, a way of getting society into a healthier, purer state'. Indeed Forgacs points out that

> these people did not think of themselves as neo-barbarians but as the new civilisers of the Thousand Year Reich. At worst, despite intentions to the contrary, the anti-modernity or barbarism chapter can provide Fascism with an ideological justification by portraying it as a sort of atavistic relapse, an aberration from the normal state of things, a coming to the surface of innate aggressive drives or instincts, and therefore as something that 'could not be helped', rather than as the product of historically particular ways of organising society and sexual difference. (Forgacs, 1994: 19–20)

Forgacs attributes the opposite position, whereby fascism is viewed as the logical consequence of modernization to Adorno and Horkheimer; here the controlled violence of fascism is a culmination of Enlightenment rationality developing along its dark side; the domination of nature and society by science and technology, bureaucratization and mass culture. But while this position helps us understand the medicalization of violence in fascist discourse, for Forgacs it 'goes too far because it makes it impossible to disentangle modernity from Fascism . . . civilisation as a whole, far from 'lapsing' into barbarism, progresses towards it. The negativity of this vision of modernity is overwhelming' (Forgacs, 1994: 20).

The thoughts of Deleuze and Guattari are helpful here in their discussion of Virilio's analysis of fascism:

> Totalitarianism is quintessentially conservative. Fascism on the other hand, involves a war machine. When fascism builds itself a totalitarian State, it is not in the sense of a State army taking power, but of a war machine taking over the State . . . in fascism, the State is far less totalitarian than it is *suicidal*. There is in fascism a realized nihilism. Unlike the totalitarian State, which does its utmost to seal all possible lines of flight, fascism is constructed on an intense line of flight, which it transforms into a line of pure destruction and abolition. (Deleuze and Guattari, 1988: 230)

As Michel Foucault explains, it is the 'tracking down of all varieties of fascism, from the enormous ones that surround and crush us to the petty ones that constitute the tyrannical bitterness of our everyday lives' (Foucault in preface to Deleuze and Guattari, 1983: xiv), which is central to Deleuze and Guattari's project of 'answering the global question: Why does desire desire its own repression, how can it desire its own repression?' (Deleuze and Guattari, 1988: 215). Fascism as such is read as reactive and life-negating.

Steve Goodman

Critical Humanism and Violence: the Great Family of Man

Postwar humanist discourse, as Burton points out, is weighted with the gravity of the reality of Aushwitz, Hiroshima and My Lai, the realities of war, genocide, torture and imminent destruction (Burton, 1980: 128).

A radical humanism, which indicts liberalism for the humanism of its discourse and the structural violence of its practice is that of Merleau-Ponty in *Humanism and Terror*. Despite playing the politics of irony, the text remains locked on the same humanist terrain. Discussing the possibility of a socialist humanism through revolutionary violence, he postulates that proletarian violence is only justified if it is a violence 'which recedes with the approach of man's future' (Merleau-Ponty, 1969: xviii). While the Marxist critique of capitalism still holds, communist practice he argues had moved away from its original humanist intentions towards the violence of cunning politics. The dilemma of violence, which is constitutive of decision and action is then to choose, to rank degrees and forms of violence – 'we ought to prefer revolutionary violence because it has a future of humanism.'

This is a moralistic humanism in which we are ontologically condemned to violence. Both capitalist institutional and party purges are graded against a scale of actual and potential humanism. Violence as in the liberal state may be put outside the law and in effect suppressed in the commerce of ideas though maintained in daily life in the form of colonization, unemployment and wages (Merleau-Ponty, 1969: 180).

Creative violence is less cautiously expounded in Sartre and Fanon in a mode more reminiscent of Sorel: in response to a fear of the contingency of history which renders politics ambivalent, here we have the mythology of catharsis in full flow. While Sartre in his preface to Fanon's *Wretched of the Earth* (1967) refers to Sorel's 'Fascist utterances', we have seen above the points of divergence between revolutionary syndicalism and the fascist cult of violence. But the mythology of catharsis pervades; in Fanon, the fracturing of colonial domination at the level of subjectivity is achieved in violence simultaneously with territorial liberation. Violence restores a humanity to the degraded colons by substituting group cohesion for serial oppression. But Fanon does more than condemn colonial terror and torture, more than mock liberalism's rhetoric, more than re-write another philosophical anthropology. Yes, his work is obviously saturated with a moral and political philosophy, but his reflections on the relation between psychiatry and criminology go beyond critical humanism. His discussion of violence is specific and he draws on psychoanalysis as a repudiation of psychiatry which essentializes the Algerian 'propensity to violence'. He rejects the colonial psychiatry attributing a semiology of Algerian criminality, that is as a frequent, savage, irrational, predatory killer. Fanon conveys instead the social pathology of everyday life of the masses during colonial repression with a descriptive psycho-pathology revealing the effects of violence on the mentality of the torturer, the tortured, the perpetrator and victim. Thus the cathartic role of violence is tempered, emphasizing a socialized, revolutionary, disciplined and party-controlled violence. More significantly, Fanon confronts the pathological effects of violence while refusing to psychologize their origins – and by facing this contradiction of the politics of violence, he questions the facile conceptions of subjectivity of humanist philosophy.

Since the Second World War, the decolonization of the European empires has been accompanied by the attempt to decolonize European thought and its forms of history. In this project, Fanon's *Wretched of the Earth* of 1961 was central. Setting himself against Sartre's contention in the *Critique of Dialectical Reason* that 'men are self-conscious agents who create the totality of history' (see Laing and Cooper, 1964), Fanon argues that the men and women who are objects of this history are condemned to immobility and silence. It is to them that his book is addressed. He indicts Europe not just for the violent history of colonial appropriation; more interestingly, colonialism, justified against the value framework of Western humanism, dehumanizes the native. As Fanon emphasizes:

> Leave this Europe where they are never done talking of Man, yet murder men everywhere they find them, at the corner of everyone of their own streets, in all the corners of the globe. For centuries they have stifled almost the whole of humanity in the name of a so called experience. . . . That same Europe where they were never done talking of Man, and where they never stopped proclaiming that they were only anxious for the welfare of Man: today we know with what sufferings humanity has paid for every one of their triumphs of mind. (Fanon, 1967: 251)

Even though Sartre attempts to reject the humanist notion of an ahistorical essence of man, his project ultimately floundered because he persisted in placing European Man at the centre of history. But in his preface to Fanon's book, he does at least recognize the complicity of humanism with the violent negativity of colonialism. Young summarizes the problematic well:

> The formation of the ideas of human nature, humanity and the universal qualities of the human mind as the common good of an ethical civilization occurred at the same time as those particularly violent centuries in the history of the world now known as the era of Western colonialism. The effect was to dehumanize the various subject-peoples: in Sartre's words, 'to wipe out their traditions, to substitute our language for theirs and to destroy their culture without giving them ours'. (Sartre, 1967: 1 in Young, 1992: 245)

Fanon notes that 'Decolonization which sets out to change the order of the world is, obviously, a programme for complete disorder' (Fanon, 1967: 27). This refers not just to the chaos of withdrawal from the outside, but also to European humanist values, an internal chaos stimulated by the 'striptease of our humanism' (Sartre, 1967: 21). And it is this seductive undressing/unmasking undertaken by a variety of recent thinkers and commonly known as *anti-humanism* to which my discussion will now turn (see also Descombes, 1980).

As Young points out,

Few politico-intellectual projects have generated as much controversy, hostility, and, ironically but perhaps symptomatically, intolerance. What is striking is that few of those defending humanism ever ask where anti-humanism came from. The standard definition states that it is derived from the critique of Marxist humanism initiated by Levi-Strauss and Althusser against Sartre and others such as Garaudy in the French Communist party. But this account hardly tells us more than that the critique of Marxist humanism came from the anti-humanists. (Young, 1992: 245)

Althusser's conflation of humanisms perhaps washed over the attempts of, for example, Lukacs, Sartre and Merleau-Ponty to devise a new historical humanism, escaping 'the Enlightenment's conception of man's unchanging nature, [for a view] that would see "man as a product of himself and of his own activity in history"' (Young, 1992: 245). And it is against these revisionist humanisms' complicity in the history of colonialism that Fanon's anti-humanism positions itself: 'The colonialist bourgeoisie, in its narcissistic dialogue, expounded by the members of its universities, had in fact deeply implanted in the minds of the colonized intellectual that the essential qualities remain eternal in spite of all the blunders men may make: the essential qualities of the West of course' (Fanon, 1967: 36). The slippage of the 'human' into identification with European values is glaring in the Marxist conception of history 'which states that if history is the product of human actions, then it can only be said to begin properly when "primitive" societies give way to (European) civilisation' (Young, 1992: 246).

Crucially then, and this applies to recent philosophically nihilistic postures, to be anti-humanist is not necessarily a position devoid of ethical spirit but perhaps the opposite. Instead, the problematization of the 'human' as an explanatory category that pretends to provide a rational explication of 'man', unmasks in a fundamentally Nietzschean mode – how an assumed universal was founded on the exclusion and marginalization of his Others, such as 'woman' (see Lloyd, 1983) or 'the native'.

A short essay by Roland Barthes in *Mythologies* is instructive here. Humanity, or 'the Family of Man' projects the myth of a global human community in two stages: initially, there is an emphasis on difference, that is a multiplicity of exotic (and usually erotic, see de Groot, 1989) varieties of everyday activities of work, play, birth, death etc. are noted, but in effect only in order to be dismissed under the sign of an underlying homogeneity and unity signifying that at some (deep) level all such experiences are identical in spite of wide cultural and historical differences – a common human nature or essence. And while such humanisms are undeniably comforting in a sentimental way, Barthes argues that such perspectives serve to circumnavigate

'differences' which we shall here quite simply call 'injustices'. . . . Any classic humanism postulates that in scratching the history of men a little, the relativity of their institutions or the superficial diversity of their skins (but why not ask the parents of Emmet Till, the young Negro assassinated by the Whites what *they* think of The Great Family of Man?), one very quickly reaches the solid rock of a universal human nature. (Barthes, 1972: 101)

Barthes points out that the global reality of, for instance, births and deaths, is not at issue – however out of their historical and cultural context, any discussion of them can only be tautological. For Barthes therefore, the universal values of humanism are illuminated in their true juxtaposition to the facts of Western colonialism and racism. It is important therefore, as Young requests, to see the French critique of humanism as, from the outset, part of a political critique of colonialism. 'The anti-humanists charged that the category of the human, however exalted in its conception, was too often invoked in order to put the male before the female, or to classify other "races" as subhuman and therefore not subject to the ethical prescriptions applicable to "humanity" at large' (Young, 1992: 247). This double bind of humanism is perhaps most dramatically evoked by Fanon: 'The violence with which the supremacy of white values is affirmed and the aggressiveness which has permeated the victory of these values over the ways of life and of thought of the native mean that, in revenge, the native laughs in mockery when Western values are mentioned infront of him' (Fanon, 1967: 33).

In common with Arendt and Camus (see Isaac, 1992), Sartre and Merleau-Ponty's writings are deeply permeated by their assessment of the historical moment, a postwar period shrouded by the annihilation of concentration camps, gulags and nuclear technology. This is crucial for understanding the compulsion they all displayed to fix their thought to some kind of humanism.

Nihilism, Postmodernity, Violence

The End of Man

The structuralist critique of humanism was produced in the context of the general refusal to recognize that violence was intrinsic to Western culture and not just accidental to it. Its decentring of the subject could be seen as an ethical activity born of the suspicion that the ontological categories of 'human' and 'human nature' were inextricably intertwined with the violence of Western history. Problematizing the 'subject', structuralism was more concerned to conceptualize it not in terms of a unitary essence, but as the product of conflicting libidinal (schizo-flows) and political economies. Reasserting the importance of linguistics, the 'I' of modern humanism is replaced by a multiplicity of grammatical positions. And as Young puts it, 'It is precisely this inscription of alterity within the self that can allow for a new relation to ethics: the self has to come to terms with the fact that it is also a second and third person' (Young, 1992: 248). So, for example, Foucault argued that the self, once engaged in linguistic activity is displaced, decentred and variously positioned as a subject according to different systems, institutions, forms of classification and hierarchies of power. With decolonization, the First World had to acclimatise to the fact that it is no longer always situated in the first person in relation to the Second and Third Worlds. The refusal to come to terms with the violence intrinsic to Western culture is particularly central to discussions of 'Fascism and the Holocaust which are often presented as if they were a unique aberration, a dark perversion of Western rationalism or a particular effect of German culture' (Young, 1992: 249). Young suggests that here we can see one of the major divergences between French thought and the Frankfurt school which he claims has strangely neglected the problem of colonialism: 'it took a Cesaire or a Fanon to point out that Fascism was simply colonialism brought home to Europe' (Young, 1992: 249).

Incalculable Justice and De(con)struction

To tie the structuralist and subsequently post-structuralist positions into this discussion of nihilism and the twentieth-century appreciation of violence it is useful to look at Jacques Derrida's reading of a controversial text written by Walter Benjamin in 1921 entitled the *Critique of Violence*. As Sergio Cotta has argued, the 'civilization' of the nineteenth century had relied on the law, and the ordering and measure which it asserts into the realm of social and political life for eliminating violence. The 'recourse' to violence which I have been examining is in part characterized in a rejection of this measure by an anti-legalism. In Benjamin's text, 'the nexus between antilegalism and violence is clearly brought to light' (Cotta, 1985: 98). As Drucilla Cornell has pointed out Derrida's engagement with Benjamin 'has been interpreted as further evidence of the inherent danger in upholding the position that law is always deconstrutable. It is this position that makes possible the "on strike"[7] posture toward any legal system. But it is a strike that supposedly never ends. Worse yet, it is a strike that supposedly cannot give us principles to legitimately curtail violence' (Cornell, 1992: 156). That deconstruction does not provide us with 'new law tables' leads some prematurely to neglect its ethical, political and juridical significance.

Introducing his topic, Benjamin points out that, in a precise sense, the concept of violence belongs to the symbolic order of law, politics and morals, and it is only to this extent that it can give rise to critique, 'critique implying decision in the form of judgement and question with regard to the right to judge'. Simultaneously, he denied that the question could be resolved on the basis of the value and justice of the agent's purpose, a claim common to both natural and positivist law traditions (Benjamin, 1979: 132). As Derrida points out, Benjamin makes use of three sets of binary oppostions:

first, there is the distinction between two kinds of violence in law . . . the founding violence, the one that institutes and positions law (. . . 'law making violence') and the violence that conserves, the one that maintains, confirms, insures the permanence and enforeablity of law (. . . 'law preserving violence'). . . . Next there is the distinction between founding violence of law termed 'mythic' . . . and the annihilating violence of destructive law . . . which is termed 'divine'. . . . Finally, there is the distinction between justice . . . as the principle of all divine positioning of the end . . . and power . . . as principle of mythical positioning of *droit*'. (Derrida, 1992: 31, my emphasis)

As Derrida goes on to argue, these distinctions are ultimately unsustainable. Before showing why, it will first be useful to summarize Benjamin's argument briefly.

Citing the usual chapter of the monopoly of force by the juridical organization, Benjamin claims that violence is considered by law to be a menace not because of the ends it pursues, but simply because it exists outside the law. The crux of the matter is that between violence and law there is an opposition of essence, which is therefore permanent, and not of ends, which would be contingent. Giving the examples of the revolutionary strike and war, Benjamin attributes the opposition to the fact that violence is in a position to found and modify juridical relations, even though the sentiment of justice may be hurt. But Benjamin does not base his criticism of violence on the unjust manner in which violence creates law, but on the pure and simple fact that it creates a juridical order. He therefore views the opposition of the law to violence as nothing but opposition between two diverse sources of norms – one power and the other violence. Benjamin's chapter is radical; he views this opposition as lacking in theoretical foundation because for him, everything in the law is always already violence, from its origins to its modes of conflict resolution, since in order to impose its own rule the law is forced to resort to violence, punishment.

It follows that the only sure foundation for a serious critique of violence lies precisely in the fact that it creates laws. Paradoxically, the fundamental fault of violence is identified by that which discloses its contingency, its instability, and marks its end because of the laborious prevalence of regularity and sense of measure. This is the structural meaning of the rise of a new juridical order following a destructive event. Hence for Benjamin, criticism of violence must begin with criticism of the violence that is law, however it arises.

This double bind is illuminated with reference to another. Drawing from Sorel, Benjamin characterizes the revolutionary strike as 'pure means of agreement', which lacks violence and is equivalent to nothing more than 'conversation'. It is notable here that he is not limiting his approval of the revolutionary strike to the justice of its cause, but rather because he sees it to be a non-violent means of negotiating an agreement. Benjamin runs with his initial paradox in judging the proletarian strike to be non-violent in its anarchy, since this logically follows from his initial premise that the law is violent. The political strike, on the other hand, he judges to be violent (and here he departs from Sorel) because in its reformism, it puts into being another law.

Benjamin's discussion culminates in the conclusion that there is violence only where a law is created or preserved; there is no violence where there is no law. To substantiate this, he makes use of the distinction between mythical violence and divine violence. He condemns the first and celebrates the second; while mythical violence establishes the law and sets limits and boundaries, inculpates and punishes, is impendant, is bloody; divine violence nullifies it in that it destroys limitlessly, it purges and expiates, it is fulminant, lethal and bloodless.[8] For Benjamin, therefore, criticism of violence not only begins with, but totally resolves itself into criticism of the law, for the law, in imposing rules and limits to action, monitors it. Contrarily, criticism of violence resolves itself into self-rehabilitation, providing that it is analogous to divinity, that is purity, immediacy, catharsis, and is unlimited. Here Benjamin is interested in the genre of pure revolutionary violence that is capable of 'making the continuum of history explode' (Benjamin, 1979: 253).

And in this respect we return full circle via my discussion of the mythology of catharsis in philosophies of emancipatory violence to Nietzsche's discussion of active nihilism as a 'violent force of destruction'. We have seen in the above discussion how this notion is instated as a distinct metaphysical position, that is the radicalized version of modern man as God, as unlimited power – in Marx's words man as 'sun unto himself' and put into praxis. In a section entitled 'On the Blissful Islands', Nietzsche remarks that man does not tolerate not being God; this makes it necessary for him to deny the law because the mere presence of it attests to his not being God, not pure goodness, nor omnipotence (Nietzsche, 1969: 109–12). It returns us to the dilemma of modernity and nihilism perhaps most succinctly posed by Dostoevsky's Ivan Karamazov in the statement 'if God does not exist is everything permitted?'

To navigate this impasse, I will now turn to Derrida's reading. Proposing the deconstructability of law, Derrida questions the positivist conception of stable grounded law. Instead, the undecidability of law merely reflects the origin of authority to *enforce* the law in a violence without ground; 'a silence is walled up in the violent structure of the founding act. Walled up, walled in because silence is not exterior to language' (Derrida, 1992: 14). For Derrida, justice is the unrepresentable, and as such always exists outside the law, hence making law always deconstructable, where to deconstruct is to constantly open up the aporias which signify a marginality, a violence at work. Such conceptualizations are crucial to new moves in legal theory which work beyond the distinction between just force and violence.[9] Concerning Benjamin's text however, in the same way that Derrida contests a pure foundation or a pure position of law, he also cannot hold Benjamin's distinction between a pure founding violence and a purely conservative violence because 'position is already iterability, a call for self-conserving repetition' (Derrida, 1992: 38). Moreover, that divine violence is instated in Benjamin's philosophy of history as pure rupture, as that which permits critique and decidability is for Derrida the most provocative paradox of the *Critique*; 'all undecidability . . . is situated, blocked in, accumulated on the side of [law], that is to say the violence that founds and conserves [law]. But on the other hand all decidability stands on the side of the divine violence that destroys [the law]' (Derrida, 1992: 38). The divine nature of pure revolutionary violence, Benjamin acknowledges demands a judgment, a decision not accessible to man since divine violence as the most decidable

> does not lend itself to any human determination, to any knowledge or decidable 'certainty' on our part . . . to be schematic, there are two violences . . . on one side, decision (just, historical, political and so on), justice beyond [law] and the state, but without decidable knowledge, on the other, decidable knowledge and certainty in a realm that structurally remains that of the undecidable, of the mythic [law] of the state. On one side the decision without decidable certainty, on the other the certainty of the undecidable but without decision. In any case, in one form or another, the undecidable is on each side, and is the violent condition of knowledge or action. (Derrida 1992: 56)

Importantly, it is this characteristic of post-structuralism in its various forms to ponder the violence of representation (see Foucault, 1984; Armstrong and Tennerhouse, 1989; Derrida, 1990) (not just in its ideological deviations and deceptions but ubiquitously in discourse as a system of differences), which perhaps best reflects the chaos which remains as modern differentiation becomes aware of its violent origins and self-de(con)structs. However, Derrida's reluctance to instate some kind of metaphysical principles of justice reflects his undermining of philosophy and its claims to truth as literature, and hence his debunking of the philosophical anthropology at the foundation of metaphysical conceptions of justice.

And it is in the face of the 'danger' that the recognition of the violence of interpretation can lead to the nihilistic levelling of all perspectives that some have emphasized the affinity of Derridian deconstruction with French anthropologist Rene Girard's theory of the scape-goat (see Girard, 1978, 1986, 1987). The formal and structural resemblance which McKenna (among others) points to, consists of a notion of *sacrifice* as restoring order by instating difference. Whereas Girard focuses on the victim and the community, Derrida's immediate focus is on writing; it was the capacity of writing to represent anything (like the arbitrarily selected scape-goat) deriving from the fact that it represents nothing in particular, which caused Plato to exclude it from his Republic – Plato condemned writing as mimesis as it represents the dynamics of the crowd or the mob whose violence is quelled only by the arbitrary expulsion of one of its members. And the violence of all against all in the melée of appropriative rivalry yields at a certain point to the violence of all against one, against the victim. This restores calm to the group, instates a before–after and an inside–outside, that is an order of time and space. While the victim is the matrix of difference for Girard, it is writing which is the matrix of difference for Derrida. Both produce philosophical and cultural institutions whose survival and credibility depends on the concealing of their violent origins to ambivalent moral effect. Girard points out that 'it is the knowledge of violence, along with the violence itself, that the act of expulsion succeeds in shunting outside the realm of consciousness' (McKenna, 1992: 28–34).

Girard's anthropology is therefore read as thematizing the moral impulse of deconstruction. His 'victimary hypothesis' postulates the sacrificial nature of the origins of all institutions. The victim then signifies, like the Derridean trace, the truth of the violent origin. In his discussion of Foucault's *Madness and Civilisation*, Derrida argues that what is expelled by the cogito as language (which Foucault places on trial) is madness as indifferentiation: the emergence of the cogito as language, as rationality, as philosophy consists in the rejection of the violence it performs in the performance of the violence it rejects. Language is the representation of violence, the chaos, the indifferentiation it rejects, in its oblivion, in forgetting or erasing the traces of its violent origin, it emerges from crisis and perpetuates itself as philosophy. But there is never a total erasure since this would lead to a loss of sense of identity. And it is this simultaneous mindfulness and forgetfulness of an originary violence that is the paradox which Girard suggests is evident in sacrifice. Foucault identifies madness as the sacrificial victim; the surrogate which must remain close enough to be named as violence and far enough to be named as a violence other than the one which expels it (see Derrida, 1990).[10]

Girard's anthropology recognizes the post-structuralist decentring of subjectivity in its focus on the mimetic structure of desire and violence. Yet as the last ditch attempt to infuse political purpose to a post-metaphysical anthropology by instating truth in the victim, what the theory of the scape-goat resembles most is an ashtray chaotically collecting the sediments of victimization, not espousing any particularly constructive political manifesto. This is merely an observation and is not intended as condemnation for reasons I will now discuss, in relation to the difficulty of projected optimism in postmodernity.

Postmodern Nihilism

The standard description of the transition from modernity to postmodernity relates the end of an era of production and industrial capitalism, and the onset of an age of simulation and a new techno-culture. The big signs of modernity (expansion, differentiation, energy, movement, interpretation of the real, power, the social) are replaced by a new language of implosion, de-differentiation and the reproduction of models of hyperreality and inertia. In his article 'On nihilism', Baudrillard describes modernity, the era of the depth models Marx and Freud wherein everything is interpreted in terms of economy or unconscious, as 'the radical destruction of appearances, the disenchantment of the world and its abandonment to the violence of interpretation and history (Baudrillard, 1984: 38). He describes the postmodern age as devoid of meaning, that is a universe of nihilism where theories float unanchored in a void; meaning is dead and exists only as frozen forms mutating in new combinations. Meaning requires depth, unseen, yet providing some kind of stability.

Baudrillard (1983b) privileges nihilism over the fantasy of meaning: 'if being nihilist is to privilege this point of inertia and the analysis of this irreversibility of systems to the point of no return, then I am a nihilist. If being nihilist is to be obsessed with the mode of disappearance, and no longer with the mode of production, then I am a nihilist. Disappearance, aphanisis, implosion, fury of the Verschwindens'. His nihilism is without joy, energy or the hope for a better future. So melancholia, rather than optimism becomes the feature of the mode of disappearance of meaning. This state is prone to contradictory emotions and responses in rapid flux; from despair to vertigo to giddiness to nostalgia to laughter. And while previous radical theory valorized negation, for Baudrillard, it is the system which assumes the role of the negation of values and is therefore nihilistic. The negation of the radical therefore becomes merely the imitation of the system's own processes and contribution to the destruction of meaning. Concerning postmodern violence, Baudrillard's recent work, in common with that of Paul Virilio, has stressed the challenge to representation mounted by terrorism on the one hand, and what Guy Debord referred to as the 'society of the spectacle' on the other (1983). In some ways terrorist acts can appear exactly as senseless and indeterminate as the system they are designed to combat; present-day terrorism, argues Baudrillard, 'offers a homologue deep down, of the silence and inertia of the masses. . . . In its deadly and indiscriminate taking of hostages, terrorism strikes at precisely the most characteristic product of the whole system: the anonymous and perfectly undifferentiated individual, the term substitutable for any other' (Baudrillard, 1983b).

It is worth comparing Baudrillard's description of postmodernity as a new stage of nihilism with Nietzsche's conception that I discussed earlier, and which he argued was the result of the collapse of Christian and metaphysical values. Like Nietzsche, Baudrillard points to the death of the values of modernity – production, *revolution*, the social and meaning. Like Nietzsche, Baudrillard also wants to derive value from appearances without appeal to depth or the supernatural. Furthermore, both appeal to aristocratic values by privileging expenditure, seduction and ritual. Baudrillard diverges however in that he does not celebrate the sense of vitalism, the celebration of life most evident in Nietzsche's *The Gay Science*. Rather, the moods of joy dissipate in Baudrillard's melancholy. In addition, while Nietzsche glorifies the sovereignty of the superior individual as a mode of transition, Baudrillard, in a more extreme form than his French contemporaries, attacks the subject itself and advocates a quite different theoretical perspective.

Postmodern Violence: the Victim Age

In modern times, binary oppositions such as order-keeping–violence, civility–barbarity and reason–passion were superimposed over controlled–uncontrolled. Modernity here is about ordering, imposition of monotony, repeatability and determination. With civility, no coercion comes by surprise – it is rationally calculable; the known necessity which Hegel celebrated as freedom. In the land of barbarity, coercion and violence is diffuse, dispersed, erratic, unpredictable and incapacitating. Since they are by definition violent, barbarians are legitimate objects of violence.

As Caygill points out, 'The border between civility and violence is no longer found at the limit of sovereign space, but now traverses that space' (Caygill, 1993: 52). Bauman makes two qualifications to this. Firstly, he points out that as modern history shows, the frontier between civility and barbarity never coincided with the borders of the nation state, even less with the circumference of the 'civilized world'. Barbarians have resided within – as the monstrosities of Auschwitz, the Gulags and Hiroshima testify. Moreover,

> there was more than a 'pinch' of barbarity sprinkled into the official iden-
> tity kits of the indolent, improvident, fickle and irresponsible poor, of the
> passion-ridden, thoughtless and frivolous female, and of any other cat-
> egory presumed to obstreperous and wayward to be safely kept at bay by
> the ordinary measure of daily coercion – be they criminals (subjects of the
> extra coercion of penology), mentally deficient (subjects of the extra coer-
> cion of psychiatry), or other degenerates. (Bauman, 1991: 147)

Most seminally, there was the wild man within every civilized one. The modern body is therefore seen as a jail, guarding the psychopath inside – however vigilance was never sufficient – the barbarian emerged with every sign of emotion, or every transgression. This fuelled the modern project of imposing order. Civility set its own rules and reserved the right to decide who was the barbarian. So the distinction was not just one clear line.

Secondly, the border between civility and violence can still to some extent be found at the limit of sovereign space. The traditional wars between 'us and them' continue under the banner of violence for peace. As mentioned earlier, it is the pacified 'sovereign territory' of civilization which perpetually creates and re-creates objects to be stigmatized or censured later as violent, and therefore the legitimate target of pacifying missions. Technological developments precede their objectives – to an increasing extent, stockpiles of weapons keep the supplies of 'barbarism outside' constant and plentiful. But with Caygill, it has to be agreed that the potential for violence is regaining its central position.

If one agrees with Levinas that 'the justification of the neighbour's pain is certainly the source of all immorality' (quoted in Bauman, 1991: 149), then one can suspend the distinction between legitimate and illegitimate violence, and point to the cruelty of all coercion. Bauman argues that there is more than a casual connec-tion between the ability to commit cruel deeds and moral insensibility. To allow the mass participation in cruelty, the 'separation of moral guilt from acts', was, he argues, facilitated by modern organization and scientific management. In *Modernity and the Holocaust*, he describes this tool of severance as 'adiaphorization' – that is, making certain actions or objects morally neutral. This is accomplished by the exclusion of some categories from the realm of moral subjects or by disguising the link between partial action and moral effect. But Bauman asks, are not bureau-cracy and technology intensifying? He points to two contemporary sources of adiaphorization.

Due to a huge exposure to images of human suffering, one could point to a desensitivization to cruelty. Elias saw the end of public executions as a sign of the civilizing process. But these were rare and festive occasions. Bakhtin described this carnival culture in terms of the periodic and spectacular reversals of the daily norms which underlined the binding routine of quotidianity. Today, media spectacles represent a constant carnival of cruelty (Bauman, 1991: 149). And as Bauman observes, a carnival which is continuous is no longer a carnival. The spillage of images of cruelty into the mainstream of everyday experience has inevitably led to a 'wearing off' impact, which demands an increasing spiral of gore to arouse and draw attention. The media presents violence in a more vivid and gripping way than reality. Staged cruelty sets the standard for what merely happens with the 'cameraman around'. For this reason, 'reality' tends to be evaluated according to the dramatic ingenuity of a crime/disaster movie or an arcade game. Moreover, the electronic mediation of 'real war' makes it easier to kill what are essentially 'dots on a screen'. With news, drama and games, the dividing lines between reality and image grow increasingly tenuous. In fact reality becomes just one more image vying for attention in the same universe of meaning (amusement). As Baudrillard never tires of repeating, this is a universe of the simulacrum where images are more real than reality, where everything is a representation. These 'realistic' images cover up for the absence of reality. And with realities melting into representations, with the 'not for real' becoming the standard of the real, adiaphorization tends towards completion.

Responsibility, which Arendt said tended to float in all bureaucracies and which drained Kafka's K. of life, is perhaps floating like never before. Technology not only mediates killing blows but also assumes the responsibility for identifying and choosing victims represented as symbols and icons. The potential for innocent victims as innocent mistakes was perhaps never as noticeable as in the Gulf War, where targets emerged at the far end of a tortuous chain of signification. Also such a war could hardly be described as combat but rather as a unilateral flow of aggression. While in the Gulf War, generals and mass media repeated ad nauseam that the object was to 'save lives', the tacit assumption was that only certain lives were worth saving. The most recent, highly developed weapons are not for combat but rather for pure slaughter (see Der Derian, 1992; Merrin, 1994). Adiaphorization, Bauman contends is alive and well in postmodernity. But under such conditions, the principle adiaphorizing mechanisms – the enabling factors of violence – shift from bureaucratic organization to the world of daily life.

Postmodernity sees a profound modification of the way in which individuality is socially constructed and of the fashion in which the bulk of the population is socially integrated and riveted into the process of systemic reproduction. Under modern conditions, Bauman argues that individuals (men) are constructed as 'producer/soldiers'. They are firstly carriers of kinetic force to be turned into creative/destructive labour, or soldiers who should ideally be immune to fatigue. In addition, modern individuals were to be disciplined actors amenable to regulation and capable of monotonous conduct. Like lego, modern individuals were incomplete when alone, in the sense that they are supposed to be confined into meaningful totalities. As such the boundaries of individuals were interfaces. Finally, the individual of modern discourse was supposed to exist in some kind of equilibrium between what s/he ought to be like and what s/he was. Here health is the key, with the capacity to perform well dependent on strength, energy, discipline and regularity (Bauman, 1991: 154–5).

Under postmodern conditions however, the individual is constructed as a consumer/player. Bauman highlights the following characteristics of the emergent subjectivities. Individuals are constructed as experiencing organisms, perpetually seeking new ones, yet immune to saturation. They are originative actors with spontaneous mobility and pliability of behaviour and are constructed as inner regulated, tending towards self-equilibration. Finally, the model of propriety is fitness rather than health, that is, the individual's bodily and spiritual capacity to absorb and creatively respond to new experience in the fast pace of change. Flaccidity is medicalized and referred for psychological counselling (Bauman, 1991: 155).

Technologies of war mean that fewer and fewer soldiers are required. Those 'productively engaged' are increasingly marginalized in the social division of labour which sees the decentring of work. The importance of panoptic and legitimizing strategies becomes, contra Habermas' legitimation crisis, redundant. Rather, the majority of the population is required to consume and therefore feed systemic reproduction, isolating a ghettoized, chaotic sub-class. The end result of this construction of postmodern subjectivity is the perfect consumer. Bauman suggests that while the modern individual was a pilgrim, the postmodern individual is a stroller, a vagabond, a tourist and a player. This splicing of life-process bars the construction of lasting networks of mutual duty and obligation. Rather than an object of moral evaluation, the Other is cast as an object of aesthetic assessment. As a hangover from the modern bureaucracy with its institutional rule of nobody, everyone avoids engagement with the fate of the Other (Bauman, 1991: 156–7).

Thanks to these new adiaphorizing modes, violence is seen to return to where the civilizing process was supposed to evict it, that is, to the family, the neighbourhood (did it ever leave?). Like Cotta, Bauman contends that there is difficulty today in distinguishing between stern parental guidance and child abuse, flirtation and harassment, sexual advances and sexual assault. The once-tolerated degree of compromise in negotiated otherness tends to be recast as undue/unendurable violence performed on the self-assertive rights. It is however important to point out that the hyperindividualist chaos which emerges is not necessarily to be mourned; the blurring of the public–private distinction achieved by the women's movement for example, has countered the de-politicization of domestic violence.

Postmodern stocks of violence are privatized, dispersed, diffuse and unfocused, in the model of the capillary. The ubiquitous presence is ambivalent: on the one hand is the exhilaration of ultimate emancipation; on the other is the gnawing fear of an anarchic, Hobbesian world. Bauman argues that this fear fuels the postmodern phenomenon of neo-tribalism. With the state ceding integrative functions to market forces, the task is left to 'postulated communities' to supply the collective guarantees of privatized identities. 'Postmodern thinking is awash with dreams of communal and local truths and certainties hoped to do the civilising job which the big truths and certainties of nation-states as spokesmen for universality, failed to perform' (Bauman, 1991: 158). Bauman points to the connections between neo-tribes and violence. In a condition of information overload, public attention is the scarcest of resources. The cogito is replaced by the 'I am noticed (I shout) therefore I exist'. Louder shouts are needed as time goes by. This upward trend in the shocking power of shocks mirrors an escalation of violence: 'it takes all the running you can do to stay in the same place' (Lewis Carroll in Bauman, 1994: 158). In addition, the existential modality of neo-tribes is as postulated communities with no estab-lished institutions and which only exist in the future tense – as a hope of coming into being. And the nervousness, bad temper and anxiety induced by the maximum of securing some brief, chimeric presence in the world is conducive to disorder (Bauman, 1991: 159).

Conclusion

This chapter has tried to show in a positive light the relevance of a post-Nietzschean theoretical terrain to understanding the dynamics and pyrotechnics of postmodern flows of violence. Undeniably and unfortunately it is is perhaps too reactive in that it is positioned against those self-conceited 'modernists' who would like, broad-brush style to brand so-called 'postmodernists' with the responsibility for all future violent holocausts. The creative–destructive ambivalence in Nietzsche's thought renders a humanist reading highly problematic. A 'gentle' Nietzsche still glows, but predictably his bourgeoisification makes him much dimmer. To set up for example a straightforward opposition between art and morality can sidetrack us from his relevance today in helping illuminate an era characterized by the aetheticization of everyday life. Against the charge of aestheticism, Nietzsche at his most radioactive attempts to understand the 'general economy of the whole': violence, cruelty and suffering as well as joy, love and happiness. His moral ambivalence reflects the turbulence of the contemporary global system.

That – because since Plato philosophy has served to oil the gears of the state – means that the task now is to rescue thought from this machinery; and when at the outset I questioned the self-evidence of the move 'beyond nihilism' and glib rejection directed at those who appear to come down from the mountain without a new law table. . .

'shatter this new law-table too! The world-weary and the preachers of death hung it up, and so did the jailers: for behold, it is also a sermon urging slavery.'

(*Zarathrustra*)

Notes

1 For elaboration of the concept of censure see recent work by Summer (e.g., 1990b, 1990c).

2 My discussion is obviously selective. The following are issues that I have been unable to develop at all or to any satisfactory degree and without which this thesis necessarily remains incomplete: Russian nihilism of the late nineteenth century; Marxist-Leninist and Trotskyist theory and praxis; anarchism; Heidegger's extended discussion of nihilism and technology; Kojeve's reading of Hegel and his *terrorist conception of history* (see Descombes, 1980); Dadaist and surrealist texts, especially Bataille's literature of transgression best evoked in the discussion of virulent nihilism in Land, 1992; the psychoanalytic dialectic of eros/thanatos; the feminist plateau which reveals the intertwining of violence and masculinity (see Siebers, 1988).

3 Here I have in mind the dismissal of post-Nietzschean terrains (e.g., in Giddens, 1985).

4 It is the interpretation of this statement in political theories of direct action which forms the problematic of this thesis. For the literary inscription of these varieties of nihilism, see Fandozzi's discussion of Stavrogin, Pyotr and Kirillov in Dostoevsky's *The Possessed* (1982) Chapter 3.

5 'German soldiers went to the front, it is reported, with the Bible in one trench-coat pocket and *Thus Spoke Zarathrustra* in the other' (Ansell-Pearson, 1994: 29).

6 In Theweleit (1987) the *mythology of catharsis* is revealed as saturated with (male) sexual anxieties about regulating bodily boundaries and controlling or eliminating dirt.

7 'There is a possibility of general strike, a right to general strike in any interpretative reading, the right to contest established law in its strongest authority, the law of the state' (Derrida, 1992: 37).

8 *Divine violence* as *bloodless* is particularly disturbing considering the techniques of the final solution.

9 See for example Cover, 1986; Sarat and Keams, 1991; Young 1994. On nihilism and law see Goodrich, 1986. On undecidability see Deleuze, 1991: Chapter 7 and McKenna, 1992: Chapter 6.

10 But Derrida questions whether Foucault can succeed in putting reason on trial since he himself questions in a rational, juridical tone, that is, Foucault denounces order from within order.

References

ABRAMSON, P. and ALDRICH, J. (1982) 'The decline of electoral participation in America', *American Political Science Review*, **76**, pp. 502–21.

ACKERMAN, N. and JAHODA, M. (1950) *Anti-Semitism and Emotional Disorder*, New York: Harper.

ADAM, P. (1992) *The Arts of the Third Reich*, London: Faber & Faber.

ADAMS, P. (1989) 'Of female bondage', in BRENNAN, T. (Ed.) *Between Feminism and Psychoanalysis*, London: Routledge.

ADORNO, T. W. (1950a) 'Prejudice in the interview material', in ADORNO, T. W., FRENKEL-BRUNSWIK, E., LEVINSON, D. J. and SANFORD, R. N. (Eds) *The Authoritarian Personality*, London: Norton.

ADORNO, T. W. (1950b) 'Types and syndromes', in ADORNO, T. W., FRENKEL-BRUNSWIK, E., LEVINSON, D. J. and SANFORD, R. N. (Eds) *The Authoritarian Personalty*, London: Norton.

ADORNO, T. W (1967) 'Sociology and psychology', *New Left Review*, **46**, pp. 67–80.

ADORNO, T. W. (1991) *The Culture Industry: Selected Essays on Mass Culture* (J. M. BERNSTEIN, Ed.), London: Routledge.

ADORNO, T. W. (1994) *The Stars Down to Earth and Other Essays on the Irrational in Culture* (S. CROOK. Ed.), London: Routledge.

ADORNO, T. W., FRENKEL-BRUNSWIK, E., LEVINSON, D. J. and SANFORD, R. N. (Eds) (1950) *The Authoritarian Personality*, London: Norton.

ADORNO, T. W. and HORKHEIMER, M. (1973) *Dialectic of Enlightenment*, London: Allen Lane.

AIZCORBE, R. (1975) *Argentina: the Peronist Myth, an Essay on the Cultural Decay in Argentina After the Second World War*, Hicksville, NY: Exposition Press.

ALEXANDER, F. (1937) 'Psychoanalysis and social disorganization', *American Journal of Sociology*, **46**, pp. 781–813.

ALEXANDER, R. J. (1951) *The Peron Era*, New York: Columbia University Press.

ALLEN, C. (1962) *A Textbook of Psychosexual Disorders*, London: Oxford University Press.

AMBROSE, S. (1989) *Nixon: The Triumph of a Politician*, New York: Simon & Schuster.

AMERICAN PSYCHIATRIC ASSOCIATION (1994) *Diagnostic and Statistical Manual of Mental Disorders* (4th edn), Washington DC: American Psychiatric Association.

ANDERSON, P. (1976) 'The antinomies of Antonio Gramsci', *New Left Review*, **100**, pp. 5–78.

References

ANDREWS, N. (1984) 'Nightmares and nasties', in BARKER, M. (Ed.) *The Video Nasties: Freedom and Censorship in the Media*, London: Pluto Press.

ANSELL-PEARSON, K. (1994) *An Introduction to Nietzsche as Political Thinker*, Cambridge: Cambridge University Press.

ARENDT, H. (1964) *Eichmann in Jerusalem: a Report on the Banality of Evil* (2nd edn), Harmondsworth: Penguin.

ARENDT, H. (1970) *On Violence*, London: Allen Lane.

ARENDT, H. (1973) *The Origins of Totalitarianism*, London: Harcourt Brace.

ARMSTRONG, N. and TENNENHOUSE, L. (Eds) (1989) *The Violence of Representation*, London: Routledge.

ARONSON, R. (1983) *The Dialectics of Disaster*, London: Verso.

ASCH, S. E. (1951) 'Effects of group pressure upon the modification and distortion of judgement', in GUETZKOW, H. (Ed.) *Groups, Leadership, and Men*, Pittsburgh: Carnegie.

ASHBEE, H. S. [Pisanus Fraxi, pseud.] (1877) *Index Librorum Prohibitorum: Being Notes Bio-Biblio-Icono-Graphical and Critical on Curious and Uncommon Books*, London: privately printed.

AXEL, L. E. (1979) 'Christian theology and the murder of the jews', Encounter, **40**, pp. 135–6.

BADCOCK, B. (1984) *Unfairly Structured Cities*, Oxford: Blackwell.

BADCOCK, C. (1992) 'Freud's findings in the context of recent evolutionary theory', in SPAIN, D. H. (Ed.) *Pshchoanalytic Anthropology after Freud: Essays Marking the Fiftieth Anniversary of Freud's Death*, New York: Psyche Press.

BALKAN, S., BERGER, R. J. and SCHMIDT, J. (1980) *Crime and Deviance in America: a Critical Approach*, California: Wadsworth, Inc.

BARKER, M. (1984) *Video Nasties: Freedom and Censorship in the Media*, London: Pluto Press.

BARKER, M. (1995) 'Violence', *Sight and Sound*, June, p. 1.

BARLOW, D. E., CARR, F. R., FERRELL, E. and JENKINS, L. B. (1993) 'Long economic cycles and the criminal justice system in the United States', *Crime, Law and Social Change*, **19**, pp. 239–67.

BARNHART, R. K. (1988) *The Barnhart Dictionary of Etymology*, London: H. W. Wilson Company.

BARON, S. (Ed.) (1991) *Degenerate Art*, New York: H. N. Abrams.

BARTHES, R. (1970) *S/Z*, Paris: du Seuil.

BARTHES, R. (1972) *Mythologies*, London: Vintage.

BARTHES, R. (1985) *The Grain of the Voice*, New York: Hill & Wang.

BARTHOLOMEW, A. A., MILTE, K. L. and GALBALLY, F. (1975) 'Sexual murder: psychopathology and psychiatric jurisprudential considerations', *Australia and New Zealand Journal of Criminology*, **8**, pp. 143–52.

BARTKY, S. L. (1990) *Femininity and Domination: Studies in the Phenomenology of Oppression*, London: Routledge.

BARTLETT, D. and STEELE, J. (1992) *America: What Went Wrong?* Kansas City: Andrews & McMeel.

BATAILLE, G. (1985) 'Nietzsche and the fascists', in STOEKL, A. (Ed.) *Visions of Excess: Selected Writings 1927–1939*, Manchester: Manchester University Press.

BAUDRILLARD, J. (1970) *La Societe de Consommation*, Paris: Gallimard.

BAUDRILLARD, J. (1983a) *In the Shadow of the Silent Majorities*, London: Semiotexte.

BAUDRILLARD, J. (1983b) *Simulations and Simulacrum*, New York: Semiotexte.

BAUDRILLARD, J. (1984) 'On nihilism', *On the Beach*, **6**, pp. 38–9.

BAUDRILLARD, J. (1987) *Forget Foucault*, New York: Columbia University Press.

BAUDRILLARD, J. (1988) *America*, London: Verso.

BAUMAN, Z. (1989) *Modernity and the Holocaust*, Cambridge: Polity.

BAUMAN, Z. (1991) *Modernity and Ambivalence*, Cambridge: Polity.

BAUMAN, Z. (1993) *Postmodern Ethics*, Oxford: Blackwell.

BAUMAN, Z. (1994) 'Violence, postmodern', unpublished paper, University of Edinburgh.

BAUMEISTER, R. F. (1991) *Escaping the Self: Alcoholism, Spirituality, Masochism, and Other Flights From the Burden of Selfhood*, New York: Basic Books.

BEARDSMORE, R. W. (1971) *Art and Morality*, London: Macmillan.

BECH, H. (1992) 'Living together in the (post)modern world', unpublished paper presented at the European Conference of Sociology, Vienna, quoted in BAUMAN, Z. (1993) *Postmodern Ethics*, Oxford: Blackwell.

BECK. T. R. and BECK, J. B. (1838) *Elements of Medical Jurisprudence*, London: Longman.

BECK, U., GIDDENS, A. and LASH, S. (1994) *Reflexive Modernization: Politics, Tradition and Aesthetics in the Modern Social Order*, Cambridge: Polity.

BECKER, H. S. (1963) *Outsiders: Studies in the Sociology of Deviance*, New York: Free Press.

BEIRNE, P. and MESSERSCHMIDT, J. (1991) *Criminology*, New York: HBJ.

BELL, D. (1980) 'Culture and religion in a post-industrial age', in KRANZBERG, M. (Ed.) *Ethics in an Age Of Pervasive Technology*, Bouldner: Westview Press.

BENJAMIN, J. (1983) 'Master and slave: the fantasy of erotic domination', in SNITOW, A., STANSELL, C. and THOMPSON, S. (Eds) *Desire: the Politics of Sexuality*, London: Virago.

BENJAMIN, W. (1979) *One Way Street and Other Writings*, London: NLB.

BENJAMIN, W. (1992) *Illuminations* (H. ARENDT, Ed.), London: Fontana.

BENJAMIN, J. and RABINBACH, A. (1989) 'Preface', in THEWELEIT, K. *Male Fantasies: Male Bodies, Psychoanalysing the White Terror*, Cambridge: Polity.

BENNETT, W. (1989) *National Drug Control Strategy*, Washington: Office of National Drug Control Policy.

BERGER, P. (1963) *Invitation to Sociology*, New York: Doubleday.

BERGLER, E. (1961) *Curable and Incurable Neurosis: Problems of Neurotic vs Malignant Masochism*, New York: Liveright.

BERGMANN, J. F. (1967) *Die Theorie des Sozialen Systems von Talcott Parsons*, Frankfurt/Main: Europaische Velaganstalt.

BERGOFFEN, D. (1990) 'Nietzsche's madman: perspectivism without nihilism', in KOELB, C. (Ed.) *Nietzsche as Postmodernist: Essays Pro and Contra*, Albany: State University of New York Press.

BERLIN, I. (1993) *Conversations with Isiah Berlin*, London: Phoenix.

BERLINER, B. (1958) 'The role of object relations in moral masochism', in *Psychoanalytic Quarterly*, **27**, pp. 38–56.

BERTRAM, J. G. [Rev. Wm. M. COOPER, pseud.] (1868) *Flagellation and the Flagellants: a History of the Rod in all Countries From the Earliest Period to the Present Time*, London: William Reeves.

BETTELHEIM, B. (1986a) *The Informed Heart: a Study of the Psychological Consequences of Living Under Extreme Fear and Terror*, Harmondsworth: Penguin.

BETTELHEIM, B. (1986b) *Surviving the Holocaust and Other Essays*, London: Fontana.

BETTELHEIM, B. (1991) *Freud's Vienna and Other Essays*, New York: Vintage.

BETTELHEIM, B. and JANOWITZ, M. (1950) *Dynamics of Prejudice*, New York: Harper.

BLANCHOT, M. (1977) 'The limits of experience: nihilism', in ALLISON, D. B. (Ed.) *The New Nietzsche*, London: MIT Press.

BLANKSTEN, G. (1953) *Peron's Argentina*, Chicago: University of Chicago Press.

BLOCH, I. (1908) *The Sexual Life of our Time and its Relations to Modern Civilization*, London: Rabman.

BLOCH, I. (1938) *Sexual Life in England Past and Present*, London: Francis Aldor.

BLONSTON, G. (1993) 'Crime fears often overshadow reality', *The Philadelphia Inquirer*, November 7.

BLOOM, H. (1987) *Friedrich Nietzsche*, New York: Chelsea House.

BOCOCK, R. (1986) *Hegemony*, London: Tavistock.

BOILEAU (1700) *Historia of the Flagellantium. De recto et perverso Flagrorum usu apud Christianos*, Paris.

BONAPARTE, M. (1953) *Female Sexuality*, London: Institute of Psychoanalysis.

BOURDIEU, P. (1977) *Outline of a Theory of Practice*, Cambridge: Cambridge University Press.

BRACHER, K. D. (1984) *The Age of Ideologies*, London: Weidenfeld & Nicholson.

BRACHER, K. D. (Ed.) (1991) *The German Dictatorship*, London: Penguin.

BRADBURY, M. (1990) 'Postmodernism', in BULLOCK, A. and STALLYBRASS, O. (Eds) *Modern Thought*, London: Fontana Press.

BRAKE, M. and HALE, C. (1992) *Public Order and Private Lives*, London: Routledge.

BRAMSTEDT, E. K. (1965) *Goebbels and National Socialist Propaganda*, East Lansing: Michigan State University Press.

BRENNAN, T. (1992) *The Interpretation of the Flesh: Freud and Femininity*, London: Routledge.

BRESLOW, N., EVANS, L. and LANGLEY, J. (1985) 'On the prevalence and roles of females in the sadomasochistic subculture: report of an empirical study', *Archives of Sexual Behaviour*, **14**, pp. 303–17.

BRITTAIN, R. P. (1970) 'The sadistic murderer', *Medicine, Science and the Law*, **10**, pp. 198–207.

BROWN, B. (1984) 'Exactly what we wanted', in BARKER, M. (Ed.) *The Video Nasties – Freedom and Censorship in the Media*, London: Pluto Press.

BROWNING, C. R. (1992) *Ordinary Men: Police Battalion 101 and the Final Solution in Poland*, New York: Harper Perennial.

BROWNSTEIN, H. (1991) 'The media and the construction of random drug violence', *Social Justice*, **18**, pp. 85–103.

BURTON, F. (1980) 'Questions of violence in party political criminology', in CARLEN, P. and COLLISON, M. (Eds) *Radical Issues in Criminology*, Oxford: Martin Robertson.

CAMPELL, D. and DILLON, M. (Ed.) (1993) *The Political Subject of Violence*, Manchester: Manchester University Press.

CAMUS, A. (1962) *The Rebel*, Harmondsworth: Penguin.

CANETTI, E. (1984) *Crowds and Power*, London: Peregrine.

CAPEL LOFT (1837) *Self-formation; or, the History of an Individual Mind.*

CAPLAN, P. (1985) *The Myth of Women's Masochism*, London: Methuen.

CARINGELLA-MACDONALD, S. (1990) 'State crisis and the crackdown on crime under Reagan', *Contemporary Crisis*, **14**, pp. 91–118.

CARMILLY-WEINBERGER, M. (1986) *Fear of Art*, New York: Bowker.

CARROLL, J. (1993) *Humanism: the Wreck of Western Culture*, London: Fontana Press.

CARSTEN, F. L. (1967) *The Rise of Fascism*, London: Methuen.

CARTER, A. (1979) *The Sadeian Woman: an Exercise in Cultural History*, London: Virago.

CARTER, M. (1994) 'SM and Meditation', unpublished essay.

CAYGILL, H. (1993) 'Violence, civility and the predicaments of philosophy', in CAMPELL, D. and DILLON, M. (Eds) *The Political Subject of Violence*, Manchester: Manchester University Press.

CECIL, R. (1972) *The Myth of the Master Race: Alfred Rosenberg and Nazi Ideology*, London: Batsford.

CHALK, F. (1990) 'Remembering the future: the impact of the holocaust and genocide on Jews and Christians', in CHALK, F. and JONASSOHN, K. (Eds) *The History and Sociology of Genocide: Analyses and Case Studies*, New Haven: Yale University Press.

CHALK, F. and JONASSOHN, K. (1990) *The History and Sociology of Genocide: Analyses and Case Studies*, New Heaven: Yale University Press.

CHAMBLISS, W. and MANKOFF, M. (1976) *Whose Law What Order? A Conflict Approach to Criminology*, New York: Wiley & Sons.

CHASSEGUET-SMIRGEL, J. (1990) 'Reflections of a psychoanalyst upon the Nazi biocracy and genocide', *International Review of Psychoanalysis*, **17**, pp. 167–76.

CHIAROMONTE, N. (1962) 'Albert Camus: on memorium', in BREE, G. (Ed.) *Camus: a Collection of Critical Essays*, New Jersey: Prentice Hall.

CHILDS, J. B. (1993) 'Towards trans-communality, the highest stage of multiculturalism: notes on the future of African Americans', *Social Justice*, **20**, pp. 35–51.

CHODOROW, N. (1989) 'The fantasy of the perfect mother', in CHODOROW, N. (Ed.) *Feminism and Psychoanalytic Theory*, Cambridge: Polity.

CLAPP, J. (1972) *Art Censorship*, New Jersey: Scarecrow Press.

COHEN, S. (1980) *Folk Devils and Moral Panics: the Creation of the Mods and Rockers*, Oxford: Blackwell.

CONNOLLY, W. (1991) *Identity/Difference: Democratic Negotiations of Political Paradox*, Ithaca: Cornell University Press.

COOPER, T. (1819) *Tracts on Medical Jurisprudence*, Philadelphia: James Webster.

COPLESTON, F. C. (1993) *Memoirs*, Kansas City: Sheed & Ward.

CORNELL, D. (1992) *The Philosophy of the Limit*, London: Routledge.

COTTA, S. (1985) *Why Violence? A Philosophical Interpretation*, Gainesville: University of Florida Press.

COUNTDOWN ON SPANNER CONFERENCE (1994) 'Consent and offences against the person': the Law Commission consultation paper on assault, 18 March 1994, Institute for Contemporary Arts, London.

COVER, R. (1986) 'Violence and the word', *Yale Law Journal*, **95**, pp. 1601–29.

CRAIB, I. (1989) *Psychoanalysis and Social Theory*, Hertfordshire: Harvester Wheatsheaf.

References

DADWIDOWICZ, L. (1982) *The Holocaust and the Historians*, Cambridge, MA: Harvard University Press.

DE BEAUVOIR, S. (1988) *The Second Sex*, London: Penguin.

DE BEAUVOIR, S. (1990) 'Must we burn Sade?' in SADE, D. A. F. *The One Hundred and Twenty Days of Sodom*, London: Arrow.

DE GROOT, J. (1989) '"Sex" and "race": the construction of language and image in the nineteenth century', in MENDUS, S. and RENDALL, J. (Eds) *Sexuality and Subordination*, London: Routledge.

DE IMAZ, J. L. (1962) *La Clasa Alta de Buenos Aires*, Buenos Aires: Editorial Universidad de Buenos Aires.

DE QUIRÓS, B. (1912) *Modern Theories of Criminality*, Boston: Little, Brown & Company.

DE RIVER, J. P. (1956) *The Sexual Criminal: a Psychoanalytical Study*, Springfield, Illinois: C.C. Thomas.

DE SADE, D. A. F. (1990) *The One Hundred and Twenty Days of Sodom*, London: Arrow.

DE SADE, D. A. F. (1991) *Juliette*, London: Arrow.

DE SADE, D. A. F. (1992) *Justine: or the Misfortunes of Virtue, and Other Early Tales*, Oxford: Oxford University Press.

DEL OLMO, R. (1990) 'The hidden face of drugs', *Social Justice*, **18**, pp. 190–206.

DEAN, M. (1994) *Critical and Effective Histories: Foucault's Methods and Historical Sociology*, London: Routledge.

DEBORD, G. (1983) *The Society of the Spectacle*, Detroit: Black & Red.

DECKER, A. (1984 and 1985) 'The legacy of shame', *Art News*, December 1984 and February 1985.

DEINHARD, H. (1970) *Meaning and Expression: Towards Sociology of Art*, Boston: Beacon Press.

DELEUZE, G. (1991) *Coldness and Cruelty*, New York: Zone Books.

DELEUZE, G. and GUATTARI, F. (1983) *Anti-Oedipus: Capitalism and Schizophrenia*, London: Athlone Press.

DELEUZE, G. and GUATTARI, F. (1988) *A Thousand Plateaus*, London: Athlone Press.

DELOLME, J. L. (1783) *The History of the Flagellants: Otherwise, of Religious Flagellations Among Different Nations and Especially Among Christians. Being a Paraphrase on the Historia Flagellantium of the Abbé Boileau*, London: G. Robinson.

DER DERIAN, J. (1992) *Antidiplomacy: Spies, Terror, Speed, and War*, Oxford: Blackwell.

DERBYSHIRE, I. (1990) *Politics in the United States from Carter to Bush*, Edinburgh: Chambers.

DERRIDA, J. (1987) 'Otobiographies: Nietzsche and the politics of the proper name', in BLOOM, H. (Ed.) *Friedrich Nietzsche*, New York: Chelsea House.

DERRIDA, J. (1990) *Writing and Difference*, London: Routledge.

DERRIDA, J. (1992) 'Force of law: the mystical foundation of authority', in CORNELL, D. (Ed.) *Deconstruction and the Possibility of Justice*, New York: Routledge.

DESCOMBES, V. (1980) *Modern French Philosophy*, Cambridge: Cambridge University Press.

DEUTSCH, H. (1930) 'The significance of masochism in the mental life of women', *International Journal of Psychoanalysis*, **11**, pp. 48–60.

DI TELLA, T. (1965) 'Populism and reform in Latin America', in VELIZ, C. (Ed.) *Obstacles to Change in Latin America*, Oxford: Oxford University Press.

DICKS, H. V. (1972) *Licensed Mass Murder*, London: Heinemann.

DIONNE, E. J. (1992) *Why Americans Hate Politics*, New York: Simon & Schuster.

DONAGHUE, E. (1993) *Passions Between Women: British Lesbian Culture 1668–1801*, London: Scarlet Press.

DOUGLAS, M. (1992) *Risk and Blame: Essays in Cultural Theory*, London and New York: Routledge.

DOWNS, A. (1973) *Opening up of the Suburbs*, New Haven: Yale University Press.

DU PREEZ, P. (1994) *Genocide: the Psychology of Mass Murder*, London: Boyars/Bowerdean.

EISLER, R. (1951) *Man into Wolf: an Anthropological Interpretation of Sadism, Masochism, and Lycanthropy*, London: Routledge & Kegan Paul.

EISSLER, K. D. (1975) 'The fall of man', *Psychoanalytic Study of the Child*, **30**, pp. 589–646.

ELLIOTT, A. (1992) *Social Theory and Psychoanalysis in Transition: Self and Society from Freud to Kristeva*, Oxford: Blackwell.

ENDELMAN, R. (1981) *Psyche and Society: Exploration in Psychoanalytic Sociology*, New York: Columbia University Press.

ERIKSON, E. (1959) *Identity and the Life Cycle*, New York: International Universities Press.

ERIKSON, E. (1964) *Insight and Responsibility*, New York: Norton.

EULENBERG, A. (1902) *Sadismus und Masochismus*, London.

FANDOZZI, P. R. (1982) *Nihilism and Technology: a Heideggerian Investigation*, Washington: University Press of America.

FANON, F. (1967) *The Wretched of the Earth*, Harmondsworth: Penguin.

FEDERN, E. (1990) *Witnessing Psychoanalysis: From Vienna Back to Vienna via Buchenwald and the USA*, London: Kamac.

FEIN, H. L. (1993) *Genocide: a Sociological Perspective*, London: Sage.

FEINGOLD, H. L. (1983) 'How Unique is the Holocaust', in GROBMAN, A. and LANDES, D. (Eds) *Genocide: Critical Issues of the Holocaust*, Los Angeles: The Simon Wiesenthal Centre.

FEST, J. C. (1970) *The Face of the Third Reich*, New York: Pantheon.

FIERZ-DAVID, L. (1988) *Women's Dionysian Initiation: the Villa of Mysteries in Pompeii*, Dallas, TX: Spring Publications.

FILLOL, T. R. (1961) *Social factors in Economic Development: the Argentine Case*, Cambridge, MA: MIT Press.

FISKE, J. and HARTLEY, J. (1978) *Reading Television*, London: Methuen.

FLYNN, P. (1978) *Brazil: a Political Analysis*, London: Ernest Benn.

FORGACS, D. (Ed.) (1990) *A Gramsci Reader*, London: Lawrence & Wishart.

FORGACS, D. (1994) 'Fascism, violence and modernity', in HOWLETT, J. and MENGHAM, R. (Eds) *The Violent Muse: Violence and the Artistic Imagination in Europe, 1910–1939*, Manchester: Manchester University Press.

FOUCAULT, M. (1961) *Madness and Civilization: a History of Insanity in the Age of Reason*, London: Routledge.

FOUCAULT, M. (1977a) *Discipline and Punish: the Birth of the Prison*, Harmondsworth: Penguin.

FOUCAULT, M. (1977b) *Language, Counter-Memory, Practice: Selected Essays and Interviews*, Oxford: Blackwell.

FOUCAULT, M. (1979) *The History of Sexuality, Volume One*, Harmondsworth: Penguin.

FOUCAULT, M. (1980a) *Herculine Barbin: Being the Recently Discovered Memoirs of a Nineteenth-Century French Hermaphrodite*, Brighton: Harvester.

FOUCAULT, M. (1980b) *Power/Knowledge*, Harmondsworth: Penguin.

FOUCAULT, M. (1984) 'Nietzsche, genealogy, history', in RABINOW, P. (Ed.) *The Foucault Reader*, London: Penguin.

FOUCAULT, M. (1987) *The Use of Pleasure: the History of Sexuality, Volume Two*, Harmondsworth: Penguin.

FOUCAULT, M. (1988) *Politics, Philosophy, Culture: Interviews and Other Writings, 1977–1984*, London: Routledge.

FOUCAULT, M. (1991) *Remarks on Marx*, New York: Columbia University Press.

FRASER, J. (1974) *Violence in the Arts*, Cambridge: Cambridge University Press.

FREIDLANDER, H. and MITTON, S. (1982) *The Holocaust: Ideology, Bureaucracy and Genocide*, New York: Kraus Milwood.

FRENKEL-BRUNSWIK, E. (1950a) 'The interviews as an approach to the prejudiced personality', in ADORNO, T. W., FRENKEL-BRUNSWIK, E., LEVINSON, D. J. and SANFORD, R. N. (Eds) *The Authoritarian Personality*, London: Norton.

FRENKEL-BRUNSWIK, E. (1950b) 'Parents, childhood, sex, people and self as seen through the interviews', in ADORNO, T. W., FRENKEL-BRUNSWIK, E., LEVINSON, D. J. and SANFORD, R. N. (Eds) *The Authoritarian Personality*, London: Norton.

FRENKEL-BRUNSWIK, E. (1950c) 'Comprehensive scores and summary of interview results', in ADORNO, T. W., FRENKEL-BRUNSWIK, E., LEVINSON, D. J. and SANFORD, R. N. (Eds) *The Authoritarian Personality*, London: Norton.

FREUD, S. (1953) *The Interpretation of Dreams*, Harmondsworth: Penguin.

FREUD, S. (1960) *Totem and Taboo*, London: Ark.

FREUD, S. (1967) *New Introductory Lectures on Psychoanalysis*, London: Hogarth Press.

FREUD, S. (1983) *The Penguin Freud Library, Volume 10, On Psychopathology* (J. STRACHEY, Ed.), Harmondsworth: Penguin.

FREUD, S. (1985) *The Penguin Freud Library, Volume 12, Civilization, Society and Religion* (J. STRACHEY, Ed.), Harmondsworth: Penguin.

FREUD, S. (1986) *The Essentials of Psychoanalysis* (P. GAY, Ed.), Harmondsworth: Penguin.

FREUD, S. (1991) 'Femininity' in *The Essentials of Psychoanalysis*, Harmondsworth: Penguin.

FRIDAY, N. (1983) *My Secret Garden*, London: Quartet.

FROMM, E. (1941) *Escape From Freedom*, London: Ark.

FROMM, E. (1942) *The Fear of Freedom*, London: Routledge & Kegan Paul.

FROMM, E. (1989) 'Psychoanalysis and sociology', in BRONNER, S. E. and KELLNER, D. (Eds) *Critical Theory and Society: A Reader*, London: Routledge.

GARLAND, D. (1990) 'Frameworks of inquiry in the sociology of punishment', *British Journal of Sociology*, **14**, pp. 1–15.

GELSTHORPE, L. and MORRIS, A. (1990) *Feminist Perspectives in Criminology*, Milton Keynes: Open University Press.

GERMANI, G. (1965) *Authoritarianism, Fascism, and National Populism*, New Jersey: Transaction Books.

GIBSON, I. (1979) *The English Vice: Beating, Sex and Shame in Victorian England and After*, London: Duckworth.

GIDDENS, A. (1985) *The Nation State and Violence*, Cambridge: Polity.

GIDDENS, A. (1990) *The Consequences of Modernity*, Cambridge: Polity.

GIDDENS, A. (1991) *Modernity and Self-Identity: Self and Society in the Late Modern Age*, Cambridge: Polity.

GIDDENS, A. (1992) *The Transformation of Intimacy: Sexuality, Love and Eroticism in Modern Societies*, Cambridge: Polity.

GIDDENS, A. (1994) 'Living in a post-traditional society', in BECK, U., GIDDENS, A. and LASH, S. (Eds) *Reflexive Modernization: Politics, Tradition and Aesthetics in the Modern Social Order*, Cambridge: Polity.

GILLIARD, D. and BECK, A. (1993) 'Prisoners in 1993', *Bureau of Justice Statistics Bulletin*, Washington, D.C.: US Department of Justice.

GILLIARD, D. (1994) 'Prisoners in 1994', *Bureau of Justice Statistics Bulletin*, Washington, D.C.: US Department of Justice.

GILMAN, S. L. (1985) *Difference and Pathology: Stereotypes of Sexuality, Race and Madness*, London: Cornell University Press.

GIMPEL, J. (1969) *The Cult of Art Against Art and Artists*, New York: Stein & Day.

GIRARD, R. (1978) *Violence and the Sacred*, Baltimore: John Hopkins University Press.

GIRARD, R. (1986) *The Scapegoat*, Baltimore: John Hopkins University Press.

GIRARD, R. (1987) *Things Hidden Since the Foundation of the World*, Stanford: Stanford University Press.

GITLIN, T. (1980) *The Whole World is Watching*, London: University of California.

GLASER, H. (1978) *The Cultural Roots of National Socialism*, London: Croom Helm.

GLICK, R. A. and MEYERS, D. I. (Eds) (1988) *Masochism: Current Psychoanalytic Perspectives*, London: Analytic Press.

GOLDING, S. (1993) 'The excess: an added remark on sex, rubber, ethics, and other impurities', *New Formations*, **7**, pp. 23–8.

GOODE, E. and BEN-YEHUDA, N. (1994) *Moral Panics: the Social Construction of Deviance*, Oxford: Blackwell.

GOODRICH, P. (1986) *Reading the Law*, Oxford: Blackwell.

GOSSELIN, C. C. (1987) 'The sadomasochistic contract', in WILSON, G. D. (Ed.) *Variant Sexuality: Research and Theory*, Baltimore, Maryland: Johns Hopkins University Press.

GOULDNER, A. (1976) *The Dialectic of Ideology and Technology*, London: Macmillan.

GRAMSCI, A. (1971) *Selections from the Prison Notebooks*, London: Lawrence & Wisehart.

GRANT, L. H. (1995) 'Populism as social control in Latin America', unpublished Mphil thesis, Cambridge University.

GREENBERG, D. (1981) *Crime and Capitalism*, New York: Mayfield Publishing Co.

GUILLEBAUD, C. W. (1942) *The Social Policy of Nazi Germany*, Cambridge: Cambridge University Press.

HABERMAS, J. (1994) *The Past as Future*, Cambridge: Polity.

HAGELL, A. and NEWBURN, T. (1994) *Young Offenders and the Media: Viewing Habits and Preferences*, London: Policy Studies Institute.

HALL, C. (1983) (compiled by) *Video, Violence and Children*, London: Casis Projects.

HALL, N. (1988) *Those Women*, Dallas, TX: Spring Publications.

HALL, S. (1979) *Drifting into a Law and Order Society*, Great Britain: Cobden Trust.

HALL, S. (1983) *The Politics of Thatcherism*, London: Lawrence & Wishart.

References

HALL, S., *et al.*, (1978) *Policing the Crisis: Mugging, the State, and Law and Order*, London: Macmillan.

HAMILTON, G. (1978) *Painting and Sculpture in Europe 1880–1940*, London: Penguin.

HAMPSHIRE, S. (1978) *Public and Private Morality*, New York: Cambridge University Press.

HANSON, J. H. (1984) 'Nazi-culture: the social uses of fantasy as repression', in LUEL, S. A. and MARCUS, P. (Eds) *Psychoanalytic Reflections on the Holocaust: Selected Essays*, New York: KTAV.

HARTMANN, H., KRIS, E. and LOEWENSTEIN, R. M. (1951) 'Some psychoanalytic comments on culture and personality', in WILBUR, G. and MUENSTERBERGER, W. (Eds) *Psychoanalysis and Culture*, New York: International Universities Press.

HAYMAN, R. (1978) *De Sade: a Critical Biography*, London: Constable.

HEBDIGE, D. (1988) *Hiding in the Light*, London: Routledge.

HEGER, H. (1980) *The Men with the Pink Triangle*, London: GMP.

HENNESSY, A. (1969) 'Populism: Its natural consequences', in IONESCU, G. and GELLNER, E. (Eds) *Populism: Its meanings and national characteristics*, London: Weidenfield and Nicolson.

HIGGINS, P. (1994) *A Queer Reader*, London: Methuen.

HILBERG, R. (1985) *The Destruction of the European Jews*, London: Holmes and Meier.

HINZ, B. (1979) *Art in the Third Reich*, Oxford: Blackwell.

HITLER, A. (1974) *Mein Kampf*, London: Hutchinson.

HODGSON, G. (1976) *America in Our Times*, Garden City: Doubleday.

HOLUB, R. (1992) *Antonio Gramsci: Beyond Marxism and Postmodernism*, London: Routledge.

HORKHEIMER, M. (1950) 'Preface', in ADORNO, T. W., FRENKEL-BRUNSWIK, E., LEVINSON, D. J. and SANFORD, R. N. (Eds) *The Authoritarian Personality*, London: Norton.

HORKHEIMER, M. (1975) 'The authoritarian state', in ARATO, A. and GEBHARDT, E. (Eds) *The Essential Frankfurt School Reader*, New York: Urizen Books.

HORKHEIMER, M. (1982) 'Egoism and the Freedom Movement: On the Anthropology of the Bourgeois Era', *Telos*, **54**, pp. 10–60.

HORNEY, K. (1937) *The Neurotic Personality of Our Time*, New York: Norton.

HOROWITZ, I. L. (1980) *Taking Lives: Genocide and State Power*, London: Transaction Books.

HOWLETT, J. and MENGHAM, R. (Eds) (1994) *The Violent Muse: Violence and the Artistic Imagination in Europe, 1910–1939*, Manchester: Manchester University Press.

HOY, D. C. (1986) *Foucault: a Critical Reader*, New York: Blackwell.

HUTCHINGS, P. (1993) *Hammer and Beyond: the British Horror Film*, Manchester: Manchester University Press.

INNIS, L. and FEAGIN, J. (1988) 'Race and ideology in the 1980s: the Black "underclass" ideology in race relations analysis', *Social Justice*, **16**(4), pp. 13–34.

IONESCO, G. and GELLNER, E. (1969) *Populism: its National Characteristics*, London: Weidenfield & Nicolson.

ISAAC, J. C. (1992) *Arendt, Camus and Modern Rebellion*, London: Yale University Press.

JAHANBEGBO, R. (1993) *Conversations with Isaiah Berlin*, London: Phoenix.

JEFFREYS, S. (1994) *The Lesbian Heresy: a Feminist Perspective on the Lesbian Sexual Revolution*, London: The Womens Press.

JESSOP, B., BONNET, K., BROMLEY, S. and LING, T. (1984) *Thatcherism: a Tale of Two Nations*, Cambridge: Polity.

JOHNS, C. (1991) 'The war on drugs: why the administration continues to pursue a policy of criminalization and enforcement', *Social Justice*, **18**, pp. 147–65.

JOSEPHS, R. (1945) *Argentine Diary*, London: Victor & Gollancz.

JUNG, C. G. (1933) *Modern Man in Search of a Soul*, London: Ark.

JUNG, C. G. (1958) *The Undiscovered Self*, London: Routledge.

KAFKA, F. (1961) 'In the penal settlement', in *Metamorphosis and Other Stories*, Harmondsworth: Penguin.

KAPLAN, H. (1994) *Conscience and Memory: Meditations in a Museum of the Holocaust*, London: University of Chicago Press.

KATZ, J. (1980) *From Prejudice to Destruction: Antisemitism, 1700–1933*, Cambridge, MA: Harvard University Press.

KATZ, S. I. (1981) 'The unique intentionality of the Holocaust', *Modern Judaism*, **1**, p. 1.

KAYE, H. L. (1991) 'A false convergence: Freud and the Hobbesian problem of order', *Sociological Theory*, **9**, pp. 87–112.

KEAT, R. and URRY, J. (1975) *Social Theory as Science*, London: Routledge & Kegan Paul.

KELLNER, D. (1984) *Herbert Marcuse and the Crisis of Marxism*, London: Macmillan.

KELLNER, D. (1989) *Jean Baudrillard: From Marxism to Postmodernism and Beyond*, Cambridge: Polity.

KIRKPATRICK, J. (1971) *Leader and Vanguard in Mass Society: a Study of Peronist Argentina*, Cambridge, MA: MIT Press.

KOLAKOWSKI, L. (1975) 'The psychoanlytic theory of culture', in BOYERS, R. (Ed.) *Psychological Men*, New York: Harper & Row.

KRAFFT-EBBING, R. von (1886) *Psychopathia Sexualis*, trans. of 7th German Ed. by CHADDOCK, C. G., Philadelphia: F. A. Davis.

KRAMER, J. and STEFFENSMEIR, D. (1993) 'Race and imprisonment decisions', *Sociological Quarterly*, **34**, pp. 367–76.

KREN, G. and RAPPOPORT, L. (1980) *The Holocaust and the Crisis of Human Behaviour*, New York: Holmes & Meier.

KROKER, A. (1992) *The Possessed Individual: Technology and Postmodernity*, London: Macmillan.

KUHNL, R. (1975) 'Problems of a theory of German Fascism: a critique of the dominant interpretations', *New German Critique*, **4**, pp. 26–50.

KUNDERA, M. (1991) 'The Hitchhiking Game', in *Laughable Loves*, London: Faber & Faber.

KUNDERA, M. (1991) *Laughable Loves*, London: Faber & Faber.

KUPER, L. (1981) *Genocide: Its Political Use in the Twentieth Century*, Harmondsworth: Penguin.

LACLAU, E. (1977) *Politics and Ideology in Marxist Theory*, London: NLB.

LAING, R. D. and COOPER, D. G. (1964) *Reason and Violence: a Decade of Sartre's Philosophy, 1950–1960*, London: Tavistock.

LAND, N. (1992) *The Thirst for Annihilation: Georges Bataille and Virulent Nihilism*, London: Routledge.

LANE, B. M. (1968) *Architecture and Politics in Germany 1918–45*, Cambridge, MA: Harvard University Press.

LAQUER, T. (1990) *Making Sex: Body and Gender from the Greeks to Freud*, Cambridge, MA: Harvard University Press.

LASH, S. and URRY, J. (1987) *The End of Organised Capitalism*, Cambridge: Polity.

LASWELL, H. D. (1933) 'The psychology of Hitlerism', *Political Quarterly*, **4**, pp. 373–84.

LAW COMMISSION (1994) *Consultation Paper No. 134, Consent and Offences Against the Person*, London: HMSO.

LEHMANN-HAUPT, H. (1954) *Art Under Dictatorship*, New York: Oxford University Press.

LEITH, J. (1965) *The Idea of Art as Propaganda in France, 1750–1799*, Toronto: Toronto University Press.

LEVI, P. (1988) *The Drowned and The Saved*, London: Abacus.

LEVINE, D. N. (1993) 'Freud, Weber, and Modern Rationales of Conscience', in PRAGER, J. and RUSTIN, M. (Eds) Psychoanalytic Sociology, Volume One, Aldershot: Albert Edgar.

LEVINE, R. M. (1970) *The Vargas Regime: the Critical Years, 1934–1938*, New York: Columbia University Press.

LEVINSON, D. J. (1950a) 'The study of anti-semitic ideology', in ADORNO, T. W., FRENKEL-BRUNSWIK, E., LEVINSON, D. J. and SANFORD, R. N. (Eds) *The Authoritarian Personality*, London: Norton.

LEVINSON, D. J. (1950b) 'The study of ethnocentric ideology', in ADORNO, T. W., FRENKEL-BRUNSWIK, E., LEVINSON, D. J. and SANFORD, R. N. (Eds) *The Authoritarian Personality*, London: Norton.

LEVINSON, D. J. (1950c) 'Projective questions in the study of personality and odeology', in ADORNO, T. W., FRENKEL-BRUNSWIK, E., LEVINSON, D. J. and SANFORD, R. N. (Eds) *The Authoritarian Personality*, London: Norton.

LEVITT, E. E., MOSER, C. and JAMISON, K. V. (1994) 'The prevalence and some attributes of females in the sadomasochistic subculture: a second report', *Archives of Sexual Behaviour*, **23**, pp. 465–73.

LIEBES, T. and KATZ, E. (1990) *The Export of Meaning*, Oxford: Oxford University Press.

LIFTON, R. J. (1984) 'Medicalized killing in Auschwitz', in LUEL, S. A. and MARCUS, P. (Eds) *Psychoanalytic Reflections on the Holocaust: Selected Essays*, New York: KTAV.

LIFTON, R. J. (1986) *The Nazi Doctors: Medical Killing and the Psychology of Genocide*, London: Macmillan.

LIFTON, R. J. (1988) 'Lift unworthy of life: Nazi racial views', in BRAHAM, R. L. (Ed.) *The Psychological Perspectives of the Holocaust and its Aftermath*, New York: Columbia University Press.

LIPSTADT, D. (1993) *Denying the Holocaust: the Growing Assault on Truth and Memory*, London: Penguin.

LLOYD, G. (1983) *The Man of Reason*, London: Methuen.

LOPEZ-REY, M. (1970) *Crime*, London: Routledge.

LUEL, S. A. and MARCUS, P. (1984a) 'Psychoanalysis and the Holocaust: an introduction', in LUEL, S. A. and MARCUS, P. (Eds) *Psychoanalytic Reflections on the Holocaust: Selected Essays*, New York: KTAV.

LUEL, S. A. and MARCUS, P. (1984b) 'Psychoanalysis and the Holocaust: a roundtable', in LUEL, S. A. and MARCUS, P. (Eds) *Psychoanalytic Reflections on the Holocaust: Selected Essays*, New York: KTAV.

LYOTARD, J.-F. (1985) *The Postmodern Condition: a Report on Knowledge*, Manchester: Manchester University Press.

MacCULLOCH, M. *et al.* (1983) 'Sadistic fantasy, sadistic behaviour and offending' *British Journal of Psychiatry*, **143**, pp. 20–9.

MADONNA (1992) *Sex*, London: Secker & Warburg.

MADRIZ, E. (1986) *Toward a Critical Theory of Social Control*, Maracaibo, Venezuela: Instituta de Criminologia, Universidad del Zuila.

MANVELL, R. and FRAENKEL, H. (1967) *The Incomparable Crime*, London: Heinemann.

MALINOWSKI, B. (1931) 'Culture', in *Encyclopaedia of the Social Sciences, volume 4*, New York: Macmillan.

MARCUS, M. (1978) *A Taste for Pain: On Masochism and Female Sexuality*, London: Souvenir Press.

MARCUSE, H. (1956) *Eros and Civilization: a Philosophical Inquiry into Freud*, London: Ark.

MARCUSE, H. (1968) *Negations: Essays in Critical Theory*, Harmondsworth: Penguin.

MASTROFSKI, S. D. (1988) 'Zero tolerance for zero-tolerance policy', *Contemporary Crisis*, **12**, pp. 187–9.

McKENNA, A. J. (1992) *Violence and Difference: Girard, Derrida and Deconstruction*, Chicago: University of Illinois Press.

McLENNAN, G. (1981) *Marxism and the Methodologies of History*, London: Verso.

McWILLIAMS, J. and KRAMER, J. (1994) 'Throw away the key: assessing the impact of minimum mandatory sentences for drug offenders', unpublished paper, presented in a public forum by the Pennsylvania State Sentencing Commission.

MEAD, G. H. (1970) *Mind, Self and Society*, Chicago: Chicago University Press.

MEDVED, M. (1992) *Hollywood vs America: Popular Culture and the War on Traditional Values*, New York: Harper Collins.

MERCK, M. (1993) 'The feminist ethics of lesbian S/M', in *Perversions: Deviant Readings*, London: Virago.

MERLEAU-PONTY, M. (1969) *Humanism and Terror*, London: Beacon Press.

MERRIN, W. (1994) 'Uncritical criticism? Norris, Baudrillard and the Gulf War', *Economy and Society*, **23**, pp. 433–58.

MESTROVIC, S. G. (1993) *The Barbarian Temperament*, London: Routledge.

MESTROVIC, S. G. (1994) *The Balkanization of the West: the Confluence of Postmodernism and Postcommunism*, London: Routledge.

METZ, C. (1990) *Psychoanalysis and Cinema: the Imaginary Signifier*, Hampshire: Macmillan.

MILGRAM, S. (1974) *Obedience to Authority*, New York: Harper.

MILLER, J. (1990) 'Carnivals of atrocity: Foucault, Nietzsche, cruelty in political theory', *Political Theory*, **18**, pp. 470–91.

MILLETT, K. (1969) *Sexual Politics*, London: Virago.

MILLON, H. A. and NOCHLIN, L. (Eds) (1978) *Art and Architecture in the Service of Politics*, Cambridge, MA: MIT Press.

MILLS, D. (1993) 'Civil Peace', *The Philadelphia Inquirer Magazine*, 18 February, p. 6.

MILOVANOVIC, D. (1992) *Postmodern Law and Disorder: Psychoanalytic Semiotics, Chaos and Juridic Exegeses*, Liverpool: Deborah Charles Publications.

MILWARD, A. S. (1965) *The German Economy at War*, London: Athlone.

MITCHELL, J. (1975) *Psychoanalysis and Feminism*, Harmondsworth: Penguin.

References

MITSCHERLICH, A., LORENZER, A., HORN, K., DAHMER, H., SCHWANENBERG, E., BREDE, K. and BERNDT, H. (1970) 'On psychoanalysis and sociology', *International Journal of Psychoanalysis*, **51**, pp. 33–48.

MIZRUCHI, E. H. (1983) *Regulating Society: Marginality and Social Control in Historical Perspective*, New York: Free Press.

MOLL, A. (1912) *The Sexual Life of the Child*, London.

MOORE, B. (1967) *Social Origins of Dictatorship and Democracy*, London: Allen Lane.

MOORE, B. (1978) *Injustice: The Social Basis of Obedience and Revolt*, London: Macmillan.

MOREY, M. (1992) *On Michel Foucault's philosophical style: Towards a critique of the Normal*, New York and London: Harvester Wheatsheaf.

MORRISON, W. (1994) 'Criminology, modernity and the truth of the human condition: reflections on the melancholy of postmodernism', in NELKEN, D. (Ed.) *Futures of Criminology*, London: Sage.

MOSSE, G. L. (1966) *Nazi Culture*, New York: Grossett and Dunlap.

MOSSE, G. L. (1978) *Toward the Final Solution*, London: J. M. Dent.

MOSSE, G. L. (1980) *Masses and Man: Nationalist and Fascist Perceptions of Reality*, New York: Howard Fertig.

MUNCH, E. (1978) *Symbols and Images*, Washington, DC: National Gallery of Art.

MYRDAL, G. (1944) *An American Dilemma*, New York: Harper.

NIETZSCHE, F. (1887) *The Gay Science*, London: Vintage.

NIETZSCHE, F. (1967) *The Will to Power*, New York: Vintage.

NIETZSCHE, F. (1969) *Thus Spoke Zarathrustra*, Harmondsworth: Penguin.

NIETZSCHE, F. (1973) *Beyond Good and Evil*, Harmondsworth: Penguin.

NIETZSCHE, F. (1983) 'On truth and lie', in SCHACHT, R. *Nietzche*, London: Routledge & Kegan Paul.

NIETZSCHE, F. (1994) *On the Genealogy of Morality*, Cambridge: Cambridge University Press.

NIN, A. (1969) *Delta of Venus*, Harmondsworth: Penguin.

NOLTE, E. (1965) *The Three Faces of Fascism*, London: Methuen.

NOVA, F. (1986) *Alfred Rosenberg: Nazi Theorist of the Holocaust*, New York: Hippocrene Books.

NORWOOD, R. (1986) *Women Who Love Too Much*, London: Arrow.

ORCUTT, J. and TURNER, B. (1993) 'Shocking numbers and graphic accounts: quantified images of drug problems in the print media', *Social Problems*, **40**, pp. 190–206.

PAGLIA, C. (1992) *Sex, Art and American Culture*, London: Penguin Books.

PARK, R. (1968) *The City*, Chicago: University of Chicago Press.

PARSONS, T. (1951) *Theories of Society, Volume One*, New York: Free Press.

PARSONS, T. (1952) *Social Structure and Personality*, New York: Free Press.

PARSONS, T. (1970) *The Social System*, London: Routledge & Kegan Paul.

PEARL, D., BONTHILET, L. and LAZAR, J. (Eds) (1982) *Television and Behavior*, Washington, DC: National Institute of Mental Health.

PEARSON, G. (1983) *Hooligan: a History of Respectable Fears*, Hampshire: Macmillan.

PEPINSKY, H. E. (1991) *The Geometry of Violence and Democracy*, Bloomington and Indianapolis: Indiana University Press.

PERÓN, J. D. (1950) *The Voice of Perón*, Buenos Aires: Subsecretaria de Infommaciones dela Presidencia de la Nacion Argentina.

PHILLIPS, E. (1995) 'The criminalisation of consensual sex', conference paper, presented at the British Criminology Conference, Loughborough University, 18–21 July 1995.

PHILLIPS, J. R. (1974) *The Reformation of Images: Destruction of Art in England. 1535–1660*, Berkeley: University of California Press.

PHILLIPS, K. (1990) *The Politics of Rich and Poor: Wealth and the American Electorate in the Reagan Aftermath*, New York: Harper Collins.

PINTHUS, K. (1940) 'Inside culture, inside Nazi Germany', *American Scholar*, **9**, pp. 483–95.

PLANT, S. (1992) *The Most Radical Gesture: the Situationist International in the Postmodern Age*, London: Routledge.

PLATT, T. (1987) *Crime and Social Justice*, **29**, p. 58.

PLATT, T. (1993) 'Rethinking race', *Social Justice*, **20**, pp. i–vii.

PLATT, T. (1994) 'The politics of law and order', *Social Justice*, **21**, pp. 3–13.

POLLOCK, F. (1975) 'State capitalism: its possibilities and limitations', in ARATO, A. and GEBHARDT, E. (Eds) *The Essential Frankfurt School Reader*, New York: Urizen Books.

POSTER, M. (1978) *Critical Theory of the Family*, London: Pluto Press.

POULANTZAS, N. (1978) *State Power Socialism*, London: Verso.

POWER, D. J. (1976) 'Sexual deviation and crime', *Medicine, Science and the Law*, **16**, pp. 111–28.

PRAGER, J. and RUSTIN, M. (1993) 'Introduction', in PRAGER, J. and RUSTIN, M. (Eds) *Psychoanalytic Sociology, Volume One: Social Theory*, Aldershot: Edward Elgar.

PRINZHORN, H. (1932) *Psychotherapy*, tr. and Ed. EILOART, A., London: Jonathan Cape.

QUENAU, R. (1965) *Bâtons, Chiffres et Lettres*, Paris: Gallimard.

QUINNEY, R. (1974) *Critique of Legal Order*, Boston: Little, Brown & Company.

QUINNEY, R. (1977) *Class, State, and Crime*, New York: Longman.

RAJCHMAN, J. (1991) *Truth and Eros: Foucault, Lacan, and the Question of Ethics*, London: Routledge.

RANSOME, P. (1992) *Antonio Gramsci*, New York: Harvester Wheatsheaf.

RÉAGE, P. [pseud. Aury, D.] (1954) *The Story of O*, New York: Ballantine Books.

REEMSTMA, J. P. (1993) 'Die "signatur des johrbunderts" ein kataleptischer irritum', *Mittelweg*, **36**(5), p. 9.

REICH, W. (1933) *Character Analysis*, New York: Noonday Press.

REICH, W. (1970) *The Mass Psychology of Fascism*, London: Souvenier Press.

REICHMANN, E. G. (1950) *Hostages of Civilization: the Social Sources of National Socialist Anti-Semitisms*, London: Victor Gollancz.

REIMAN, J. (1979) *The Rich Get Richer and the Poor Get Prison*, New York: Yale University Press.

REIMAN, J. (1991) *Justice and Modern Moral Philosophy*, London: Yale Press.

REITLINGER, G. (1956) *The SS: Alibi of a Nation*, London: Heinemann.

RICOEUR, P. (1981) *Hermeneutics and the Human Sciences: Essays on Language, Action and Interpretation*, Cambridge: Cambridge University Press.

RIEFF, P. (1964) *Psychoanalysis in American History and the Social Sciences*, New York: Harper & Row.

ROBERTS, P. (1993) 'Social control and the censure(s) of sex', *Crime, Law and Social Change*, **19**, pp. 171–86.

ROCK, P. (1973) *Deviant Behaviour*, London: Hutchinson.

ROCK, P. (1977) 'Review Article', *British Journal of Criminology*, **17**, pp. 392–5.

ROCK, P. (Ed.) (1994) *Latin America in the 1940s*, London: University of Califomia Press.

ROSE, J. (1986) *Sexuality in the Field of Vision*, London: Verso.

ROSENBERG, A. (1970) *Selected Writings*, London: Jonathan Cape.

ROTHMAN, G. (1971) *The Riddle of Cruelty*, New York: Philosophical Library.

ROXBOROUGH, I. (1987) 'Populism and Class Conflict: Latin American Populism' in ARCHETTI, E. P., CAMMACK, P. and ROBERTS, B. (Eds) *Latin America*, Basingstoke: Macmillan.

RUBENSTEIN, R. L. (1978) *The Cunning of History: the Holocaust and the American Future*, New York: Harper & Row.

RUMMEL, R. J. (1994) *Death by Government*, London: Transaction.

RUSTIN, M. (1991) *The Good Society and the Inner World: Psychoanalysis, Politics and Culture*, London: Verso.

SABINI, J. P. and SILVER, M. (1980) 'Destroying the innocent with a clear conscience: a sociopsychology of the Holocaust', in DIMSDALE, J. E. (Ed.) *Survivors, Victims, and Perpetrators: Essays on the Nazi Holocaust*, New York: Hemisphere.

SABOL, W. J. (1989) 'Racially disproportionate prison populations in the United States: an overview of historical patterns and review of contemporary issues', *Contemporary Crisis*, **13**, pp. 405–32.

SALT, H. S. (1916) *The Flogging Craze: a Statement of the Case Against Corporal Punishment*, London: Allen & Unwin.

SANFORD, R. N. (1950) 'The contrasting ideologies of two college men: a preliminary review', in ADORNO, T. W., FRENKEL-BRUNSWIK, E., LEVINSON, D. J. and SANFORD, R. N. (Eds) *The Authoritarian Personality*, London: Norton.

SANFORD, R. N., ADORNO, T. W., FRENKEL-BRUNSWIK, E. and LEVINSON, D. J. (1950) 'The measurement of implicit antidemocratic trends', in ADORNO, T. W., FRENKEL-BRUNSWIK, E., LEVINSON, D. J. and SANFORD, R. N. (Eds) *The Authoritarian Personality*, London: Norton.

SARAT, A. and KEARNS, T. (1991) 'A journey through forgetting', in SARAT, A. and KEARNS, T. (Eds) *The Fate of Law*, Ann Arbor, MI: University of Michigan Press.

SARTRE, J-P. (1967) 'Preface', in FANON, F. *The Wretched of the Earth*, London: Routledge & Kegan Paul.

SARTRE, J-P. (1968) *On Genocides*, Boston: Beacon Press.

SARTRE, J-P. (1973) *Existentialism and Humanism*, London: Methuen.

SARTRE, J-P. (1988) *Saint Genet*, London, Heinemann.

SARTRE, J-P. (1995) *Being and Nothingness*, London: Routledge.

SARUP, M. (1993) 'Lacan and Film', in SARUP, M. (Ed.) *Jacques Lacan*, New York: Harvester Wheatsheaf.

SCARRY, E. (1985) *The Body in Pain: the Making and Unmaking of the World*, New York: Oxford University Press.

SCHAPIRO, L. (Ed.) (1983) *Totalitarianism*, London: Macmillan.

SCHILLER, F. (1967) *On the Aesthetic Education of Man in a Series of Letters*, tr. WILKINSON, E. and WILLOUGHBY, J., Oxford: Oxford University Press.

SCHWENDINGER, H. and SCHWENDINGER, J. (1981) 'Social class and the definition of crime', in PLATT, T. and TAKAGI, P. (Eds) *Crime and Social Justice*, London: Macmillan.

SCOTT, G. R. (1938) *The History of Corporal Punishment: a Survey of Flagellation in its Historical, Anthropological and Sociological Aspects*, London: Torchstream Books.

SERENY, G. (1972) *The Case of Mary Bell*, London: Methuen.

SERENY, G. (1974) *Into That Darkness*, London: Andre Deutsch.

SIEBERS, T. (1988) *The Ethics of Criticism*, Ithaca: Cornell University Press.

SINCLAIR, P. R. (1976) 'Fascism and crisis in capitalist society', *New German Critique*, **9**, pp. 87–112.

SINGER, J. and SINGER, D. (1981) *Television. Imagination and Aggression: a Study of Pre-schoolers*, New Jersey: Lawrence Erlbaum Associates.

SKIDMORE, T. E. (1967) *Politics in Brazil*, New York: Oxford University Press.

SLATTERY, B. (1990) 'The myth of retributive justice', in The Canadian Section of the International Society of Law and Social Philosophy (Eds) *Retribution and Its Critics*, Stuttgart: FS Verlag.

SMELSER, N. J. (1967) 'Sociology and the other social sciences' in LAZARSFELD, P. F., SEWELL, W. H. and WILENSKY, H. L. (Eds) *The Uses of Sociology*, New York: Basic.

SMELSER, N. J. (1993) 'The psychoanlytic mode of inquiry in the context of the behavioral and social sciences', in PRAGER, J. and RUSTIN, M. (Eds) *Psychoanalytic Sociology: Volume One*, Aldershot: Edward Elgar.

SOREL, G. (1961) *Reflections On Violence*, New York: Collier-Macmillan.

SPARKS, R. (1983) *Fictional Representations of Crime and Law: Enforcement on British Television*, Cambridge: Institute of Criminology.

SPARKS, R. (1992) *Television and the Drama of Crime: Moral Tales and the Place of Crime in Public Life*, Buckingham: Open University Press.

SPENGLER, A. (1983) 'Manifest sadomasochism of males', in WEINBERG, T. and KAMEL, G. W. L. (Eds) *S and M: Studies in Sadomasochism*, Buffalo: Prometheus.

SREBENY MOHAMMADI, M. (1992) 'The global and the local in international communications', in CURRAN, J. and GUREVITCH, M. (Eds) *Mass Media and Society*, London: Edward Arnold.

STAUB, E. (1989) *The Roots of Evil: the Origins of Genocide and Other Group Violence*, Cambridge: Cambridge University Press.

STEIN, S. (1987) 'Social Control', in ARCHETTI, E. P., CAMMACK, P. and ROBERTS, B. (Eds) *Latin America*, Basingstoke: Macmillan.

STEINER, J. M. (1976) *Power Politics and Social Change in National Socialist Germany*, The Hague: Monton.

STERN, F. (1971) 'The German past, the American present', *Columbia Forum, New York*.

STERN, F. (1981) *The Politics of Despair: a Study in the Rise of Germanic Ideology*, Berkeley: University of California Press.

STERNELL, Z. (1994) *The Birth of Fascist Ideology*, Princeton: Princeton University Press.

STOLLMAN, R. (1978) 'Fascist politics as a total work of art: tendencies of the aesthetizaion political life in National Socialism', *New German Critique*, **14**, pp. 41–60.

STORR, A. (1991) *Human Destructiveness: the Roots of Genocide and Human Cruelty*, London: Routledge.

STROMBERG, R. N. (1968) *European Intellectual History Since 1789*, New York: Meredith.

SUMNER, C. S. (1976) 'Marxism and deviancy theory', in WILES, P. (Ed.) *Sociology of Crime and Delinquency*, London: Martin Robertson.

SUMNER, C. S. (1982) 'The ideological nature of the law', in BEIRNE, P. and QUINNEY, R. (Eds) *Marxism and Law*, New York: Wiley & Sons.

SUMNER, C. S. (Ed.) (1990a) *Censure, Politics and Criminal Justice*, Buckingham: Open University Press.

SUMNER, C. S. (1990b) 'Foucault, gender and the censure of deviance', in GELSTHORPE, L. and MORRIS, A. (Eds) *Feminist Perspectives in Criminology*, Buckingham: Open University Press.

SUMNER, C. S. (1990c) 'Rethinking deviance: towards a sociology of censure', in SUMNER, C. (Ed.) *Censure, Politics And Criminal Justice*, Milton Keynes: Open University Press.

SUMNER, C. S. (1994) *The Sociology of Deviance: an Obituary*, Buckingham: Open University Press.

SURVEY OF STATE PRISON INMATES, (1991), Washington DC, Bureau of Justice Statistics.

SURVEY OF STATE PRISON INMATES, (1992), Washington DC, Bureau of Justice Statistics.

TANNAHILL, R. (1981) *Sex in History*, London: Abacus.

TARANTINO, Q. (1995) *True Romance*, London: Faber & Faber.

TAYLOR, A. J. P. (1954) *The Struggle for Mastery in Europe, 1848–1918*, Oxford: Clarendon Press.

TAYLOR, B. and VAN DER WILL, W. (1990) *The Nazification of Art*, Winchester: Winchester Press.

THEWELEIT, K. (1987) *Male Fantasies: Women, Floods, Bodies, History*, Cambridge: Polity.

THEWELEIT, K. (1989) *Male Fantasies: Male Bodies, Psychoanalysing the White Terror*, Cambridge: Polity.

THOMAS. C. Y. (1984) *The Rise of the Authoritarian State in Peripheral Societies*, New York: Monthly Review Press.

THOMPSON, J. B. (1990) *Ideology and Modern Culture: Critical Social Theory in the Era of Mass Communication*, Cambridge: Polity.

THOMPSON, M. (1991) *Leatherfolk*, Boston: Alyson Publications.

THOMPSON, W. (1994) *Sadomasochism: Painful Perversion or Pleasurable Play?*, London: Cassel.

TOCH, H. and ADAMS, K. (1989) *The Disturbed Violent Offender*, New Haven: Yale University Press.

TREVOR-ROPER, H. (1970) *The Plunder of the Arts in the Seventeenth Century*, London: Thames & Hudson.

TURNER, C. and CARTER, E. (1986) 'Political somatics: notes on Klaus Theweleit's "Male Fantasies"', in BURGIN, V., DONALD, J. and KAPLAN, C. (Eds) *Formations Of Fantasy*, London: Methuen.

TWITCHELL, J. (1989) *Preposterous Violence: Facts of Aggression in Modern Culture*, New York: Oxford University Press.

TYDEMAN, J. and JAKES KELM, E. (1986) *New Media in Europe: Satellites, Cable, VCRs, Videotex*, Maidenhead: McGraw.

URIEL, T. (1975) *Christians and Jews in Germany: Religion, Politics and Ideology, 1870–1914*, Ithaca: Cornell University Press.

VALENTIN, V. (1946) *The German People: Their History and Civilization from the Holy Roman Empire to the Third Reich*, New York: Knopf.

VAN DEN HAAG, E. (1975) *Punishing Criminals*, New York: Basic Books.

VOGLER, R. (1991) *Reading the Riot Act: the Magistracy, the Police and the Army in Civil Disorder*, Milton Keynes: Open University Press.

VON BROCKDORF, E. (1972) *Artistry of the Mentally Ill*, New York: Springer.

VON KRAFFT-EBING, R. (1965) *Psychopathia Sexualis: Aberrations of Sexual Life, a Medico-Legal Study for Doctors and Lawyers*, London: Panther.

VON SACHER-MASOCH (1991) 'Venus in Furs', in DELEUZE, G. (Ed.) *Coldness and Cruelty*, New York: Zone Books.

WALLACE, H. S. (1993) 'Mandatory minimums and the betrayal of sentencing', *Federal Bar News and Journal*, **11**, p. 1.

WALLERSTEIN, R. S. and SMELSER, N. J. (1969) 'Psychoanalysis and sociology: articulations and applications', *International Journal of Psychoanalysis*, **50**, pp. 693–710.

WALLIMANRH, I. and DOBKOWSKI, M. N. (Eds) (1987) *Genocide and the Modern Age*, London: Greenwood Press.

WALTER, R. J. (1968) *Student Politics in Argentina: the University Reform and its Effects, 1918–1964*, New York: Basic Books.

WANGH, M. (1963) 'National Socialism and the genocide of the jews: a psychoanalytic study of a historical event', *International Journal of Psychoanalysis*, **45**, pp. 386–95.

WARNOCK, M. (1995) 'Introduction', in SARTRE, J-P. *Being and Nothingness*, London: Routledge.

WASKO, J. (1994) *Hollywood in the Information Age: Beyond the Silver Screen*, Cambridge: Polity.

WEBER, M. (1968) *Economy and Society*, New York: Bedminster Press.

WEINSTEIN, F. and PLATT, G. M. (1973) *Psychoanalytic Sociology: an Essay on the Interpretation of Historical Data and the Phenomena of Collective Behavior*, London: John Hopkins University Press.

WEINSTEIN, F. and PLATT, G. M. (1975) 'The coming crisis of psychohistory', *Journal of Modern History*, **47**, pp. 202–28.

WEST, C. (1993) *Race Matters*, Boston: Beacon Press.

WHITAKER, A. P. and JORDAN, D. C. (1966) *Nationalism in Contemporary Latin America*, New York: Free Press.

WIESEL, E. (1981) *Night*, Harmondsworth: Penguin.

WILES, P, (1969) 'A syndrome, not a doctrine: Some elementary theses on populism', in IONESCO, G. and GELLNER, E. (Eds) *Populism: its National Characteristics*, London: Weidenfield & Nicolson.

WILLIAMS, L. (1992) 'Submission and reading: feminine masochism and feminist criticism', *New Formations*, **6**, pp. 9–19.

WILSON, J. Q. (1975) *Thinking about Crime*, Boston: Harvard University Press.

WILSON, W. J. (1987) *The Truly Disadvantaged*, Chicago: University of Chicago Press.

WING LO, T. (1993) *Corruption and Politics in Hong Kong and China*, Buckingham: Open University Press.

WISTRICH, R. S. (1991) *Anti-Semitism: the Longest Hatred*, London: Thames Mandarin.

WOLLHEIM, R. (1991) *Freud*, London: Fontana Press.

WORLD HEALTH ORGANISATION (1992) *International Statistical Classification of Diseases and Related Health Problems*, 10th revision, Geneva: WHO.

References

WRONG, D. H. (1961) 'The oversocialized conception of man in modern sociology', *American Sociological Review*, **26**, pp. 183–93.

WRONG, D. H. (1976) *Skeptical Sociology*, London: Heinemann.

YOUNG, A. (1994) 'Caveat sponsa: violence and the body in law', in BRETTLE, J. and RICE, S. (Eds) *Public Bodies/Private States*, Manchester: Manchester University Press.

YOUNG, R. (1992) 'Colonialism and humanism', in DONALD, J. and RATTANSI, A. (Eds) *Race, Culture and Difference*, London: Sage.

ZEMAN, Z. A. B. (1964) *Nazi Propaganda*, New York: Oxford University Press.

ZIMABARDO, P. G., HANEY, C., BANKS, W. C. and JAFFE, D. (1973) 'A pirandellian prison: the mind is a formidable jailer', *New York Times Magazine*, April 8, pp. 38–60.

ZIMRING, F. and HAWKINS, G. (1990) 'What kind of drug war?', *Social Justice*, **18**, pp. 104–21.

ZIV, A. (1994) 'The pervert's progress: an analysis of "Story of O" and the "Beauty Trilogy"', *Feminist Review*, **44**, pp. 3–17.

Notes on Contributors

Anthony Amatrudo is a member of the Institute of Historical Research. He took a degree in Sociology before obtaining Master's degrees in Ancient Philosophy and Patristic Theology at the University of London and Criminology at the University of Cambridge. He is currently a Research Fellow in the Department of Sociology at Warwick University.

David Craig studied Psychology at Manchester University before taking the M.Phil. in Criminology in Cambridge. He is currently studying for the Bar.

Steven Goodman has an LLB in Law and Philosophy from the University of Edinburgh and an M.Phil. in Criminology from the University of Cambridge. He is currently researching for a Ph.D. on post-modern violence in the Cybernetic Culture Research Unit, University of Warwick. His current interests are cybernetics, jungle warfare, hyperurban meltdown and the transhuman condition.

Laurence Grant has a BA in Applied Social Studies from Sheffield Hallam University and a Master's in Criminology from Cambridge. He is now studying the social censure of evil for a doctorate in the School of Law at the University of East London.

Victoria Harbord has a degree in Philosophy and Literature from Middlesex University, a Diplome d'études universitaires générales II in the same area, and an M.Phil. in Criminology from Cambridge. She is currently editor of the Home Office magazine *Civil Protection* and is a contributor to *Crime Prevention News*.

Ethan Raup has a BA in History and Political Science from Brown University and an M.Phil. in Criminology from Cambridge. He has worked in Washington State as Research Director for the US Senate race in 1994 and as Deputy Campaign Manager for a gubernatorial campaign in 1996. In his current position on policy staff for the Mayor of Seattle, he is working on a major local initiative to prepare for the consequences of federal 'welfare reform'.

Colin Summer is Professor and Head of Department in the School of Law at the University of East London. Formerly a lecturer in Criminology at the Cambridge Institute of Criminology, he has published several books: *Reading Ideologies* (1979); *Crime, Justice and Underdevelopment* (1982); *Crime, Justice and the Mass Media* (1982); *Censure, Politics and Criminal Justice* (1990) and *The Sociology of Deviance: an Obituary* (1994). He is co-Editor of a new international journal, *Theoretical Criminology* and has a book on *Social Control and Political Order* (edited with Roberto Bergalli) in press.

Claire Valiér is a Munro research student at Queen's College, Cambridge.

Index